—— THE ——
GREATEST

THE GREATEST

MARK MEGNA

To order additional copies of this book, contact:
Xlibris LLC
1-888-795-4274
www.Xlibris.com
Orders@Xlibris.com
614334

CONTENTS

Dedication

To Dick Megna, Vince Megna, and Don Brill

All of them share a great passion for baseball

Dick Megna was a terror on and off the field. He was quick on the bases, good with the glove and hit for power with a big bat. If there was one player that he could be compared with that would have to be Billy Martin.

Vince Megna held the little league record for homers of 14 in 20 games for many years. Three of his teammates from that team went on to play in the major leagues. He was also MVP his senior year and known for his power with the use of a Mac 44 bat and his golden glove at first base.

Don Brill hit near .400 his sophomore year while batting from both sides of the plate. His gold glove at third base was modeled after that of Ron Santo. Famous for his legendary "Road to Wrigley" trips. People are still asking "Who is Don Brill." Well Known Unknown.

Introduction—

An "Absolute Numbers" Theory. A theory of baseball which compares how well a player has performed relative to his era. All rankings in this book are based on this objective theory.

What if we could know what every baseball players ranking is within the entire history of baseball at any time? That is what this book is all about. I have created the "Absolute Numbers" in which every player's ability can be compared with the entire history of baseball. When you know what a players "Absolute Number" is for a single season or for his entire career you know not only how he ranks within the current league but also among the entire history of baseball. Therefore, we know longer have to guess at who is the best player. His "Absolute Number" tells us.

Unfortunately, to some this may be one the most disturbing baseball books that you will ever read. Forget what you thought you knew about what makes up a good hitter. All of us were wrong. As it turns out this book is completely biased towards the power hitter. Believe me, this was never my intention but the raw data has become impossible to dismiss. You will find that a lot of players that have been inducted into the Hall of Fame should not be there. Or, a lot of players passed over for the Hall of Fame should be inducted. This book proves it. As Ricky always said to Lucy on "I love Lucy"—"Lucy you got some 'splainin to do".

This book is a statistical book but it is very simple. The question in my mind since I was about 10 years old was who the greatest hitter of all time was? So finally now at the age of 51, I took 456 hitters and compared their relative success in their era and created a ratio of how much better or worse they each were relative to the average player in their career so that I could then put all of the players on one list as if they all played in the same era. By no means is this an all-inclusive book of every player in baseball history but is only a comparison of the ones that I chose to look at. I took the slugging percentage of each guy for his career and compared it to the exact years in which each player played in. This way we could start to make a comparison between a Tris Speaker, Ty Cobb, Babe Ruth, Ted Williams, Willie Mays, Rod Carew, Mark McGuire, Barry Bonds, and Ryan Braun. As it turned out this was my big mistake. Picking the slugging percentage as that statistic that I was going to use for my comparison. I only picked it since it is the most important statistic not because I had a bias towards a power hitter over a chronic singles hitter. Slugging percentage is a hitters total bases divided by total at bats. It therefore calculates "almost" everything that you need to know about a hitter into one simple number. It's only short fall is that it doesn't incorporate walks or stolen bases into it. As it turns out some weird things start to develop when you do something like this. The results showed that the best hitters are the ones that could hit for both power and average primarily. I think everyone would agree with that expectation. But, It also showed that a solely power hitter is more valuable than a chronic singles hitter. This is where the major problem came in. Some of the best batting average hitters in baseball history were way down on my list of the greatest hitters of all time. There had to be something wrong so I started to investigate and apparently this has been a problem for a long time. This can't be the case since we all hail the guy that can hit

.330 as being the "best hitter in the league" don't we? At one point in history this was so disturbing to statisticians that were trying to analyze baseball hitters that they decided to come up with something called the "on base slugging percentage" or OPS. This is done by merely adding the slugging percentage and their on base percentage together. The idea caught on so well that you started hearing some baseball announcers use the term and even the Topps baseball card started printing it on the back of cards. There is one problem though. By doing this you are double counting. A players on base percentage is largely already factored in the slugging percentage. So you in effect count the amount of hits twice when you add the on base percentage and the slugging percentage together. The more hits you get the higher your slugging percentage goes. It's not my fault that hitting a home run is four times better than someone "chinking" a single to right. Don't get me wrong. I think that hitting a major league pitcher is the hardest thing to do in any sport. But, it is simply a fact. If I was running in a straight line and went 90 feet. I simply went 90 feet. I can't mysteriously say that I went 90 feet once and then 90 feet again and add them together. You still only went 90 feet!

There was one short fall in my initial calculation of only using the slugging percentage as my main number. It did not include walks or stolen bases. Therefore, I came up with an "adjusted slugging percentage" which included these divided by total plate appearances and then adjusted for how well each player did relative to his era. Now we can say that it does calculate everything there is to know about a players hitting. There is thus no need for the "double counting" of the OPS #. Therefore, I made a list of the greatest hitters in the history of baseball using this information. There is no subjectivity in this analysis. The numbers are what they are. After all, given that every player gets almost 10,000 at bats each in his career we can feel pretty confident that the numbers don't lie.

Some people are going to say that this adjusted slugging percentage or the relative era adjustment that I used is not the best way to do this analysis. I disagree. This is a very simple objective way of comparing the eras. Yes, it is true that there were many differences in the eras and that is exactly why comparing how a player performed within his era relative to everyone else is the only way to make an objective comparison. There was the dead ball era of Frank Baker, and the live ball era of Babe Ruth, and the anemic decade during world war II, the big stadiums with 440 to center, the pitchers era in the 1960's when the mound was raised, domed stadiums, and the enhanced vitamin era of the 1990's and 2000's. Yet, this is all factored into the relative performance of each era.

Other people will say that you simply can't compare the eras. Obviously the physical athlete of today is so much superior to that of the 1890's. I agree. But, again, this takes out all of those preconceived biases that we may have one way or another.

All everyone has to do is use these "Absolute Numbers" ("era adjusted slugging percentage "in the case of offensive players) from now on and we will always know who the best hitter in baseball is not only in each of the current years but also relative to the entire history of baseball instantly as well. It will be the same as when people used to ask what is someone's batting average which is not an extremely good way of determining how good of an overall hitter someone is. This way there won't be any more errors made with the Hall of Fame or the MVP voting or the All Star game or anything else for that matter. Granted this doesn't include the defensive aspect of the game. I agree, but, as far as evaluating a hitter goes this is all you need. Moreover, you can use these methods for determining the best defensive players are as well so in effect we do have everything in an objective sense.

It's funny how in football everyone asks what someone's quarterback rating is yet they have no idea how it is calculated. This is not like that. This is simple.

Again, forget about the "OPS" (adding slugging percentage to on base percentage) number that people have been using. It is simply wrong for the reason that I stated that you are double counting numbers and creating a new almost meaningless number. I'm sure that this all came about with good intentions not to offend the "chronic singles hitters" or come up with some way to even out the numbers so that the guys that were on top of the highest batting average list were included in an "overall production" number list but this "OPS" number is simply wrong.

Let's face facts. The average person isn't just sitting around wondering who the greatest hitter of all time is or within a single year is and a way to calculate it. But, when the ability to do it like this is right at our fingertips it's stupid not to do it. All major league baseball, Topps, the announcers, and the news agency have to do is use it. Once it is incorporated the general public will be fascinated by how easy all this was for people to understand. At the very least let's get people back to talking about the slugging percentage number or the adjusted slugging percentage number which includes walks and stolen bases. Even if we don't buy into my notion about adjusting this for someone's performance relative to their era we can at least talk about a simple calculation that actually makes sense and incorporates into it everything that you need to know about someone's offensive production I just want to keep the integrity of the game in tact for what increasingly seems like a tarnished reputation.

Unfortunately, I don't even want to tell you where some of the greatest "chronic singles hitters" rank on the all-time list in this book because I know it will offend you and you won't want to read on any further.

With that said I had to proceed on with the list and publish this book. It is too important. Again, the facts are what they are no matter what our preconceived notions are of who the greatest hitters are in baseball history or within a single season. I did not try to "cook the books" with a flawed "OPS" number for example to try to include players that I thought should have been or must be towards the top.

These rankings are averages based on per at bat performances so you can argue that someone who performed at a high level for many years should be ranked higher than someone who had a short career. I will give you that and that is why I considered total number of years that each player played. Even my daughter Jessica could see that needs to be a consideration. This seems to somewhat correspond more to how the Hall of Fame voting has gone over the years by weighting heavily on players that had lengthy careers. Yet, no matter which list (a pure ranking without regard to years played or one weighted for years played) you use you can see that a lot of errors have been made by the Hall of Fame voters because in a lot of ways bias has set in over what constitutes a great baseball player and sometimes even an outright popularity contest prevailed.

I didn't want to bore the reader with a lot of statistics even though this is a statistical game and a statistical book. So I tried to keep the amount of numbers to a minimum. I'm sure many of you have already seen a lot of printouts of a complete players' batting history or worse yet a complicated analysis of what the numbers all mean in an attempt to calculate overall production statistics. The important thing is that we can all agree that the concept of evaluating hitters in this fashion is sound. Therefore, if we know a players "Absolute Numbers" we will instantly know where that person ranks now and within the entire history of baseball all at the same time.

So, without wasting everyone's time I am going to start out with the actual bottom line findings of the book first listing the greatest players of all time based on "absolute player" rankings factoring in offense, defense, and longevity and then build my case from there.

I included the "Glossary of Terms" section early on in the book because it is central to the book on how these objective calculations were made. The bottom line of it all is that each player is ranked according to our well they each played in their era using the adjusted slugging percentage which included walks and stolen bases for offense evaluations, ERA for pitching, and fielding percentage times range for defense all compared to the averages of their time.

Best Absolute Team of All-Time

	1st Team	2nd Team	3rd Team	4th Team
C	Johnny Bench	Roy Campanella	Joe Torre	Gabby Hartnett
1B	Jimmy Foxx	Lou Gehrig	Dan Brouthers	Stan Musial
2B	Rogers Hornsby	Nap Lajoie	Joe Morgan	Eddie Collins
SS	Honus Wagner	Alex Rodriguez	George Davis	Bill Dahlen
3B	Mike Schmidt	Richie Allen	Harmon Killebrew	Eddie Mathews
OF	Babe Ruth	Willie Mays	Hank Aaron	Billy Hamilton
OF	Barry Bonds	Ty Cobb Tris	Speaker Shoeless	Joe Jackson
OF	Ted Williams	Mickey Mantle	Frank Robinson	Ed Delahanty
P	Walter Johnson	Greg Maddux	Carl Hubbell	Randy Johnson
P	Grover Alexander	Cy Young	Christy Mathewson	Tom Seaver
P	Ed Walsh	Whitey Ford	Smokey Joe Wood	ube Waddell
P	Roger Clemons	Pedro Martinez	Lefty Grove	Dizzy Dean
R	Mariano Rivera	Hoyt Wilhelm	John Hiller	Rich Gossage

Glossary of Terms—Offensive Player

Slugging Percentage = Total Bases / At Bats
ie - 400/600 = .666

Slugging Percentage Ratio = Slugging Percentage / League Average Slugging Percentage
Ie - .666/.375 = 1.77

Adjusted Slugging Percentage = Total Bases + Walks + Stolen Bases / Plate Appearances
Ie - 500/700 = .714

Absolute Adjusted Slugging Percent Ratio = Adjusted Slugging Percentage / League Slugging Percentage
Ie - .714 /.375 = 1.90

Absolute Adjusted Slugging = Absolute Adjusted Slugging Percentage Ratio x .375
Ie - 1.90 x .375 = .712

(.375 is the average slugging percentage in the history of the league.)

The "Absolute" best offensive players were determined by ranking this number in order.

Glossary of Terms—Defensive Player

Absolute Fielding = (Fielding Percentage/ League Fielding Percentage) x (Range/League Range)
Ie - (.980/.970) x (2.4/2) = 1.21

All Defensive Players in this book were ranked by using this number.

Range = Put-outs + Assists

Catchers
Absolute Fielding = (Fielding Percentage/ League Fielding) x (Caught Stealing % / League %)

Ie - .980/.970 x .35/.30 = 1.17

All Catchers were ranked using this number for defensive

Glossary of Terms—Absolute Player

Absolute Player = Absolute Adjusted Slugging x Absolute Fielding x Longevity Factor

Ie - .700 x 1.1 x 1.05 = .808

The best overall player was determined by ranking this number

Longevity Factors

Players career lasting 20 or more years = 1.05
Players career lasting 15 to 19 years = 1.0
Players career lasting 10 to 14 years = .95
Players career lasting 5 to 9 years = .90

Glossary of Terms—Pitching

Absolute ERA Ratio = ERA / League ERA
Ie - 3.00 / 4.00 = .75

Absolute ERA = Absolute ERA Ration x 3.75

(3.75 is the average era over the history of baseball)

Absolute Adjusted ERA = Absolute ERA x Longevity Factor

All pitchers were ranked by this number to determine the best pitcher of all-time.

Best Absolute Player Rankings of all time

This includes offense, defense, and longevity

Hall of Fame members are in bold

Refer to the back of the book for a listing without regard to defense or longevity

Rank	Abs plyr	Player (yrs)	Yrs	Slg ratio	Po	GG	2B	3B	HR	RBI	SB	BB	BA	OBP	SLG
1	0.741	**Babe Ruth+ (22)**	22	**1.82**	of		33	9	46	144	8	133	0.342	0.474	0.690
2	0.701	Barry Bonds (22)	22	**1.48**	of	8	33	4	41	108	28	139	0.298	0.444	0.607
3	0.690	**Ted Williams+ (19)**	19	**1.65**	of		37	5	37	130	2	143	0.344	0.482	0.634
4	0.685	**Willie Mays+ (22)**	22	**1.47**	of	12	28	8	36	103	18	79	0.302	0.384	0.557
5	0.683	**Ty Cobb+ (24)**	24	**1.45**	of		39	16	6	103	48	67	0.366	0.433	0.512
6	0.677	**Jimmie Foxx+ (20)**	20	**1.56**	1b		32	9	37	134	6	102	0.325	0.428	0.609
7	0.663	**Honus Wagner+ (21)**	21	**1.38**	ss		37	15	6	100	42	56	0.328	0.391	0.467
8	0.650	**Lou Gehrig+ (17)**	17	**1.58**	1b		40	12	37	149	8	113	0.340	0.447	0.632
9	0.640	**Mickey Mantle+ (18)**	18	**1.46**	of	1	23	5	36	102	10	117	0.298	0.421	0.557
10	0.638	**Rogers Hornsby+ (23)**	23	**1.51**	2b		39	12	22	114	10	74	0.358	0.434	0.577
11	0.637	**Hank Aaron+ (23)**	23	**1.47**	of	3	31	5	37	113	12	69	0.305	0.374	0.555
12	0.635	**Tris Speaker**	22	**1.40**	of		46	13	7	89	25	80	0.345	0.428	0.500
13	0.634	**Stan Musial+ (22)**	22	**1.47**	1b		39	9	25	104	4	86	0.331	0.417	0.559
14	0.625	**Frank Robinson+ (21)**	21	**1.43**	of	1	30	4	34	105	12	82	0.294	0.389	0.537
14	0.625	**Mike Schmidt+ (18)**	18	**1.38**	3b	10	27	4	37	107	12	102	0.267	0.380	0.527
15	0.623	**Nap Lajoie+ (21)**	21	**1.37**	2b		43	11	5	104	25	34	0.338	0.380	0.466
16	0.617	**Billy Hamilton**	14	**1.18**	of		25	10	4	75	93	121	0.344	0.455	0.432
17	0.616	Shoeless Joe Jackson	13	**1.54**	of		37	20	7	95	25	63	0.356	0.423	0.517

18	0.614	**Mel Ott+ (22)**	22	**1.38**	1b		29	4	30	110	5	101	0.304	0.414 0.533
19	0.612	**Ed Delahanty+ (16)**	16	**1.39**	of		46	16	9	129	40	65	0.346	0.411 0.505
20	0.610	Dick Allen (15)	15	**1.44**	3b		30	7	33	104	12	83	0.292	0.378 0.534
21	0.607	**Hank Greenberg+ (13)**	13	**1.55**	1b		44	8	38	148	7	99	0.313	0.412 0.605
22	0.605	**Joe DiMaggio+ (13)**	13	**1.51**	of		36	12	34	143	3	74	0.325	0.398 0.579
23	0.605	**Joe Morgan**	22	**1.14**	2b	5	27	6	16	69	42	114	0.271	0.392 0.427
24	0.604	**Willie McCovey+ (22)**	22	**1.37**	1b		22	3	33	97	2	84	0.270	0.374 0.515
11	0.637	**Dan Brouthers+ (19)**	19	**1.48**	1b		45	20	10	125		81	0.342	0.423 0.519
26	0.599	**Willie Stargell+ (21)**	21	**1.41**	1b		29	4	33	106	1	64	0.282	0.360 0.529
27	0.598	Mark McGwire (16)	16	**1.44**	1b	1	22	1	50	122	1	114	0.263	0.394 0.588
28	0.598	**Ricky Henerson**	25	**1.04**	of	1	27	3	16	59	74	115	0.279	0.401 0.419
29	0.598	Ken Griffey (22)	22	**1.30**	of	10	32	2	38	111	11	80	0.284	0.370 0.538
30	0.596	**Johnny Mize+ (15)**	15	**1.46**	1b		32	7	31	115	2	74	0.312	0.397 0.562
31	0.592	**Roger Conner**	18	**1.37**	1b		36	19	11	107	13	81	0.316	0.397 0.486
32	0.592	**Hugh Duffy**	17	**1.26**	of		30	11	10	121	54	62	0.326	0.386 0.451
33	0.590	**Eddie Collins**	25	**1.19**	2b		25	11	3	75	42	86	0.333	0.424 0.429
34	0.589	Jim Thome (22)	22	**1.33**	1b		29	2	39	108	1	111	0.276	0.402 0.554
-		-												
35	0.586	**Johnny Bench**	17	**1.27**	c	10	29	2	29	103	5	67	0.267	0.342 0.476
35	0.586	**Joseph Kelly**	17	**1.27**	of		31	17	6	104	39	80	0.317	0.402 0.451
38	0.586	**Reggie Jackson**	21	**1.29**	of		27	3	32	98	13	79	0.262	0.356 0.490
39	0.584	Albert Pujols (13, 33)	13	**1.44**	1b	2	43	1	41	124	8	88	0.321	0.410 0.599
40	0.583	Alex Rodriguez (20, 37)	20	**1.33**	ss	2	33	2	41	124	20	78	0.299	0.384 0.558
41	0.582	**Fred Clarke**	21	**1.23**	of		26	16	5	73	37	63	0.312	0.386 0.429
42	0.579	**Frank Chance**	17	**1.17**	1b		25	10	3	75	51	70	0.296	0.394 0.394
43	0.579	Charlie Keller (13)	13	**1.39**	of		23	10	26	105	6	109	0.286	0.410 0.518
44	0.577	**Duke Snider**	18	**1.39**	of		27	6	31	101	7	73	0.295	0.380 0.540
45	0.575	**Harmon Killebrew**	22	**1.34**	3b		19	2	38	105	1	104	0.256	0.376 0.509
46	0.572	Larry Walker (17)	17	**1.37**	of	7	38	5	31	107	19	74	0.313	0.400 0.565
47	0.571	**Eddie Mathews**	17	**1.33**	3b		24	5	35	98	5	98	0.271	0.376 0.509
48	0.567	**Al Simmons**	20	**1.36**	of		39	11	22	134	6	45	0.334	0.380 0.535
49	0.566	Cesar Cedeno (17)	17	**1.16**	of	5	35	5	16	79	44	54	0.285	0.347 0.443
50	0.564	**Carl Yastremski**	23	**1.23**	of	7	32	3	22	90	8	90	0.285	0.379 0.462
51	0.564	Darrel Evans	21	**1.13**	3b		20	2	25	82	6	97	0.248	0.361 0.431
52	0.562	**Max Carey**	20	**1.05**	of		27	10	5	52	48	68	0.285	0.361 0.386

53	0.560	Tim Raines	23	**1.06**	of		28	7	11	63	52	86	0.294	0.385	0.425
54	0.560	**George Brett**	21	**1.27**	3b	1	**40**	**8**	**19**	**96**	**12**	**66**	**0.305**	**0.369**	**0.487**
55	0.560	**Al Kaline+ (22)**	22	**1.26**	of	1	**28**	**4**	**23**	**90**	**8**	**73**	**0.297**	**0.376**	**0.480**
56	0.559	**Jesse Burkett**	16	**1.24**	of		**25**	**14**	**6**	**75**	**30**	**81**	**0.338**	**0.415**	**0.446**
57	0.558	Reggie Smith (17)	17	**1.31**	of	1	30	5	26	89	11	73	0.287	0.366	0.489
58	0.558	**Frank Thomas+ (19)**	19	**1.33**	1b		**35**	**1**	**36**	**119**	**2**	**116**	**0.301**	**0.419**	**0.555**
46	0.573	**Cap Anson**	22	**1.28**	1b		**37**	**9**	**6**	**133**	**11**	**63**	**0.334**	**0.394**	**0.447**
60	0.555	**Roy Campanella+ (10)**	10	**1.29**	c		**24**	**2**	**32**	**114**	**3**	**71**	**0.276**	**0.360**	**0.500**
61	0.554	**Joe Torre+ (18)**	18	**1.28**	c	1	**25**	**4**	**18**	**87**	**2**	**57**	**0.297**	**0.365**	**0.452**
62	0.554	Jeff Bagwell (15)	15	**1.29**	1b	1	37	2	34	115	15	106	0.297	0.408	0.540
63	0.554	Dwight Evans (20)	20	**1.23**	of	8	30	5	24	86	5	86	0.272	0.370	0.470
64	0.554	Fred Lynn (17)	17	**1.26**	of	4	32	4	25	91	6	71	0.283	0.360	0.484
65	0.553	**Ron Santo**	15	**1.24**	3b	5	**26**	**5**	**25**	**96**	**3**	**80**	**0.277**	**0.362**	**0.464**
66	0.552	Eric Davis (17)	17	**1.19**	of	3	24	3	28	93	35	74	0.269	0.359	0.482
67	0.552	Bobby Bonds (14)	14	**1.26**	of	3	26	6	29	90	40	80	0.268	0.353	0.471
68	0.552	Ken Williams (14)	14	**1.40**	of		33	9	23	106	18	66	0.319	0.393	0.530
69	0.550	Norm Cash (17)	17	**1.30**	1b		19	3	29	86	3	81	0.271	0.374	0.488
70	0.550	Jim Wynn (15)	15	**1.18**	of		24	3	25	81	19	103	0.250	0.366	0.436
71	0.549	**Sam Crawford**	19	**1.35**	of		**29**	**20**	**6**	**98**	**24**	**49**	**0.309**	**0.362**	**0.452**
72	0.548	Frank Howard (16)	16	**1.33**	1b		21	3	33	96	1	67	0.273	0.352	0.499
73	0.548	Bill Dahlen	21	**1.09**	ss		27	11	6	82	36	71	0.272	0.358	0.382
74	0.547	Lance Berkman (15, 37)	15	**1.28**	1b		36	3	32	106	7	104	0.293	0.406	0.537
75	0.546	**Ralph Kiner+ (10)**	10	**1.43**	of		**24**	**4**	**41**	**112**	**2**	**111**	**0.279**	**0.398**	**0.548**
76	0.546	Jim Edmonds (17)	17	**1.25**	of	8	35	2	32	97	5	80	0.284	0.376	0.527
77	0.545	Rafael Palmeiro (20)	20	**1.26**	1b	3	33	2	33	105	6	77	0.288	0.371	0.515
78	0.545	Jack Clark (18)	18	**1.24**	of		27	3	28	96	6	103	0.267	0.379	0.476
79	0.544	**Dave Windfield**	22	**1.22**	of	7	**29**	**5**	**25**	**100**	**12**	**66**	**0.283**	**0.353**	**0.475**
80	0.542	Bob Johnson (13)	13	**1.33**	of		34	8	25	112	8	93	0.296	0.393	0.506
81	0.540	David Ortiz (17, 37)	17	**1.31**	1b		43	1	35	118	1	89	0.287	0.381	0.549
82	0.540	**Larry Doby**	13	**1.26**	of		**26**	**5**	**27**	**103**	**5**	**92**	**0.283**	**0.386**	**0.490**
83	0.540	Orlando Cepeda+ (17)	17	**1.33**	1b		32	2	29	104	11	45	0.297	0.350	0.499
84	0.539	**Joe Cronin**	20	**1.21**	ss		**39**	**9**	**13**	**109**	**7**	**81**	**0.301**	**0.390**	**0.468**
85	0.539	**Jacob Beckley**	20	**1.23**	1b		**32**	**17**	**6**	**107**	**21**	**42**	**0.308**	**0.361**	**0.436**
86	0.539	Manny Ramirez (19, 41)	19	**1.39**	of		38	1	39	129	3	94	0.312	0.411	0.585
87	0.539	Sammy Sosa (18)	18	**1.29**	of		26	3	42	115	16	64	0.273	0.344	0.534

88	0.539	Jeff Heath (14)	14	**1.35**	of		33	12	23	104	7	69	0.293	0.370	0.509
89	0.538	**Ryne Sandberg**	16	1.15	2b	9	30	6	21	79	26	57	0.285	0.344	0.452
90	0.537	Todd Helton (17, 39)	17	**1.29**	1b	3	43	3	27	101	3	96	0.316	0.414	0.539
91	0.536	**Elmer Flick**	13	**1.32**	of		29	18	5	83	36	65	0.313	0.389	0.445
92	0.536	Gary Sheffield (22)	22	**1.24**	of		29	2	32	105	16	93	0.292	0.393	0.514
93	0.536	**Roberto Clemente**	18	**1.27**	of	12	29	11	16	87	6	41	0.317	0.359	0.475
94	0.536	**Paul Waner**	20	**1.22**	of		38	12	7	83	7	69	0.333	0.404	0.473
95	0.535	**Chuck Klein+ (17)**	17	**1.39**	of		37	7	28	111	7	56	0.320	0.379	0.543
96	0.534	Dolph Camilli (12)	12	**1.29**	1b		28	9	26	103	7	103	0.277	0.388	0.492
97	0.534	Hank Sauer (15)	15	**1.30**	of		23	2	33	101	1	65	0.266	0.347	0.496
98	0.534	Vladimir Guerrero (16)	16	**1.31**	of		36	3	34	113	14	56	0.318	0.379	0.553
99	0.533	**Hack Wilson+ (12)**	12	1.37	1b		32	8	29	128	6	81	0.307	0.395	0.545
100	0.532	**Eddie Murray**	21	**1.21**	1b	3	30	2	27	103	6	71	0.287	0.359	0.476
101	0.532	Gil Hodges (18)	18	**1.26**	1b	3	23	4	29	100	5	74	0.273	0.359	0.487
102	0.532	Albert Belle (12)	12	**1.38**	of		41	2	40	130	9	72	0.295	0.369	0.564
103	0.531	Darryl Strawberry (17)	17	**1.26**	of		26	4	34	102	23	84	0.259	0.357	0.505
104	0.531	Edgar Martinez (18)	18	**1.25**	3b		41	1	24	99	4	101	0.312	0.418	0.515
105	0.531	**Andre Dawson**	21	**1.23**	of	8	31	6	27	98	19	36	0.279	0.323	0.482
106	0.530	Kirk Gibson (17)	17	**1.18**	of		26	5	25	86	28	71	0.268	0.352	0.463
107	0.529	Juan Gonzalez (17)	17	**1.36**	of		37	2	42	135	2	44	0.295	0.343	0.561
108	0.529	**Sam Thompson**	15	1.41	of		39	18	14	150		52	0.331	0.384	0.505
109	0.529	**Tony Perez**	23	1.23	1b		29	5	22	96	3	54	0.279	0.341	0.463
110	0.529	Boog Powell (17)	17	**1.24**	1b		21	1	27	94	2	79	0.266	0.361	0.462
111	0.528	Bill Nicholson (16)	16	**1.23**	of		26	6	23	92	3	77	0.268	0.365	0.465
112	0.528	**Paul Molitar**	21	**1.13**	3b		37	7	14	79	30	66	0.306	0.369	0.448
113	0.527	Miguel Cabrera (11, 30)	11	**1.37**	1b		40	1	36	123	4	78	0.321	0.399	0.568
114	0.527	Tip O'Neill (10)	10	1.35	of		34	14	8	117		65	0.326	0.392	0.458
115	0.526	**Harry Heilmann**	17	**1.37**	of		41	11	14	116	9	65	0.342	0.410	0.520
116	0.526	Fred McGriff (19)	19	**1.24**	1b		29	2	32	102	5	86	0.284	0.377	0.509
117	0.525	**Joe Medwick**	17	**1.33**	of		44	9	17	113	3	36	0.324	0.362	0.505
118	0.525	Bobby Abreu (17)	17	**1.14**	of	1	39	4	20	93	28	100	0.292	0.396	0.477
119	0.525	Hal Trosky (11)	11	**1.35**	1b		40	7	27	122	3	66	0.302	0.371	0.522
120	0.525	**Earl Averill**	13	**1.34**	of		39	12	23	113	7	75	0.318	0.395	0.534
121	0.525	**Gabby Hartnett**	20	**1.23**	c		32	5	19	96	2	57	0.297	0.370	0.489
122	0.524	Keith Hernandez (17)	17	**1.13**	1b	11	33	5	13	83	8	83	0.296	0.384	0.436

#		Player			Pos										
123	0.524	Greg Luzinski (15)	15	**1.26**	of		31	2	27	100	3	75	0.276	0.363	0.478
124	0.523	**Ernie Banks+ (19)**	19	1.31	ss	1	**26**	**6**	**33**	**105**	**3**	**49**	**0.274**	**0.330**	**0.500**
125	0.523	**Home Run Baker+ (13)**	13	**1.29**	3b		**32**	**11**	**10**	**102**	**24**	**49**	**0.307**	**0.363**	**0.442**
126	0.523	**Edd Roush**	18	**1.20**	of		**28**	**15**	**6**	**81**	**22**	**40**	**0.323**	**0.369**	**0.446**
127	0.523	Pedro Guerrero (15)	15	**1.24**	1b		28	3	23	95	10	64	0.300	0.370	0.480
128	0.523	**Charlie Geringher**	19	**1.22**	2b		**40**	**10**	**13**	**100**	**13**	**83**	**0.320**	**0.404**	**0.480**
129	0.522	Carlos Delgado (17)	17	**1.29**	of		38	1	38	120	1	88	0.280	0.383	0.546
130	0.522	Craig Nettles	22	**1.11**	3b	2	20	2	23	79	2	65	0.248	0.329	0.421
131	0.522	Rick Monday (19)	19	**1.18**	of		20	5	20	63	8	75	0.264	0.361	0.443
132	0.522	**Lefty O'Doul (11)**	11	**1.35**	of		**29**	**7**	**19**	**91**	**6**	**56**	**0.349**	**0.413**	**0.532**
133	0.522	Dale Murphy (18)	18	**1.21**	of	5	26	3	30	94	12	73	0.265	0.346	0.469
134	0.521	Ellis Burks (18)	18	**1.24**	of	1	33	5	29	98	15	64	0.291	0.363	0.510
135	0.520	Rico Carty (15)	15	**1.25**	of		27	2	20	87	2	63	0.299	0.369	0.464
136	0.520	**Pete Browning (13)**	13	**1.33**	of		**40**	**12**	**6**	**90**		**64**	**0.341**	**0.403**	**0.467**
137	0.520	**Bill Williams**	18	**1.32**	of		**28**	**6**	**28**	**96**	**6**	**68**	**0.290**	**0.361**	**0.492**
138	0.520	**Buck Ewing**	18	**1.29**	c		**31**	**22**	**9**	**109**		**48**	**0.303**	**0.351**	**0.456**
139	0.520	**Goose Goslin**	18	**1.25**	of		**35**	**12**	**18**	**114**	**12**	**67**	**0.316**	**0.387**	**0.500**
140	0.520	Tony Oliva (15)	15	**1.29**	of	1	32	5	21	92	8	43	0.304	0.353	0.476
141	0.519	**Carlton Fisk**	24	**1.20**	c	1	**27**	**3**	**24**	**86**	**8**	**55**	**0.269**	**0.341**	**0.457**
142	0.519	**George Sisler+ (15)**	15	**1.24**	1b		**34**	**13**	**8**	**93**	**30**	**37**	**0.340**	**0.379**	**0.468**
143	0.519	Babe Herman (13)	13	**1.34**	of		42	11	19	104	10	54	0.324	0.383	0.532
144	0.519	Brian Giles (15)	15	**1.19**	of		36	5	25	95	10	104	0.291	0.400	0.502
145	0.518	Cy Williams (19)	19	**1.26**	of		25	6	20	81	9	56	0.292	0.365	0.470
146	0.518	Al Rosen (10)	10	**1.28**	3b		26	3	30	111	6	91	0.285	0.384	0.495
147	0.518	**Zach Wheat**	19	**1.25**	of		**32**	**12**	**9**	**84**	**14**	**44**	**0.317**	**0.367**	**0.450**
148	0.518	Tommy Henrich (11)	11	**1.28**	of		34	9	23	100	5	90	0.282	0.382	0.491
149	0.517	Bob Allison (13)	13	**1.25**	of		23	6	27	84	9	84	0.255	0.358	0.471
150	0.517	**Roger Bresnahan**	17	**1.07**	c		**24**	**8**	**3**	**59**	**24**	**80**	**0.279**	**0.386**	**0.377**
151	0.517	Jason Giambi (19, 42)	19	**1.24**	1b		29	1	32	104	1	98	0.278	0.400	0.519
152	0.517	George Foster (18)	18	**1.26**	of		25	4	29	102	4	55	0.274	0.338	0.480
153	0.516	Bernie Williams (16)	16	**1.14**	of	4	35	4	22	98	11	83	0.297	0.381	0.477
154	0.516	Ivan Rodriguez (21)	21	**1.11**	c	13	36	3	20	85	8	33	0.296	0.334	0.464
155	0.516	Bobby Grich	17	**1.11**	2b	4	26	4	18	70	8	88	0.266	0.371	0.424
156	0.516	Dave Kingman (16)	16	**1.26**	1b		20	2	37	101	7	51	0.236	0.302	0.478
157	0.515	Ted Kluszewski (15)	15	**1.28**	1b		27	3	26	97	2	46	0.298	0.353	0.498

158	0.515	Mark Teixeira (11, 33)	11	**1.27**	1b	5	38	2	37	119	2	81	0.278	0.368	0.525
159	0.515	Rocky Colavito (14)	14	**1.28**	of		25	2	33	102	2	84	0.266	0.359	0.489
160	**0.514**	**Jackie Robinson**	**10**	**1.22**	**2b**		**32**	**6**	**16**	**86**	**23**	**87**	**0.311**	**0.409**	**0.474**
161	0.514	Chipper Jones (19)	19	**1.26**	3b		36	2	30	105	10	98	0.303	0.401	0.529
162	0.514	Carlos Beltran (16, 36)	16	**1.18**	of	3	35	6	28	104	24	73	0.283	0.359	0.496
163	**0.514**	**Barry Larkin**	**19**	**1.08**	**ss**	**3**	**33**	**6**	**15**	**71**	**28**	**70**	**0.295**	**0.371**	**0.444**
164	0.513	Rusty Staub (23)	23	**1.15**	of		27	3	16	80	3	69	0.279	0.362	0.431
165	0.513	Oscar Gamble (17)	17	**1.20**	of		19	3	20	68	5	62	0.265	0.356	0.454
166	0.513	Bobby Murcer (17)	17	**1.18**	of	1	24	4	21	89	11	73	0.277	0.357	0.445
167	0.513	Ryan Braun (7, 29)	7	**1.38**	of		41	5	36	117	22	57	0.312	0.374	0.564
168	**0.512**	**Bill Dickey**	**17**	**1.25**	**c**		**31**	**7**	**18**	**109**	**3**	**61**	**0.313**	**0.382**	**0.486**
169	**0.512**	**Tony Gwynn+ (20)**	**20**	**1.14**	**of**	**5**	**36**	**6**	**9**	**76**	**21**	**52**	**0.338**	**0.388**	**0.459**
170	0.512	Andruw Jones (17)	17	**1.16**	of	10	28	3	32	95	11	66	0.254	0.337	0.486
171	0.512	Vern Stephens (15)	15	**1.23**	ss		29	4	23	111	2	65	0.286	0.355	0.460
172	0.512	Jose Canseco (17)	17	**1.27**	of		29	1	40	121	17	78	0.266	0.353	0.515
173	0.511	John Mayberry (15)	15	**1.17**	1b		21	2	26	88	2	88	0.253	0.360	0.439
174	0.511	Ryan Howard (10, 33)	10	**1.32**	1b		30	3	43	132	2	81	0.271	0.361	0.545
175	0.511	Ken Singleton (15)	15	**1.15**	of		25	2	19	83	2	98	0.282	0.388	0.436
176	0.510	Reggie Sanders (17)	17	**1.16**	of		31	5	28	90	28	61	0.267	0.343	0.487
177	**0.510**	**King Kelly**	**16**	**1.29**	**of**		**40**	**11**	**8**	**106**		**61**	**0.308**	**0.368**	**0.438**
178	0.510	Roy Sievers (17)	17	**1.22**	1b		25	4	27	98	1	72	0.267	0.354	0.475
179	0.510	Gary Matthews (16)	16	**1.15**	of		25	4	19	78	15	75	0.281	0.364	0.439
180	0.510	Scott Rolen (17)	17	**1.17**	3b	8	41	3	25	102	9	71	0.281	0.364	0.490
181	0.510	Joey Votto (7, 29)	7	**1.33**	1b		41	2	29	96	9	103	0.314	0.419	0.541
182	0.509	Minnie Minoso (17)	17	**1.19**	of		30	7	16	90	18	72	0.298	0.389	0.459
183	0.509	Gorman Thomas (13)	13	**1.18**	of		24	1	30	88	6	79	0.225	0.324	0.448
184	**0.509**	**Kiki Cuyler**	**18**	**1.19**	**of**		**34**	**14**	**11**	**92**	**28**	**58**	**0.321**	**0.386**	**0.474**
185	0.509	Will Clark (15)	15	**1.22**	1b	1	36	4	23	99	5	77	0.303	0.384	0.497
186	0.509	Alan Trammel	20	**1.06**	ss	4	29	4	13	71	17	60	0.285	0.352	0.415
187	0.508	Moises Alou (17)	17	**1.24**	of		35	3	28	107	9	61	0.303	0.369	0.516
188	0.508	Kevin Mitchell (13)	13	**1.30**	of		30	3	31	101	4	65	0.284	0.360	0.520
189	0.508	Vic Wertz (17)	17	**1.21**	of		25	4	23	102	1	72	0.277	0.364	0.469
190	**0.508**	**Yogin Berra**	**19**	**1.25**	**c**		**25**	**4**	**27**	**109**	**2**	**54**	**0.285**	**0.348**	**0.482**
191	0.507	Jay Buhner (15)	15	**1.21**	of	1	26	2	34	106	1	87	0.254	0.359	0.494
192	0.507	Bob Elliott (15)	15	**1.17**	3b		31	8	14	98	5	79	0.289	0.375	0.440

#		Name			Pos									AVG	OBP	SLG
193	0.507	**Cal Ripken**	21	**1.11**	ss	2	33	2	23	91	2	61		**0.276**	**0.340**	**0.447**
194	0.507	**Rod Carew**	19	**1.14**	2b		29	7	6	67	23	67		**0.328**	**0.393**	**0.429**
195	0.507	Ryan Klesko (16)	16	**1.19**	1b		32	3	26	92	8	76		0.279	0.370	0.500
196	0.507	**Sam Rice**	20	**1.12**	of		34	12	2	73	24	48		**0.322**	**0.374**	**0.427**
197	0.507	Jimmy Ryan (18)	18	**1.23**	of		36	13	9	88		65		0.308	0.375	0.444
198	0.506	Ken Boyer (15)	15	**1.21**	3b	5	25	5	22	91	8	57		0.287	0.349	0.462
199	0.506	**Flash Gordon**	11	**1.23**	2b		27	5	26	101	9	79		**0.268**	**0.357**	**0.466**
200	0.506	Harold Baines (22)	22	**1.16**	of		28	3	22	93	2	61		0.289	0.356	0.465
201	0.506	Joe Adcock (17)	17	**1.25**	of		24	3	28	93	2	49		0.277	0.337	0.485
202	0.506	Brian Downing	20	**1.11**	of		25	2	19	74	3	83		0.267	0.370	0.425
203	0.505	Javy Lopez (15)	15	**1.17**	c		29	2	28	93	1	38		0.287	0.337	0.491
204	0.505	Bill White (13)	13	**1.20**	1b	7	27	6	20	84	10	58		0.286	0.351	0.455
205	0.504	Ron Gant (16)	16	**1.14**	of		27	4	28	89	21	68		0.256	0.336	0.468
206	0.503	David Wright (10, 30)	10	**1.22**	3b		41	3	26	103	22	79		0.301	0.382	0.506
207	0.503	Danny Tartabull (14)	14	**1.25**	of		33	3	30	107	4	88		0.273	0.368	0.496
208	0.502	Alfonso Soriano (15, 37)	15	**1.21**	2b		40	3	34	96	24	42		0.272	0.321	0.504
209	0.502	Dave Parker (19)	19	**1.23**	of	3	35	5	22	98	10	45		0.290	0.339	0.471
210	0.502	**Chick Hafey**	13	**1.32**	of		43	8	21	105	9	47		**0.317**	**0.372**	**0.526**
211	0.502	**James Bottemley**	16	**1.25**	1b		38	12	18	116	5	54		**0.310**	**0.369**	**0.500**
212	0.501	Matt Williams (17)	17	**1.20**	3b	4	29	3	33	106	5	41		0.268	0.317	0.489
213	0.501	**Lou Brock**	19	**1.09**	of		30	9	9	56	58	47		**0.293**	**0.343**	**0.410**
214	0.501	Matt Holliday (10, 33)	10	**1.28**	of		42	3	28	109	11	67		0.311	0.387	0.531
215	0.500	Dave Orr (8)	8	**1.47**	1b		41	22	8	128		20		0.342	0.366	0.502
216	0.500	Eric Chavez (16, 35)	16	**1.14**	3b	6	32	2	27	92	5	65		0.268	0.342	0.476
217	0.499	Sid Gordon (13)	13	**1.23**	of		24	5	22	88	2	80		0.283	0.377	0.466
218	0.499	Robin Ventura (16)	16	**1.08**	3b	6	26	1	23	92	2	84		0.267	0.362	0.444
219	0.499	Wally Berger (11)	11	**1.31**	of		36	7	29	108	4	52		0.300	0.359	0.522
220	0.498	Roger Maris (12)	12	**1.26**	of	1	22	5	30	94	2	72		0.260	0.345	0.476
221	0.498	Bob Horner (10)	10	**1.29**	3b		27	1	35	109	2	59		0.277	0.340	0.499
222	0.498	Ted Simmons (21)	21	**1.15**	c		32	3	16	92	1	56		0.285	0.348	0.437
223	0.497	Ron Fairly	21	**1.09**	of		20	2	14	69	2	70		0.266	0.360	0.408
224	0.497	**Robin Yount**	20	**1.12**	ss	1	33	7	14	80	15	55		**0.285**	**0.342**	**0.430**
225	0.497	Willie Horton (18)	18	**1.23**	of		23	3	26	93	2	50		0.273	0.332	0.457
226	0.497	Ron Cey (17)	17	**1.16**	3b		26	2	25	89	2	79		0.261	0.354	0.445
227	0.496	Paul O'Neill (17)	17	**1.16**	of		36	2	22	100	11	70		0.288	0.363	0.470

228	0.496	Ben Oglivie (16)	16	**1.18**	of		26	3	22	83	8	52	0.273	0.336	0.450
229	0.496	**Jim Rice**	16	**1.30**	of		29	6	30	113	4	52	0.298	0.352	0.502
230	0.495	Pete Rose	24	**1.09**	of	2	34	6	7	60	9	71	0.303	0.375	0.409
231	0.495	Carlos Gonzalez	6	**1.31**	of	3	35	7	29	98	25	53	0.300	0.357	0.530
232	0.495	Jim Ray Hart (12)	12	**1.27**	3b		21	4	24	83	2	55	0.278	0.345	0.467
233	0.495	Bob Watson (19)	19	**1.19**	1b		27	4	16	87	2	58	0.295	0.364	0.447
234	0.495	Derrek Lee (15)	15	**1.18**	1b	3	36	3	28	90	9	73	0.281	0.365	0.495
235	0.495	Vada Pinson	18	**1.18**	of	1	32	8	17	77	20	38	0.286	0.327	0.442
236	0.495	David Justice (14)	14	**1.22**	of		28	2	31	102	5	91	0.279	0.378	0.500
237	0.494	Troy Tulowitzki (8, 28)	8	**1.24**	ss	2	35	4	29	103	10	67	0.295	0.367	0.509
238	0.494	Ray Lankford (14)	14	**1.15**	of		34	5	23	83	25	79	0.272	0.364	0.477
239	0.494	Larry Hisle (14)	14	**1.20**	of		26	4	22	91	17	63	0.273	0.347	0.452
240	0.493	Adam Dunn (13, 33)	13	**1.19**	of		27	1	38	96	5	108	0.238	0.366	0.495
241	0.493	Adrian Gonzalez (10, 31)	10	**1.21**	1b	3	38	1	29	103	1	70	0.294	0.367	0.501
242	0.493	Kent Hrbek (14)	14	**1.23**	1b		29	2	27	101	3	78	0.282	0.367	0.481
243	0.492	Chili Davis (19)	19	**1.13**	of		28	2	23	91	9	79	0.274	0.360	0.451
244	0.491	Andres Galarraga (19)	19	**1.23**	1b	2	32	2	29	102	9	42	0.288	0.347	0.499
245	0.491	Dusty Baker (19)	19	**1.14**	of	1	25	2	19	80	11	61	0.278	0.347	0.432
246	0.491	Cecil Cooper (17)	17	**1.22**	1b	2	35	4	21	96	8	38	0.298	0.337	0.466
247	0.491	Walker Cooper (18)	18	**1.23**	c		26	4	19	89	2	34	0.285	0.332	0.464
248	0.490	Steve Garvey (19)	19	**1.17**	1b	4	31	3	19	91	6	33	0.294	0.329	0.446
249	0.490	Johnny Callison (16)	16	**1.17**	of		28	8	19	72	6	56	0.264	0.331	0.441
250	0.490	Ken Griffey (19)	19	**1.12**	of		28	6	12	66	15	56	0.296	0.359	0.431
251	0.490	**Jimmy Collings**	14	1.18	3b		33	11	6	92	18	40	0.294	0.343	0.409
252	0.490	Shawn Green (15)	15	**1.17**	of	1	37	3	27	89	13	62	0.283	0.355	0.494
253	0.490	Lee May (18)	18	**1.23**	1b		27	2	28	97	3	38	0.267	0.313	0.459
254	0.489	**Arky Vaughn**	14	1.18	ss		32	11	9	83	11	84	0.318	0.406	0.453
255	0.489	**Kirby Puckett**	12	1.21	of	6	38	5	19	99	12	41	0.318	0.360	0.477
256	0.489	Hanley Ramirez (9, 29)	9	**1.23**	ss		40	4	26	86	37	67	0.302	0.373	0.506
257	0.489	Mo Vaughn (12)	12	**1.26**	1b		29	1	35	114	3	78	0.293	0.383	0.523
258	0.488	Magglio Ordonez (15)	15	**1.19**	of		37	2	26	108	8	57	0.309	0.369	0.502
259	0.487	**Gordon Cochrane**	13	1.20	c		36	7	13	91	7	94	0.320	0.419	0.478
260	0.487	**Ernie Lombardi**	17	1.21	c		24	2	17	87	1	38	0.306	0.358	0.460
261	0.487	Doug DeCinces (15)	15	**1.16**	3b		31	3	23	86	6	61	0.259	0.329	0.445
262	0.487	Torii Hunter (17, 37)	17	**1.11**	of	9	34	3	24	95	15	47	0.279	0.335	0.466

#	Score	Name			Pos								AVG	OBP	SLG
263	0.487	George Scott (14)	14	**1.17**	1b	8	24	5	22	84	5	56	0.268	0.333	0.435
264	0.486	**Bid Mcphee**	18	1.04	2b		23	14	4	81		74	**0.272**	**0.355**	**0.373**
265	0.486	Bobby Bonilla (16)	16	**1.16**	3b		31	5	22	90	3	70	0.279	0.358	0.472
266	0.486	**Willie Keeler**	19	**1.19**	of		18	11	3	62	38	40	**0.341**	**0.388**	**0.415**
267	0.486	**Roberto Alomar**	17	**1.08**	2b	1	34	5	14	77	32	70	**0.300**	**0.371**	**0.443**
268	0.486	Jesse Barfield (12)	12	**1.21**	of	2	25	3	27	81	7	63	0.256	0.335	0.466
269	0.485	Gary Maddox	15	**1.08**	of	8	31	6	11	70	23	30	0.285	0.320	0.413
270	0.485	**Robert Doerr**	14	**1.22**	2b		33	8	19	108	5	70	**0.288**	**0.362**	**0.461**
271	0.485	Luis Gonzalez (19)	19	**1.15**	of		37	4	22	90	8	72	0.283	0.367	0.479
272	0.484	**John Evers**	18	0.99	2b		20	6	1	49	29	71	**0.270**	**0.356**	**0.334**
273	0.484	**Tony Lazerri**	14	**1.17**	2b		31	11	17	111	14	81	**0.292**	**0.380**	**0.467**
274	0.483	Lave Cross	21	**1.08**	3b		29	10	3	98	22	33	0.292	0.329	0.383
275	0.483	Andrew McCutch	5	**1.21**	of	1	36	7	23	84	28	80	0.296	0.380	0.489
276	0.483	**Bill Terry+ (14)**	14	**1.27**	1b		35	11	14	101	5	51	**0.341**	**0.393**	**0.506**
277	0.483	Smoky Burgess (18)	18	**1.16**	c		22	3	12	64	1	46	0.295	0.362	0.446
278	0.483	**Roderick Wallace**	25	1.03	ss		27	10	2	76	14	53	**0.268**	**0.332**	**0.358**
279	0.482	John Olerud (17)	17	**1.13**	1b	3	36	1	18	89	1	92	0.295	0.398	0.465
280	0.482	Bobby Veach (14)	14	**1.22**	of		35	13	6	104	17	51	0.310	0.370	0.442
281	0.482	Richie Zisk (13)	13	**1.23**	of		27	3	23	88	1	59	0.287	0.353	0.466
282	**0.481**	**Wade Boggs**	18	**1.11**	3b	2	38	4	8	67	2	94	**0.328**	**0.415**	**0.443**
283	0.481	Craig Bigio	20	**1.05**	2b	4	38	3	17	67	24	66	0.281	0.363	0.433
284	0.481	Dick Stuart (10)	10	**1.28**	1b		23	4	33	108	0	44	0.264	0.316	0.489
285	0.481	**James O'Rourke**	19	**1.26**	of		38	12	5	98		42	**0.310**	**0.352**	**0.422**
286	0.481	Jeff Kent (17)	17	**1.19**	2b		39	3	27	107	7	56	0.290	0.356	0.500
287	0.481	Matt Stairs (19)	19	**1.14**	of		25	1	23	77	3	61	0.262	0.356	0.477
288	0.481	Don Mattingly (14)	14	**1.20**	1b	9	40	2	20	100	1	53	0.307	0.358	0.471
289	0.480	Jim Gentile (9)	9	**1.27**	1b		20	1	31	95	1	82	0.260	0.368	0.486
290	0.480	**Richie Ashburn**	15	0.98	of		23	8	2	43	17	89	**0.308**	**0.396**	**0.382**
291	0.480	Julian Franco	23	1.03	ss		26	3	11	77	18	59	0.298	0.365	0.417
292	0.480	Tim Salmon (14)	14	**1.19**	of		33	2	29	98	5	94	0.282	0.385	0.498
293	0.480	**Joe Tinker**	15	1.07	ss		24	10	3	70	30	37	**0.262**	**0.308**	**0.353**
294	0.480	**Brooks Robinson**	23	1.06	3b	16	27	4	15	76	2	48	**0.267**	**0.322**	**0.401**
295	0.479	Curtis Granderson	10	**1.18**	of		27	11	30	83	17	70	0.261	0.340	0.488
296	0.479	Joe Carter (16)	16	**1.16**	of		32	4	29	107	17	39	0.259	0.306	0.464
297	0.479	**Heinie Manush**	17	1.20	of		40	13	9	95	9	41	**0.330**	**0.377**	**0.479**

298	**0.479**	**Harry Hooper**	**17**	**1.08**	**of**		**27**	**11**	**5**	**57**	**26**	**80**	**0.281** **0.368** **0.387**
299	0.479	Al Oliver (18)	18	**1.20**	of		36	5	15	91	6	37	0.303 0.344 0.451
300	0.479	Jorge Posada (17)	17	**1.07**	c		23	2	27	80	3	104	0.241 0.369 0.449
301	0.479	Andy Pafko (17)	17	**1.18**	of		23	5	19	85	3	49	0.285 0.350 0.449
302	0.478	J.D. Drew (14)	14	**1.16**	of		28	5	25	82	9	89	0.278 0.384 0.489
303	0.478	Jose Bautista (10, 32)	10	**1.18**	of		28	2	31	85	7	86	0.254 0.361 0.487
304	0.478	Ruben Sierra (20)	20	**1.10**	of		32	4	23	98	11	45	0.268 0.315 0.450
305	0.478	**Enos Slaughter**	**19**	**1.18**	**of**		**28**	**10**	**12**	**89**	**5**	**69**	**0.300 0.382 0.453**
306	0.477	Bob Meusel (11)	11	**1.24**	of		42	11	18	123	16	43	0.309 0.356 0.497
307	0.477	**Frank Frisch**	**19**	**1.09**	**2b**		**33**	**10**	**7**	**87**	**29**	**51**	**0.316 0.369 0.432**
308	0.477	George Hendrick (18)	18	**1.17**	of		27	2	21	88	5	45	0.278 0.329 0.446
309	0.477	Paul Konerko (17, 37)	17	**1.17**	1b		29	1	31	99	1	65	0.281 0.356 0.491
310	0.476	Devon White	17	**1.03**	of	7	32	6	17	71	29	45	0.263 0.319 0.419
311	0.476	**Lou Boudreou**	**15**	**1.11**	**ss**		**38**	**6**	**7**	**78**	**5**	**78**	**0.295 0.380 0.415**
312	0.476	**Cary Carter**	**19**	**1.14**	**c**	**3**	**26**	**2**	**23**	**86**	**3**	**60**	**0.262 0.335 0.439**
313	0.475	Bill Robinson (16)	16	**1.17**	of		25	3	18	71	8	29	0.258 0.300 0.438
314	0.475	Chet Lemon (16)	16	**1.15**	of		32	5	18	72	5	61	0.273 0.355 0.442
315	0.475	Mike Cameron (17)	17	**1.05**	of		32	5	23	80	25	72	0.249 0.338 0.444
316	0.474	**Luke Appling**	**18**	**1.03**	**ss**		**29**	**7**	**3**	**75**	**12**	**87**	**0.310 0.399 0.398**
317	0.474	Cecil Fielder (13)	13	**1.20**	1b		22	1	35	111	0	76	0.255 0.345 0.482
318	0.473	Tony Clark (15)	15	**1.15**	1b		24	1	26	86	1	55	0.262 0.339 0.485
319	0.473	Travis Hafner (12, 36)	12	**1.20**	1b		34	2	29	100	2	82	0.273 0.376 0.498
320	0.473	Josh Hamilton (7, 32)	7	**1.30**	of		37	4	33	115	9	57	0.295 0.354 0.530
321	0.473	Prince Fielder (9, 29)	9	**1.28**	1b		33	1	35	107	2	89	0.286 0.389 0.527
322	0.473	Chase Utley (11, 34)	11	**1.20**	2b		36	5	27	99	16	67	0.287 0.373 0.498
323	0.471	Troy Glaus (13)	13	**1.16**	3b		31	1	34	100	6	90	0.254 0.358 0.489
324	0.471	Evan Longoria (6, 27)	6	**1.26**	3b	2	41	2	33	111	8	76	0.275 0.357 0.512
325	0.471	Del Ennis (14)	14	**1.22**	of		30	6	25	109	4	51	0.284 0.340 0.472
326	0.471	Sixto Lezcano (12)	12	**1.15**	of		23	4	19	74	5	72	0.271 0.360 0.440
327	0.471	Rob Deer (11)	11	**1.13**	of		21	2	32	84	6	81	0.220 0.324 0.442
328	0.470	Mike Piazza (16)	16	**1.30**	c		29	1	36	113	1	64	0.308 0.377 0.545
329	0.470	Mike Sweeney (16)	16	**1.15**	1b		36	1	24	101	6	58	0.297 0.366 0.486
330	0.470	Dante Bichette (14)	14	**1.22**	of		38	3	26	108	14	34	0.299 0.336 0.499
331	0.469	Nomar Garciaparra (14)	14	**1.23**	ss		42	6	26	106	11	46	0.313 0.361 0.521
332	0.469	**Earle Coombs**	**12**	**1.16**	**of**		**34**	**17**	**6**	**70**	**11**	**75**	**0.325 0.397 0.462**

333	0.469	**Monte Irvin**	8	1.22	of		21	7	21	94	6	74	0.293 0.383 0.475
334	0.469	**Pie Traynor**	17	1.10	3b		31	14	5	106	13	39	0.320 0.362 0.435
335	0.468	Felipe Alou	17	1.15	of		28	4	16	66	8	33	0.286 0.328 0.433
336	0.468	Ken Caminiti	15	1.10	3b	3	32	2	22	90	8	67	0.272 0.347 0.447
337	0.467	Buddy Bell	18	1.06	3b	6	29	4	14	74	4	56	0.279 0.341 0.406
338	0.466	Tino Martinez	16	1.13	1b		29	2	27	102	2	62	0.271 0.344 0.471
339	0.465	Tony Fernandez	17	1.00	ss	4	31	7	7	63	18	52	0.288 0.347 0.399
340	0.465	Mark Grace	16	1.08	1b	4	37	3	12	83	5	78	0.303 0.383 0.442
341	0.465	Dixie Walker	18	1.09	of		32	8	9	87	5	69	0.306 0.383 0.437
342	0.465	Matt Kemp	8	1.20	of	2	30	5	26	94	27	52	0.293 0.350 0.493
343	0.465	Richie Sexson	12	1.19	of		31	2	36	112	2	70	0.261 0.344 0.507
344	0.465	Tony Conigliaro	8	1.28	of		26	4	31	95	4	53	0.264 0.327 0.476
345	0.463	Gary Gaetti	20	1.09	3b	4	29	3	23	87	6	41	0.255 0.308 0.434
346	**0.463**	**Ross Youngs**	10	1.17	of		32	12	6	79	20	74	0.322 0.399 0.441
347	0.463	**Hugh Jennings**	17	1.09	ss		29	11	2	106	45	44	0.312 0.391 0.406
348	0.462	Adrian Beltre	16	1.14	3b	4	35	2	27	93	8	45	0.282 0.334 0.478
349	0.462	Paul Blair	17	1.02	of	8	23	5	11	52	14	37	0.250 0.302 0.382
350	0.462	Don Baylor	19	1.14	of		26	2	24	90	20	57	0.260 0.342 0.436
351	0.462	Willie Wilson	19	0.97	of	1	21	11	3	44	50	32	0.285 0.326 0.376
352	0.462	Raul Ibanez	18	1.12	of		33	4	23	92	4	53	0.276 0.338 0.471
353	0.462	Bill Freehan	15	1.11	c	5	22	3	18	69	2	57	0.262 0.340 0.412
354	0.461	Steve Finley	19	1.07	of	5	28	8	19	73	20	53	0.271 0.332 0.442
355	0.461	Joe Mauer	10	1.13	c		39	3	14	87	6	85	0.323 0.405 0.468
356	0.461	Bill Madlock	15	1.14	3b		31	3	15	77	16	54	0.305 0.365 0.442
357	0.461	Bill Buckner	22	1.07	1b		32	3	11	78	12	29	0.289 0.321 0.408
358	0.461	**Pee Wee Reese**	16	0.98	ss		25	6	9	66	17	90	0.269 0.366 0.377
359	0.460	Johnny Damon	18	1.03	of		34	7	15	74	27	65	0.284 0.352 0.433
360	0.460	Raul Mondesi	13	1.14	of	2	34	5	29	91	24	50	0.273 0.331 0.485
361	0.459	Derek Jeter	19	1.06	ss	5	33	4	16	79	22	65	0.312 0.381 0.446
362	0.459	Russell Branyan	14	1.15	3b		22	1	30	71	2	62	0.232 0.329 0.485
363	0.458	Kevin Youkilis	10	1.15	1b		39	3	23	94	4	82	0.281 0.382 0.478
364	0.457	Richie Hebner	18	1.16	3b		23	5	17	76	3	58	0.276 0.352 0.438
365	0.457	Mickey Tettleton	14	1.13	c		23	2	27	80	3	104	0.241 0.369 0.449
366	0.457	Ripper Collins	9	1.25	1b		31	10	20	98	3	53	0.296 0.360 0.492
367	0.456	Zeke Bonura	7	1.23	1b		41	5	21	124	3	71	0.307 0.380 0.487

368	0.456	Larry Parrish	15	**1.12**	3b		31	3	22	85	3	45	0.263	0.318	0.439
369	0.455	Chris Davis	6	**1.26**	1b		33	1	35	98	3	49	0.266	0.327	0.512
370	0.453	**George Kell**	15	**1.09**	3b		35	5	7	79	5	56	**0.306**	**0.367**	**0.414**
371	0.451	Bill Skowron	14	**1.19**	1b		24	5	21	87	2	37	0.282	0.332	0.459
372	0.451	Vernon Wells	15	**1.10**	of	3	35	3	25	90	10	44	0.270	0.319	0.459
373	0.451	Vinny Castilla	16	**1.14**	3b		30	2	28	97	3	37	0.276	0.321	0.476
374	0.450	Curt Flood	15	**1.03**	of	7	25	4	8	59	8	41	0.293	0.342	0.389
375	0.450	Thurman Munson	11	**1.09**	c	3	26	4	13	80	5	50	0.292	0.346	0.410
376	0.450	Justin Morneau	11	**1.16**	1b		36	2	27	107	1	64	0.277	0.347	0.482
377	0.450	Nelson Cruz	9	**1.20**	of		34	2	32	99	13	50	0.268	0.327	0.495
378	0.449	Aramis Ramirez	16	**1.20**	3b		37	2	30	107	2	49	0.285	0.345	0.501
379	0.449	Elston Howard	14	**1.12**	c	2	22	5	17	77	1	38	0.274	0.322	0.427
380	0.448	**George Kelly**	16	**1.08**	1b		35	5	7	79	5	56	**0.306**	**0.367**	**0.414**
381	0.448	Dean Palmer	14	**1.14**	3b		28	2	33	101	6	60	0.251	0.324	0.472
382	0.448	**Ozzie Smith**	19	**0.83**	ss	13	25	4	2	50	37	67	**0.262**	**0.337**	**0.328**
383	0.448	Justin Upton	7	**1.16**	of		32	6	25	80	16	70	0.275	0.356	0.473
384	0.447	Joe Pepitone	12	**1.17**	1b		18	4	25	84	5	35	0.258	0.301	0.432
385	0.447	**Billy Herman**	15	**1.06**	2b		41	7	4	71	6	62	**0.304**	**0.367**	**0.407**
386	0.446	Willie Davis	18	**1.05**	of	3	26	9	12	70	27	28	0.279	0.311	0.412
387	0.445	Davey Johnson	13	**1.09**	2b	3	27	2	15	69	4	63	0.261	0.340	0.404
388	0.445	Willie Randolph	18	**0.91**	2b		23	5	4	51	20	91	0.276	0.373	0.351
389	0.445	Brian Jordan	15	**1.08**	of		30	4	20	91	13	39	0.282	0.333	0.455
390	0.444	Jermaine Dye	14	**1.15**	of	1	33	2	30	99	4	55	0.274	0.338	0.488
391	0.442	**Deacon White**	15	**1.17**	3b		28	10	2	103		32	**0.312**	**0.346**	**0.393**
392	0.441	Bert Campaneris	19	**0.91**	ss		22	6	5	45	45	43	0.259	0.311	0.342
393	0.440	**Luis Aparicio**	18	**0.91**	ss	9	25	6	5	49	32	46	**0.262**	**0.311**	**0.343**
394	0.439	**Travis Jackson**	15	**1.09**	ss		28	8	13	91	7	40	**0.291**	**0.337**	**0.433**
395	0.439	Shane Victorino	10	**1.05**	of	4	30	9	14	64	30	49	0.277	0.342	0.432
396	0.438	Willie Mcgee	18	**0.99**	of	3	26	7	6	63	26	33	0.295	0.333	0.396
397	0.437	Jimmy Rollins	14	**1.02**	ss	4	38	9	17	69	35	57	0.269	0.327	0.426
398	0.437	Omar Visquel	24	**0.85**	ss	11	25	4	4	52	22	56	0.272	0.336	0.352
399	0.436	Tim Wallach	17	**1.06**	3b	3	32	3	19	82	4	48	0.257	0.316	0.416
400	0.436	Corey Hart	9	**1.18**	1b		36	6	26	87	14	46	0.276	0.334	0.491
401	0.435	Mike Napoli	8	**1.22**	c		28	1	32	88	5	73	0.259	0.357	0.502
402	0.435	Miguel Tejada	16	**1.09**	ss		35	2	23	97	6	41	0.285	0.336	0.456

403	0.435	Edwin Encarnacion	9	**1.16**	3b		33	1	29	91	7	65	0.265	0.348	0.479
404	0.435	Garret Anderson	17	**1.09**	of		38	3	21	99	6	31	0.293	0.324	0.461
405	0.434	Robinson Cano	9	**1.22**	2b	2	44	3	24	97	4	41	0.309	0.355	0.504
406	0.432	Ryan Zimmerman	9	**1.16**	3b		39	2	26	96	5	65	0.286	0.352	0.477
407	0.432	Wes Parker	9	**1.02**	1b	6	24	4	8	59	8	67	0.267	0.351	0.375
408	0.430	**Richard Ferrell**	18	**0.94**	c		28	4	2	63	2	80	0.281	0.378	0.363
409	0.428	**Fred Lindstom**	13	**1.12**	3b		34	9	12	88	9	38	0.311	0.351	0.449
410	0.428	Eric Hinske	12	**1.04**	3b		28	2	16	61	7	53	0.249	0.332	0.430
411	0.428	**Lloyd Waner**	18	**1.01**	of		23	10	2	49	5	34	0.316	0.353	0.393
412	0.427	**Tom McCarthy**	13	**1.05**	of		24	7	6	93		68	0.292	0.364	0.375
413	0.426	Dustin Pedroia	8	**1.10**	2b		46	2	16	79	19	67	0.302	0.370	0.454
414	0.425	Dave Conception	19	**0.93**	ss	5	25	3	7	62	21	48	0.267	0.322	0.357
415	0.425	Richard Hidalgo	9	**1.15**	of		35	3	28	92	8	59	0.269	0.345	0.490
416	0.425	**David Bancroft**	16	**0.94**	ss		27	7	3	50	12	70	0.279	0.355	0.358
417	0.425	Geoff Jenkins	11	**0.95**	of		31	11	5	98	42	60	0.295	0.362	0.405
418	0.424	Carlos Quentin	8	**1.19**	of		35	1	31	98	3	58	0.255	0.350	0.492
419	0.424	Lyle Overbay	13	**1.04**	1b		38	1	16	71	2	67	0.267	0.348	0.434
420	0.424	**Rabbit Maranville**	23	**0.90**	ss		23	11	2	54	18	51	0.258	0.318	0.340
421	0.423	Travis Fryman	13	**1.07**	3b	1	33	4	21	98	7	57	0.274	0.336	0.443
422	0.423	Bob Boone	19	**0.90**	c	7	22	2	8	59	3	47	0.254	0.315	0.346
423	0.422	Yadier Molina	10	**0.98**	c	6	30	0	12	73	5	44	0.284	0.339	0.404
424	0.421	Dan Uggla	8	**1.11**	2b		30	2	30	90	3	79	0.246	0.340	0.458
425	0.421	**Red Schoendist**	19	**1.01**	2b		31	6	6	57	7	44	0.289	0.337	0.387
426	0.420	BJ Surhoff	19	**1.00**	c		31	3	13	81	10	45	0.282	0.332	0.413
427	0.419	Maury Wills	14	**0.89**	ss	2	15	6	2	38	49	46	0.281	0.330	0.331
428	0.418	Vic Power	12	**1.06**	1b	7	29	5	13	66	4	28	0.284	0.315	0.411
429	0.418	Tommy Davis	18	**1.02**	of		22	3	12	85	11	31	0.294	0.329	0.405
430	0.418	Edgar Renteria	16	**0.95**	ss	2	33	2	11	69	22	54	0.286	0.343	0.398
431	0.415	Frank White	18	**1.00**	2b	8	28	4	11	62	12	29	0.255	0.293	0.383
432	0.415	**Joe Sewell**	14	**1.04**	ss		37	6	4	90	6	72	0.312	0.391	0.413
433	0.413	Bobby Thomson	15	**1.01**	of		24	7	24	93	3	51	0.270	0.332	0.462
434	0.413	Bret Boone	14	**1.05**	2b	4	33	3	23	93	9	50	0.266	0.325	0.442
435	0.411	**Bill Mazorowski**	17	**0.97**	2b	8	22	5	10	64	2	33	0.260	0.299	0.367
436	0.408	Chris Speier	19	**0.91**	ss		22	4	8	52	3	61	0.246	0.327	0.349
437	0.406	**John Ward**	17	**0.99**	ss		20	9	2	77		37	0.275	0.314	0.341

Rank	Abs plyr	Player	Yrs		Po	GG	2B	3B	HR	RBI	SB	BB	BA	OBP	SLG
438	0.405	**Ray Schalk**	18	0.85	c		18	5	1	55	16	59	0.253	0.340	0.316
439	0.405	Brian McCann	9	1.15	c		33	0	26	97	3	61	0.277	0.350	0.473
440	0.398	Orlando Cabrera	15	0.93	ss	2	37	3	10	70	18	42	0.272	0.317	0.390
441	0.397	**Phil Rizzuto**	13	0.93	ss		23	6	4	55	15	63	0.273	0.351	0.355
442	0.392	Zoilo Versalles	12	0.98	ss	2	27	7	11	55	11	37	0.242	0.290	0.367
443	0.391	Victor Martinez	11	1.12	c		39	0	19	102	0	63	0.303	0.369	0.464
444	0.389	Tony Pena	18	0.92	c	4	24	2	9	58	7	37	0.260	0.309	0.364
445	0.389	Sandy Alomar Jr	20	0.99	c	1	29	1	13	69	3	25	0.273	0.309	0.406
446	0.387	**Nellie Fox**	19	0.94	2b	3	24	8	2	54	5	49	0.288	0.348	0.363
447	0.383	Placido Polanco	16	0.95	2b	3	29	3	9	61	7	36	0.297	0.343	0.397
448	0.383	Mark Belanger	18	0.75	ss	8	14	3	2	31	13	46	0.228	0.300	0.280
449	0.382	Mark Grudzielanek	15	0.93	2b	1	35	3	8	58	12	33	0.289	0.332	0.393
450	0.381	Manny Trillo	17	0.90	2b	3	22	3	6	52	5	41	0.263	0.316	0.345
451	0.377	Larry Bowa	16	0.84	ss	2	19	7	1	38	23	34	0.260	0.300	0.320
452	0.364	Ichiro Suzuki	13	0.92	of	10	28	4	11	62	12	29	0.255	0.293	0.383
453	0.340	Bobby Richardson	12	0.87	2b	5	22	4	4	45	8	30	0.266	0.299	0.335

Commentary on players of interest

Babe Ruth is the greatest player of all time hands down. He is the "gold standard" by which to judge all other players. For the first 4 years of his career he pitched and is ranked among the top 50 pitchers of all time on an "absolute" basis as well. His "absolute slugging ratio" is 1.82 which means he was 82% better than the average player his entire 22 year career. In a prorated 162 game season he averaged 33 doubles, 9 triples, 46 home runs, 144 rbi's, 133 walks, .342 batting average and the all-time leading .690 slugging percentage. His performance in 1920 ranks as the greatest "absolute" single season ever. It was so good relative to the average player that he would have hit 141 home runs as opposed to Barry Bonds 73 home run year in which he would have only hit 43 home runs on a relative basis. In 1920 the league took 133 at bats to hit a home run on average. In 2001 the league was hitting a home run every 30 at bats on average. Hall of Fame.

Year	G	R	H	2B	3B	HR	RBI	SB	BB	SO	BA	SLG
1914	5	1	2	1	0	0	2	0	0	4	0.2	0.3
1915	42	16	29	10	1	4	21	0	9	23	0.315	0.576
1916	67	18	37	5	3	3	15	0	10	23	0.272	0.419
1917	52	14	40	6	3	2	12	0	12	18	0.325	0.472
1918	95	50	95	26	11	11	66	6	58	58	0.3	0.56
1919	130	103	139	34	12	29	114	7	101	58	0.322	0.66
1920	142	158	172	36	9	54	137	14	150	80	0.376	0.85
1921	152	177	204	44	16	59	171	17	145	81	0.378	0.85
1922	110	94	128	24	8	35	99	2	84	80	0.315	672
1923	152	151	205	45	13	41	131	17	170	93	0.393	0.76

Year												
1924	153	143	200	39	7	46	121	9	142	81	0.38	0.74
1925	98	61	104	12	2	25	66	2	59	68	0.29	0.543
1926	152	139	184	30	5	47	153	11	144	76	0.372	0.74
1927	151	158	192	29	8	60	164	7	137	89	0.356	0.77
1928	154	163	173	29	8	54	142	4	137	87	0.323	0.71
1929	135	121	172	26	6	46	154	5	72	60	0.345	0.7
1930	145	150	186	28	9	49	153	10	136	61	0.359	0.73
1931	145	149	199	31	3	46	163	5	128	51	0.373	0.7
1932	133	120	156	13	5	41	137	2	130	62	0.341	0.661
1933	137	97	138	21	3	34	103	4	114	90	0.301	0.582
1934	125	78	105	17	4	22	84	1	104	63	0.288	0.537
1935	28	13	13	0	0	6	12	0	20	24	0.181	0.431
22 Yrs	2503	2174	2873	506	136	714	2220	123	2062	1330	0.34	0.69
162 Game Avg.	162	141	186	33	9	46	144	8	133	86	0.34	0.69

Barry Bonds added 8 gold gloves to his hitting for power and average and stole 28 bases per year. He could do it all. He averaged 33 doubles, 41 home runs, 108 rbi's,139 walks, .298 batting average, and a .607 slugging percentage during a time that averaged a relatively high .411 slugging percentage over a 22 year career. His 2001 year in which he hit 73 home runs ranks as the 5th best single best year of all time by this book. He also had 7 MVP awards. **Not in the Hall of Fame.**

Ted Williams played ½ of his career during a relatively low period of baseball in the 1940's in which the average slugging percentage was only .367. He averaged 37doubles, 37 home runs, 130 rbi's, a staggering .344 batting average, and a .634 slugging percentage. His 1941 year in which he hit .406 ranks as the 4th greatest single season of all-time. Hall of Fame.

Willie Mays played ½ of his career during the low statistical decade for hitting in the 1960's. The average batting average during that decade was only .248 which is the lowest in the history of baseball possibly due to the fact that the mound was raised which aided pitchers. Again, with use of the calculations of "absolute adjusted slugging percentage" and "absolute fielding" we are able to determine that Mays is the 4th best overall player of all time. He also had 6 gold gloves and 2 MVP awards. Hall of Fame.

Ty Cobb is the 5th best all-around player despite playing ½ of his career during the dead ball era between 1910 and 1919 when the average slugging percentage in the league was only .337. Cobb had a .512 slugging percentage for his career while averaging 39 doubles, 16 triples, only 6 hr's, 103 rbi's, 48 stolen bases, and a whopping all-time best .366 batting average. It is a myth to think that all players had high batting averages back then. In the decade of 1910 to 1919 the average batting average was only .256 and later jumped up to .285 in the decade of the 1920's. His 1911 year in which he hit .420 ranks as the 6th best single season of all-time. Hall of Fame.

Jimmy Foxx is the first non-outfielder to top the all-time list at #6. He primarily played during 2 decades of the 1920's and 30's which had relatively high average slugging percentages of .396 and .399. His slugging percentage was .609 for his career. He averaged 32 doubles, 9 triples, 37 hr's, 134 rbi's, and an outstanding .325 batting average. Hall of Fame.

Honus Wagner is the highest ranked shortstop in baseball history and # 7 overall on our absolute ranking system. He had a 1.38 "absolute slugging percentage ratio" over the average player of his career. He had a .467 slugging percentage while the average was. .338. He averaged 37 doubles, 15 triples, only 6 hr's, 42 stolen bases, and a .328 batting average at a time when the average batting average was .255 of the early 1900's. Hall of Fame.

Lou Gehrig ranks slightly lower than the previous 7 due primarily to playing during relatively high statistical years of the 1920's and 1930's and also because he only played 17 years. The prior 7 all played 20 or more years except Ted Williams who played 19. Some weight has to be given for a player that sustains a high performance over a longer period of time. On a purely percentage basis Lou Gehrig ranks slightly higher than Jimmy Foxx if you don't take number of years into account. He averaged 40 doubles, 12 triples, 37 hr's, 149 rbi's, 113 walks, and an outstanding .340 batting average. His 1927 year in which he hit 47 home runs and batted .373 ranks as the 19th best single season of all-time. Hall of Fame.

Mickey Mantle ranks #9 again like Mays playing ½ of his career during the difficult hitting period of the 1960's. He averaged 23 doubles only, 36 home runs, 117 walks, and a .298 batting average over a 18 year career. He won 1 gold glove and 3 MVP's. Hall of Fame.

Rogers Hornsby is the highest ranked second baseman in history. During the 1920's and 30's he averaged 39 doubles, 12 triples, only 22 hr's, and a tremendous .354 batting average over a 23 year career. Hall of Fame.

Hank Aaron comes in at #11 again playing ½ of his career in the 1960's. He had only 1 MVP but a surprising to some 3 gold gloves. He averaged 31 doubles, 37 home runs, 113 rbi's, .305

batting average and a .555 slugging percentage over a 23 year career. Hall of Fame.

Tris Speaker averaged 46 doubles, 13 triples, only 7 hr's, 25 stolen bases, 80 walks, and a .345 batting average. He had a .500 slugging percentage at a time when the average was .357 over a 22 year career. Hall of Fame.

We have Stan Musial listed as a first baseman in our position rankings yet he played more games in the outfield early in his career. He averaged 39 doubles, 25 hr's, .331 batting average and a .559 slugging percentage. His 1948 year in which he had a slugging percentage of .702 ranks as the 28th best "absolute" single season of all time by this book. Hall of Fame.

Frank Robinson is one of the few Triple Crown winners and won MVP awards in both leagues in addition to one gold glove. He averaged 30 doubles, 34 hr's. He had a .537 career slugging percentage over a 21 year career at a time when the average was .376. Hall of Fame.

Mike Schmidt is the greatest third baseman of all-time without question and tied at #14 with Frank Robinson. He earned 10 gold gloves, won the MVP 3 times, and won the home run title 8 times. Hall of Fame.

Nap Lajoie is the 2nd best all-around second baseman of all time. He is also the best absolute fielding second baseman of all time slightly ahead of Bill Mazoroski. He hit .426 in 1901 and had a lifetime batting average of .338. Hall of Fame.

Billy Hamilton is the 16th best overall player of all time yet most people have never heard the name. You may remember that it was Hamilton's all-time stolen base record that Lou Brock beat and, then, subsequently surpassed by Ricky Henderson. Over 14 years he averaged 75 stolen bases (which is 17 more per year than Brock), 121 walks, and hit for .344. Hall of Fame.

Shoeless Joe Jackson was kicked out of baseball in 1920 after 13 years. Despite that he is ranked as the 17th best overall player in the history of baseball. He averaged 37 doubles, 20 triples, only 7 hr's in the dead ball era, 25 stolen bases, and had a .356 batting average in a time between 1910 and 1919 when the average batting average was only .256. **Not in the Hall of Fame.**

Mel Ott is the 4th best first baseman of all time and the 18th best overall player. In his 22 years he averaged 30 hr's with a .304 batting average. Hall of Fame.

Ed Delahanty average 46 doubles, 16 triples, 129 rbi's, and a .346 batting average over a 16 year career. Had a .505 slugging percentage at a time with a relatively high .411 league average of the 1890's. Hall of Fame.

Richie Allen is the 20th best player of all-time. He could either be ranked as the 2nd best third baseman where he started his career for 5 years or the 5th best first baseman of all time. In 15 years he averaged 30 doubles, 33 hr's, 12 stolen bases, 83 walks, .292 batting average and a .534 slugging percentage when the average slugging was a low .378 of the 1960's and 1970's. Strange that a guy by the name of Deacon White was just inducted into the hall of fame in 2013 who ranked extremely lower than Allen in hitting and slightly lower than him in fielding in an absolute ranking sense. **Not in the Hall of Fame.**

Hank Greenberg averaged 44 doubles, 38 hr's, 148 rbi's, 99 walks, .313 batting average, and a .605 slugging percentage over a 13 year career. Hall of Fame.

Joe DiMaggio averaged 36 doubles, 12 triples, 34 hr's, an extremely high 143 rbi's, .325 batting average, and a .579 slugging percentage over a 13 year career. Hall of Fame.

Joe Morgan is the 3rd ranked second baseman and 23rd ranked all-around player of all-time. He averaged 27 doubles, 16 hr's, 42 stolen bases, 114 walks, and a .271 batting average. Interesting that he did earn 5 gold gloves despite him being ranked slightly below average (.99) in "absolute fielding" in this book. The stats over his 22 years show that he had slightly less than average range (put-outs plus assist per nine innings) in relation to all other second basemen of his era. Hall of Fame.

Willie McCovey is the 24th best all-around player in the history of baseball and continues the trend of dominance by outfielders and first baseman so far on the list. He had a .567 slugging during a time when the league slugging averaged .376. Hall of Fame.

Dan Brouthers was a first baseman who played 19 years from 1879 to 1896. He had a .519 slugging during a time when the average was .351. This is another good example of why our theory of "absolute numbers" relative to their era is the only way to analyze the history of baseball. He only averaged 10 hr's per year yet led the league in homers twice. He also averaged 45 doubles, an amazing 20 triples, 125 rbi's, 81 walks, and a .341 batting average at a time that only averaged .252 in th 1880's and .278 of the livelier 1890's. His 1886 year in which he hit .370 ranks as the 17th greatest single season of all-time. Hall of Fame.

Willie Stargell is the 26th best overall player in history again playing in though years of the 1960's and 1970's. He averaged 33 hr's, 106 rbi's, and a .529 slugging percentage. Hall of Fame.

Mark McGuire played 16 years known for his hitting actually received one gold glove although his overall "absolute fielding rating was slightly below average for his career at .98 with 1.0 being average. He averaged a whopping 50 hr's, 122 rbi's, 114 walks, and a .588 slugging percentage at a time that averaged .407 slugging. **Not in the Hall of Fame.**

Ricky Henderson is the 28th greatest all-around player of all time over a 25 year career. He averaged 27 doubles, 16 home runs, 74 walks, 115 walks with a .279 batting average. He gets credit for his lengthy career and his .401 on base percentage along with being the all-time leader in stolen bases. Also had one gold glove and a 1.05 absolute fielding ranking (5% better than the average outfielder). Hall of Fame.

Ken Griffey Jr is the 29th greatest of all time while playing 22 years in a career that ended in 2010. He had ten gold a 1.10 absolute fielding ranking along with averaging 32 doubles, 38 home runs, 111 rbi"s, 80 walks and a .538 slugging percentage during a time with a .414 average slugging percentage. **Not in the Hall of Fame.**

Johnny Mize averaged 32 doubles, 31 home runs, 111 rbi's, 80 walks, and had .538 slugging percentage relative to .384 slugging in his era of 15 years from 1936 to 1953 missing 3 years due to World War II. Hall of Fame.

Roger Conner is not a well-known name in baseball history yet he is the 31st best player of all time. He played 18 years at first base while averaging 36 doubles, 19 triples, only 11 home runs, 107 rbi's, 81 walks, .316 batting average and a .486 slugging percentage at a time with a relatively low slugging percentage of .354. Therefore, his "absolute slugging ratio" was 1.37 which means that he was 37% better than the average player of his time. Hall of Fame.

Hugh Duffy hit an all-time record .440 in 1894 and had a lifetime batting average of .326 while playing 17 years in the outfield. He had an "absolute slugging" ratio of 1.26 which means that he was 26% better than players in his era. He averaged 30 doubles, 11 triples, 10 hr's, 121 rbi's, and 54 stolen bases. Hall of Fame.

Eddie Collins is the 4th ranked second baseman of all-time. He had a lifetime batting average of .333. His "absolute fielding" ratio was 1.02 which means that he was only slightly better than the average second baseman in the field during his era. Hall of Fame.

Jim Thome played 22 years end in 2012 and had a 1.33 "absolute slugging percentage" ratio. His slugging was .554 at a time when the league average was .416. He averaged 29 doubles, 39 home runs, 108 rbi's, 111 walks, and a .276 batting average at first base. His "absolute fielding" ratio was .99 so he was not a liability in the field. **Not in the Hall of Fame.**

Johnny Bench is the best catcher in the history of baseball and the 35th best player of all time. He averaged 29 doubles, 29 home runs, 103 rbi's, and had a .467 slugging percentage during a time when the average was .376. Interesting that he had 10 gold gloves yet he is only ranked as the 8th best fielding catcher in this book with a 1.23 "absolute fielding" ratio over his 17 year career. Hall of Fame.

Reggie Jackson is the 38th best player of all-time over a 21 year career. He averaged 32 homeruns, 98 rbi's and a .490 slugging percentage. Hall of Fame.

Albert Pujols is the 39th best player of all time and is the best "absolute fielding" first baseman reviewed in this book of all time with a 1.11 ratio and 2 gold gloves. He averaged 43 doubles, 41 home runs, 124 rbi's, 88 walks, .321 batting average, and a .599 slugging percentage over a period that has averaged .415 slugging percentage. He will be moving up the list of all-time greats as his career progresses. He has only played 13 seasons as of the writing of this book. For purpose of the all-time great ranking I ranked him 5% lower than players that have played an average of 15 to 19 years and 10% lower than players that have played 20 or more years. If we don't downgrade him for having a short career to date he lands in the top 15 players of all-time. **Not in the Hall of Fame yet.**

Alex Rodriguez is the 40th ranked player of all-time and the second ranked shortstop of all-time over 20 years. He has averaged 33 doubles, 41 home runs, 124 rbi's, 78 walks, .299 batting average and a .558 slugging percentage at a time when the average is .419 slugging percentage. He also has 2 gold gloves and a 1.01 "absolute fielding" ratio in this book and had 3 MVP's. **Not in the Hall of Fame.**

Harmon Killebrew averaged 38 home runs, 105 rbi's, 104 walks, and a .509 slugging percentage over a 22 year career. He is ranked as the 3rd best third baseman of all-time. Hall of Fame.

Larry Walker is the 46th best player of all-time over a 17 year career ending in 2005. He averaged 38 doubles, 31 home runs, 107 rbi's, 19 stolen bases, 74 walks, plus an amazing .313 batting average and .565 slugging percentage at a time when the average slugging percentage was .412. His "absolute slugging ratio" was 1.37 therefore which means that he was a 37% better hitter than the average player in his era. He is a one-time MVP and 7 time gold glove award winner. Although he had a fantastic arm interesting that his "absolute fielding" ratio only came in at .93 due to poor range. **Not in the Hall of Fame.**

Cesar Cedeno is believe it or not the 49th best player of all-time according to this book. Over 17 years he averaged 35 doubles, 16 home runs, 44 stolen bases, and had a .443 slugging percentage at a time when the average was .381. He had 5 gold gloves and a 1.16 "absolute fielding" ratio. I have his "absolute player" ranking ranked higher than 26 current members of the hall of fame in the outfield as of this date. **Not in the Hall of Fame.**

Darrel Evans again believe it or not is the 51st best "absolute player" of all-time and the 5th best third baseman according to this book. He averaged 20 doubles, 25 home runs, 82 rbi's, 97 walks, and a .431 slugging percentage when the average was .381. Although he only hit 248 for his career he had a .366 on base percentage. I have him as the best "absolute fielding" third baseman of all time with an "absolute fielding" ratio of 1.11 which was higher than even Mike Schmidt at 1.10 despite Schmidt having 10 gold gloves. **Not in the Hall of Fame.**

Tim Raines is the 53rd best "absolute player" of all time. Over 23 years he averaged 28 doubles, 7 triples, 52 stolen bases, 86 walks, and a .294 batting average. Again, I have him ranked higher than 24 current members of the hall of fame in the outfield at this time. **Not in the Hall of Fame.**

Reggie Smith is the 57th best player of all-time over a 17 year career. He averaged 30 doubles, 26 home runs, 89 rbi's, 11 stolen bases, 73 walks, .287 batting average and a .489 slugging percentage at a time when the average was .373. His "absolute slugging" ratio was 1.31 therefore or 31% better than the average player in his era. He had one gold glove and an "absolute fielding" ratio of 1.08. **Not in the Hall of Fame.**

Roy Campanella is the 60th best player of all-time and the 2nd best catcher despite playing only 10 years. He is one example to prove that you do not necessarily have to have a long career to get into the hall of fame yet it is rare. He averaged 24 doubles, 32 home runs, 114 rbi's, 71 walks, 2.76 batting average, and a .500 slugging percentage. Defensively I have him as the 4th best defensive catcher of all-time by throwing out 57% of runners. Hall of Fame.

Joe Torre was inducted into the hall of fame as a manager yet is the 61st best player and 3rd best catcher who threw out 41% of all runners. Over 18 years he averaged 25 doubles, 18 home runs, 87 rbi's, .297 batting average, and a .452 slugging percentage at a time when .352 was the average. He had one gold glove and one MVP. Hall of Fame.

Jeff Bagwell is the 62nd best player of all-time over a 15 year career. He averaged 37 doubles, 34 home runs, 115 rbi's, 15 stolen bases, 106 walks, .297 batting average and .540 slugging at a time that averaged .417 slugging. He has one gold glove and one MVP. In his outstanding year in 1994 he hit .366 and is ranked as the 50th best "absolute" single season of all-time by this book. **Not in the Hall of Fame.**

Dwight Evans is the 63rd best player of all-time. Over 20 years he averaged 37 doubles, 24 home runs, 86 rbi's, 86 walks, .370 on base percentage, and a .470 slugging percentage during an era that averaged 383. Therefore, his "absolute slugging" ratio was 1.23. Despite having 8 gold gloves and a cannon for an arm he came in at only .93 for an "absolute fielding" ratio due to lack of range (put-outs plus assist per nine innings) relative the average outfielder of his era. **Not in the Hall of Fame.**

Fred Lynn is the 64th best player of all-time who had 4 gold gloves and one MVP. He averaged 32 doubles, 25 home runs, 91 rbi's, 71 walks, .360 on base percentage and a .484 slugging percentage at a time with a .385 average **Not in the Hall of Fame.**

Ron Santo is considered the 65th best player of all-time and the 7th best third baseman. In his 15 years he averaged 26 doubles, 25 home runs, 96 rbi's, 80 walks, .277 batting average, .362 on base percentage, and a .464 slugging percentage at a time that averaged .373. He was therefore, 24% better than the average hitter in the league. He had 5 gold gloves and is ranked as the 5th best fielding 3rd baseman of all-time with an "absolute fielding" ratio of 1.07 since he had both above average range and fielding percentage. His best single season was in 1964 when he hit 33 doubles, an amazing 13 triples, 30 home runs, 114 rbi's, 86 walks, .313 batting average, .398 on base percentage, and a .564 slugging percentage in a year that had only a .378 average slugging percentage. Hall of Fame.

Eric Davis is the 66th best player of all time. On a pro rata 162 games played (All numbers are adjusted as if each played a full 162 games for comparison purposes) over 17 years he averaged 24 doubles, 28 home runs, 93 rbi's, 35 stolen bases, 74 walks,

.359 on base percentage and a .482 slugging percentage. He also had 3 gold gloves and an "absolute fielding" ratio of 1.08. In 1997 he was diagnosed with colon cancer yet still went on to have 3 of his 6 remaining seasons with a slugging percentage over .500. This book has him ranked over 20 current outfielders currently in the hall of fame. **Not in the Hall of Fame.**

Bobby Bonds is the 67th best player of all-time. Over 14 seasons he had 26 doubles, 29 home runs, 90 rbi's, 40 stolen bases, 80 walks, .353 on base percentage, and a .471 slugging percentage. If he would have continued on with his career this book would have ranked him in the top 40 players of all time. He had 3 gloves despite having a 1.0 "absolute fielding" ratio by this book. He is also ranked above 20 current hall of famers. **Not in the Hall of Fame.**

Ken Williams is an unknown player that excelled during the 1920's. Over 14 years averaged 33 doubles, 9 triples, 23 home runs, 106 rbi's, 18 stolen bases, .319 batting average, .393 on base percentage, and a .530 slugging percentage during his career that averaged .379**. Not in the Hall of Fame.**

Norm Cash is the 69th best player of all time and the 18th best first baseman. Over 17 years he averaged 29 home runs, 86 rbi's, 81 walks, .374 on base percentage, and a .488 slugging percentage during an era that averaged .375. In 1961 he hit 41 home runs, 132 rbi's, 124 walks, .361 batting average, .487 on base percentage, and .662 slugging percentage in a year that averaged .388 slugging. Possibly that year got overshadowed by Maris and Mantle's chase of Ruth's home run record of 60. **Not in the Hall of Fame.**

Jim Wynn is the 70th best player of all time. Over 15 years he averaged 24 doubles, 25 home runs, 81 rbi's, 19 stolen bases, 103 walks, .366 on base percentage, and a .436 slugging at a time that averaged .370**. Not in the Hall of Fame.**

Frank Howard, over 16 years, averaged 21 doubles, 33 home runs, 96 rbi's, 67 walks, .352 on base percentage, and a .499 slugging percentage at time that averaged .375. Therefore, his "absolute slugging" ratio was 1.33. **Not in the Hall of Fame.**

Lance Berkman has played 15 years as of the date of this book. He has averaged 36 doubles, 32 home runs, 106 rbi's, 104 walks, and a .406 on base percentage. **Active player currently not in the Hall of Fame.**

Ralph Kiner led the league in homers seven straight years over a 10 year career. He is another example and proof that you don't necessarily have to have a long career to get into the hall of fame. He averaged 24 doubles, 41 home runs, 112 rbi's, an amazing 111 walks, .398 on base percentage, and a .548 slugging at a time with an average slugging of .384. He, therefore, had an "absolute slugging" ratio of 1.43 which means that he was a 43% better hitter than the average player during his career. Hall of Fame.

Jim Edmonds is the 76th best player of all time and 7th best defensive outfielder in the history of the game. Over 17 years he had 8 gold gloves, and averaged 35 doubles, 32 home runs, 97 rbi's, 80 walks, .284 batting average, .376 on base percentage, and a .527 slugging percentage during a career that averaged a high .422 slugging percentage. This book has him ranked higher than 19 outfielders currently in the hall of fame. **Not in the Hall of Fame.**

Raphael Palmeiro is the 77th best player of all time and a high ranking defensive player who had 3 gold gloves. Over a 20 year career he averaged 33 doubles, 33 home runs, 105 rbi's, 77 walks, 2.88 batting average .371 on base percentage, and a .515 slugging during an era that averaged a .410 slugging percentage. This gives him an "absolute slugging" percentage ratio of 1.26. Compare that to hall of famer unknown first baseman George Kelly for example who played 16 years, is ranked 380th as the all-time best player and only had an "absolute slugging" ratio of 1.08. So Palmeiro was a 26% better hitter than the average player of his era and had 3 gold gloves over 20 years compared to a George Kelly who was only a 8% better hitter than his peers. Therefore, once again, you can see what a joke the hall of fame has become. **Not in the Hall of Fame.**

Jack Clark is the 78th best player over 18 years. He averaged 27 doubles, 28 home runs, 96 rbi's, 103 walks, .379 on base percentage, and a .476 slugging while the league average was .385. We have him ranked higher than 7 first baseman currently in the hall of fame. **Not in the Hall of Fame.**

Dave Winfield is the 79th best player of all time. He averaged 29 doubles, 25 home runs, 100 rbi's, .283 batting averaged, and a .475 slugging percentage over 22 years. His "absolute slugging" ratio was 1.22. He also had 7 gold gloves despite our having his "absolute fielding" ratio at .90 due to poor range? Hall of Fame.

David Oritz has currently played 17 years at first base. He has averaged an amazing 43 doubles, 35 home runs, 118 rbi's, 89 walks, .381 on base percentage, and a .549 slugging percentage during an era that averaged .411 slugging percentage. That puts him at 1.31 ratio. **Active player currently not in the Hall of Fame.**

Orlando Cepeda is the 83rd best all time player. Over 17 years he averaged 32 doubles, 29 home runs, 104 rbi's, and a .499 slugging percentage during a time that averaged .375. That puts his "absolute slugging" ratio at 1.33. We have him ranked higher than 7 current first baseman in the hall of fame. **Not in the Hall of Fame.**

Manny Ramirez is the 86th best player of all time. Over 19 years he has averaged 38 doubles, 39 home runs, 129 rbi's, 94 walks, and a .534 slugging percentage during an era that averaged .420 slugging percentage. That puts his ratio at 1.39 plus when you add in all the walks he gets it puts his "absolute adjusted slugging percentage" and player ranking even higher. In the year 2000 for example he hit 38 home runs, .351 batting average, and a .697 slugging. **Active player not in the Hall of Fame.**

Sammy Sosa is the 87th best player of all time. Over 18 years he averaged 26 doubles, 42 home runs, 115 rbi's, 16 stolen bases, and a .534 slugging percentage while the average was .413. His year in 2001 when he hit 64 home runs we have ranked as the 82nd best single season of all time on a relative basis. **Not in the Hall of Fame.**

Ryne Sandberg is the 89th best player of all time and the 5th best second baseman. Over 16 years he averaged 30 doubles, 21 home runs, only 79 rbi's, 26 stolen bases, and a .452 slugging percentage during an era that averaged .394. That put his "absolute slugging" ratio at 1.15 relative to all other players. He had 8 gold gloves. **Hall of Fame.**

Todd Helton is the 90th best player of all time. Currently in his 17th season he has averaged 43 doubles, 27 home runs, 101 rbi's, 96 walks, .316 batting average, an amazing .414 on base percentage, and a .534 slugging percentage during an era of .418. He also had 3 gold gloves. How are they going to keep him out of the hall of fame. Hitter friendly park? **Active player not in the Hall of Fame.**

Gary Sheffield is the 92nd best player whose career ended in 2009. Over 22 years he averaged 29 doubles, 32 home runs, 105 rbi's, 16 stolen bases, 93 walks, .292 batting average, .393 on base percentage, and .514 slugging percentage during an era that averaged .413. That put his "absolute slugging" ratio at 1.24 but his overall player ranking was increase by 5% due to playing over 20 years, and his high level of walks took his "absolute player" ranking therefore to .536 which put him at the 92nd spot all time. We have him ranked higher than 16 current outfielders currently in the hall of fame. **Currently not in the hall of fame.**

Roberto Clemente is the 93rd best player of all time. Many people would say that he should be towards the top of the all-time list yet his lack of power and walks keep him relatively low. Also, despite the fact that he had 12 gold gloves it isn't enough to tip the scales that much. He only averaged 2.18 put-outs and assists per 9 innings for his career. That is consistent with what an outfielder gets and when you consider that there are 27 outs in a game it shows that it is not that significant. Over 18 years he averaged 29 doubles, 11 triples, 16 home runs, 87 rbi's, 6 stolen bases, 41 walks, .317 batting average, and only a .359 on base percentage and .475 slugging during an era that averaged .374. That puts his "absolute slugging" ratio at a relatively modest 1.27. **Hall of Fame.**

Vladimir Guerrero is the 98th best player of all time. During his 16 years he averaged 36 doubles, 34 home runs, 113 rbi's, 14 stolen bases, only 56 walks, .318 batting average, .395 on base percentage and a .545 slugging during a time that averaged .421 slugging. Therefore, his "absolute slugging" ratio was 1.31. He was somewhat of a liability in the field with an "absolute fielding" ratio of .94. Yet, he is still better than 13 current members of the hall of fame that played outfield. **Not in the Hall of Fame.**

Hack Wilson is the 99th best player over a short career of 12 years. Another example which proves that you don't not need a lengthy career to get inducted. He averaged 32 doubles, 29 home runs, 128 rbi's, 81 walks, .307 batting average, 395 on base percentage, and .545 slugging during a time that averaged .399. In 1930 he had 56 homers and 191 rbi's which ranks surprisingly at only the 97th best single season of all time on a relative basis. 1930 was a year in which the average slugging percentage was an extremely high .434. Hall of Fame.

Eddie Murray is the 100th best player of all time who had 3 gold gloves and a .545 slugging percentage over a 21 year career. Hall of Fame.

Gil Hodges is the 101st best player in baseball history. He had 3 gold gloves and a .487 slugging percentage over 18 years. He is ranked higher than 4 first baseman currently in the hall of fame. **Not in the Fall of Fame.**

Darryl Strawberry is 103rd best player over 17 years. He averaged 26 doubles, 34 home runs, 102 rbi's, 23 stolen bases, 84 walks, .357 on base percentage, and a .505 slugging during a time that averaged .401 slugging. This book has him ranked higher than 13 outfielders inducted. **Not in the Hall of Fame.**

Edgar Martinez is the 104th best of all time with a .515 slugging over 18 years mostly at DH and 3 years at third base. **Not in the Hall of Fame.**

Andre Dawson is the 105th best. He had 8 gold gloves over a 21 year career. He averaged 31 doubles, 27 home runs, 98 rbi's, 19 stolen bases, only an amazingly low 36 walks, .279 batting average, a low .329 on base percentage, and a .482 slugging. He only had a modest 1.23 "absolute slugging" ratio. His low walk total kept him relatively high on the all-time list. Hall of Fame.

Kirk Gibson is the 106th best. He averaged 26 doubles, 25 hr's, 86 rbi's, 28 stolen bases, 71 walks, and a .453 slugging. He is ranked higher than 12 current outfielders inducted. **Not in the Hall of Fame.**

Juan Gonzalez is at 107. Over 17 years he averaged 37 doubles, 42 home runs, 135 rbi's, and a .561 slugging at time with an average slugging of .412 therefore a ratio of 1.36. He is also ranked higher than 12 outfielders inducted. You can see that either some inductees need to be removed from the hall of fame or these better players need to be enshrined. It makes no sense at all**. Not in the Hall of Fame.**

Sam Thompson is at 108. He played outfield for 15 years and averaged 39 doubles, 18 triples, 14 home runs, an amazing 150 rbi's, .331 batting average and a .505 slugging during a time that averaged .359. In 1894 he hit .415 which is ranked as the 84th best single season of all time. Hall of Fame.

Tony Perez is at 109. He is someone that benefited from a lengthy career of 23 years. He averaged 29 doubles, 22 home runs, 96 rbi's, 54 walks, .279 batting average, .341 on base percentage and a .463 slugging at time when the average was .377. Therefore, his "absolute slugging" ratio was only 1.24. Amazingly he did hit .357 in 1969. Hall of Fame.

Boog Powell is at 110. Over 17 years he averaged 21 doubles, 27 home runs, 94 rbi's, 79 walks, .361 on base percentage, and a .462 slugging during a time that averaged .373. That put his ratio at 1.24 plus gets a boost by a high number of walks. We have him ranked higher than 4 current inductees (Sisler, Bottemley, Bill Terry, and George Kelly). Kelly in particular is huge problem for the hall of fame at first base. He was inducted for some unknown reason in 1973 and is currently ranked as the lowly 380th best player of all time by this book. He opens the door for countless numbers of other deserving first baseman to be inducted. I almost think that the hall of fame has no other option but to rescind his nomination as crazy as that sounds. **Not in the Hall of Fame.**

Paul Molitar is at 112 and inducted as a third baseman despite only playing 792 games there. He is another player that benefited from a long career of 21 years. He averaged 37 doubles, 14 home runs, 79 rbi's, 30 stolen bases, 66 walks, .306 batting average, .369 on base %, and a .448 slugging during a time that averaged .395. Therefore, his "absolute slugging" ratio was a low 1.13. That means that he was only 13% better than the average player during his career. At third base we have him at 1.03 for his "absolute fielding" so he was only slightly better than average. Hall of Fame.

Miguel Cabrera is at 113 over his 11 year career so far. He will only rise over time. So far he has averaged 40 doubles, 36 home runs, 123 rbi's, 78 walks, .321 batting average, .399 on base percentage, and a .568 slugging at a time of .414 average giving him a 1.37 ratio. **Active player not in the Hall of Fame.**

Tip O'neil is the 114th best player of all time despite only playing 10 years. His 1887 year ranks as the 15th best single season when he hit .435. and for the triple crown. **Not in the Hall of Fame.**

Harry Heilmann is at 115. He averaged 41 doubles, 11 triples, 14 hr's, 116 rbi's, .342 batting average, .410 on base percentage, and a .520 slugging percentage during an era with a .380 average. That put his ratio at 1.37. Hall of Fame.

Fred McGriff is the 116th best player of all time. Over his 19 years he averaged 29 doubles, 32 home runs, 102 rbi's, 86 walks, .284 batting average, .362 on base percentage, and a .505 slugging at a time that averaged .410 producing a 1.24 ratio. He is ranked ahead of 3 other first baseman inducted including again George Kelly. **Not in the Hall of Fame.**

Joe Medwick is the 117th ranked. He averaged 44 doubles, 17 home runs, 113 rbi's, only 36 walks, .324 batting average, and a .505 slugging. Hall of Fame.

Bobby Abreu is the 118th player. Over his 17 seasons he averaged 39 doubles, 20 home runs, 93 rbi's, 28 stolen bases, 100 walks, .292 batting average, .396 on base percentage, and a .477 at a time when the average slugging was .420 thus producing a low ratio of 1.14. The walks and stolen bases however raise him up to an "absolute adjusted slugging percentage" of .525. He also had one gold glove and hit over

.330 twice. Currently ranked ahead of 8 lower inductees. **Not in the Hall of Fame.**

Keith Hernandez is the 122ⁿᵈ player of all time. He had 13 gold gloves and a .436 slugging. **Not in the Hall of Fame.**

Greg Luzinski is at 122. Over 15 years he averaged 31 doubles, 27 home runs, 100 rbi's, 75 walks, and a .478 slugging during an era of .379 giving a ratio of 1.26. He ends up with an "absolute adjusted slugging" of .524 after taking walks into account. **Not in the Hall of Fame.**

Ernie Banks is the 124ᵗʰ best player of all time. Over his 19 years he averaged 26 doubles, 33 home runs, 105 rbi's, only 3 stolen bases, only 49 walks, .274 batting averaged, only a .330 on base percentage and a .500 slugging percentage at a time when the average was .381 giving him a 1.31 ratio. However, due to his low stolen base and walks totals he received little benefit when looking at the absolute adjusted slugging percentage. He had one gold glove. Hall of Fame.

Home Run Baker is the 125ᵗʰ best player. Over his 13 seasons at third base he averaged 10 home runs, 3.07 batting average, and a .442 slugging while the average was .343 giving him a ratio of 1.29. Hall of Fame.

Pedro Guerrero is the 127ᵗʰ best player of all time. Over 15 years he averaged 28 doubles, 23 home runs, 95 rbi's, 64 walks, .300 batting average, .370 on base percentage, and a .480 slugging. **Not in the Hall of Fame.**

Carlos Delgado is the 129ᵗʰ best player of all time. Over 17 years he averaged 38 doubles, 38 home runs, 120 rbi's, 88 walks, .383

on base percentage, and a .546 slugging during a time with .423 as the average. This leaves him with slugging ratio of 1.29 plus the benefit of a high walk total. **Not in the Hall of Fame.**

Craig Nettles played 22 years at third base and received 2 gold gloves with a .421 slugging**. Not in the Hall of Fame.**

Rick Monday is the 131st. Over a 19 year career he had a .443. slugging at a time with a .375 average slugging giving him a 1.18 ratio plus the benefit of 75 walks per year puts his "absolute adjusted slugging" at .522. **Not in the Hall of Fame.**

Lefty O'doul is 132nd. Over 11 years he averaged 29 doubles, 19 home runs, 91 rbi's, 56 walks, .349 batting average, .413 on base percentage, and a .532 slugging at a time with a .393 giving him a ratio of 1.35 prior to adding in a relatively low walk total. Another example of a player that was inducted with only 11 years played. Hall of Fame.

Dale Murphy is the 133rd best player. Over 18 years earned 5 gold gloves and had a .469 slugging and a ratio of 1.21. **Not in the Hall of Fame.**

Ellis Burkes is at 134. Over 18 years averaged 33 doubles, 29 home runs, 98 rbi's, 15 stolen bases, and a .510 slugging with a 1.24 ration. Also earned one gold glove**. Not in the Hall of Fame.**

Rico Carty is at 135. Over 15 years he had a .464 slugging and a ratio of 1.25 **Not in the Hall of Fame.**

Billy Williams at 137. Played 18 years with a 1.32 ratio. Hall of Fame.

Tony Oliva at 140. Played 15 years with a 1.29 ratio**. Not in the Hall of Fame.**

Carlton Fisk at 141. Played 24 years with a ratio of 1.20. Had one gold glove. Hall of Fame.

George Sisler is at 142. Played 15 years with a ratio of 1.24. Hit .407 and .420 in 1920 and 1922. Hall of Fame.

Cy Williams is at 145. Had a ratio of 1.26 over 19 years. **Not in the Hall of Fame.**

Brian Giles is at 144. Over 15 years he averaged 36 doubles, 25 home runs, 95 rbi's, 104 walks, .291 batting average, and a .502 slugging and 1.19 ratio before adding in walks. **Not in the Hall of Fame.**

Jason Giambi at 151. 19 seasons with a ratio of 1.24. **Active player not in the Hall of Fame.**

George Foster at 152. Over 18 years he averaged 25 doubles, 29 home runs, 102 rbi's, and a ratio of 1.26. **Not in the Hall of Fame.**

Ivan Rodriguez at 154. Had 13 gold gloves at cather and a ratio of 1.11. **Not in the Hall of Fame.**

Bobby Grich at 155. Played 17 seasons with a ratio of 1.11 and 4 gold gloves. **Not in the Hall of Fame.**

Dave Kingman at 156. Over 16 seasons he averaged 37 home runs, 101 rbi's, with a ratio of 1.26**. Not in the Hall of Fame.**

Ted Kluszewski at 157. Over 15 years had a ratio of .128**. Not in the Hall of Fame.**

Mark Teixeira at 158.

Rocky Colivito at 159 with a ratio of 1.28 over 14 years. Averaged 33 home runs. **Not in the Hall of Fame.**

Jackie Robinson is at 160. Over 10 years had a ratio of 1.22. Here is another example of a guy that opens the door for many other players to be inducted given his short career. Hall of Fame.

Chipper Jones at 161. Over 19 years had a ratio of 1.26**. Not in the Hall of Fame.**

Carlos Beltran at 162.

Rusty Staub at 164. Over 23 years had a ratio of 1.15. **Not in the Hall of Fame.**

Oscar Gamble at 165

Bobby Murcer at 166.

Ryan Braun at 167.

Tony Gwynn at 169 with a ratio of 1.14 over 20 years. Hall of Fame.

Andruw Jones at 170 with 10 gold gloves and a ratio of 1.16 over 17 years. **Not in the Hall of Fame.**

Jose Canseco at 172. Played 17 years with a ratio of .127. **Not if the Hall of Fame.**

Ken Singleton at 175. **Not in the Hall of Fame.**

Yogi Berra at 190. Hall of Fame.

Cal Ripken at 193. Hall of Fame.

Rod Carew at 194. Had a ratio of 1.114 over 19 years. Hall of Fame.

Ryan Klesko at 195.

Ken Boyer at 198.

Harold Baines at 200. Played 22 years.

Javy Lopez at 203.

Alfonso Soriano at 208.

Dave Parker at 209. Had a ratio of 1.23 over 19 years**. Not in the Hall of Fame.**

Matt Williams at 212.

Lou Brock at 213. Hall of Fame.

Ted Simmons at 221.

Robin Yount at 224. Hall of Fame.

Ron Cey at 226.

Jim Rice at 229. Hall of Fame.

Pete Rose at 230. Had a ratio of only 1.09 over 24 years**. Not in the Hall of Fame.**

Bill Terry at 276. Hall of Fame.

Wade Boggs at 282. Had a ratio of 1.11 over 18 years. Hall of Fame.

Don Mattingly at 288. Had 9 gold gloves and a 1.20 ratio over 14 years. **Not in the Hall of Fame.**

Brooks Robinson at 294. Hall of Fame.

Harry Hooper at 298. Had a 1.08 ratio over 17 years in the outfield. Barely an above average player. Hall of Fame.

George Kelly at 380. Had a ratio of 1.08 over 16 years at first base. Should not be in the hall of fame but is. Hall of Fame.

Ozzie Smith at 382. 13 gold gloves. Hall of Fame.

Bill Herman at 385. Over 15 years had a ratio of 1.06 at second base. Barely an above average player. How do some of these guys ever even get considered. Hall of Fame.

Deacon White at 391. Had a ratio of 1.17 over 15 years at third base. Only got 32 walks per year. Was just inducted in 2013. Hall of Fame.

Lloyd Waner is a t 411. He averaged an "absolute slugging" ratio of 1.01 over 18 years in the outfield. He is a prime example of someone who opens that door to the hall of fame for almost anyone that has been a better than average player. Since the likes of him have been inducted it makes the hall of fame a complete joke. All of these marginal players have to have their inductions rescinded otherwise you have to honor most of the players in this book. The discrimination that has been exercised over these many other valid candidates is beyond belief compared to these marginal members. Hall of Fame.

Absolute Pitcher Rankings

Includes weight given for longevity and adjusted relative 3.75 all time average

Abs Adj ERA	Pitcher		ERA	Lg ERA	W	L	SO	BB	SHO	SV
2.35	Walter Johnson+ (21)	R	2.17	328	19	13	163	63	5	2
2.53	Grover Alexander (20)	R	2.56	360	20	11	115	50	5	2
2.55	Ed Walsh+ (14)	R	1.82	280	18	12	158	56	5	3
2.63	Roger Clemens (24)	R	3.13	424	17	9	224	76	2	0
2.63	Greg Maddux+ (23)	R	3.16	428	16	10	154	46	2	0
2.68	Cy Young+ (22)	R	2.63	349	20	12	111	48	3	1
2.69	Whitey Ford+ (16)	L	2.75	382	17	8	142	79	3	1
2.70	Pedro Martinez (18)	R	2.93	406	17	8	242	58	1	0
2.70	Carl Hubbell+ (16)	L	2.98	413	18	11	118	51	3	2
2.71	Christy Mathewson+ (17)	R	2.13	295	21	11	143	49	5	2
2.71	Smoky Joe Wood (14)	R	2.03	295	21	10	176	75	5	2
2.72	Lefty Grove+ (17)	L	3.06	421	19	9	144	75	2	3
2.73	Randy Johnson (22)	L	3.29	430	17	9	271	83	2	0
2.77	Tom Seaver+ (20)	R	2.86	368	16	11	190	73	3	0
2.77	Rube Waddell+ (13)	L	2.16	307	18	13	211	73	5	0
2.82	Dizzy Dean (12)	R	3.02	421	19	10	145	56	3	4
2.85	Warren Spahn+ (21)	L	3.09	386	17	12	124	69	3	1
2.85	Mordecai Brown+ (14)	R	2.06	284	20	11	115	56	5	4
2.86	Addie Joss	R	1.89	273	20	12	115	45	6	1
2.87	Sandy Koufax+ (12)	L	2.76	379	16	8	229	78	4	1
2.87	Nolan Ryan+ (27)	R	3.19	375	14	13	246	120	3	0
2.89	Kevin Brown (19)	R	3.28	425	15	10	169	64	1	0
2.89	Monte Ward+ (17)	R	2.10	272	20	13	113	31	3	0

2.92	**Jim Palmer+ (19)**	R	2.86	367	17	10	139	83	3	0
2.92	**Kid Nichols+ (15)**	R	2.96	379	21	12	108	73	3	1
2.94	**Tom Glavine (22)**	L	3.54	429	15	10	130	75	1	0
2.95	**Hal Newhouser+ (17)**	L	3.06	388	16	12	142	99	3	2
3.02	**Juan Marichal+ (16)**	R	2.89	359	18	10	169	52	4	0
3.03	**Bob Gibson+ (17)**	R	2.92	361	17	12	210	90	4	0
3.03	**Bob Feller+ (18)**	R	3.26	403	17	10	167	114	3	1
3.04	**Gaylord Perry+ (22)**	R	3.11	364	15	12	164	64	2	1
3.05	Jack Pfiester (8)	L	2.02	274	17	11	123	72	4	0
3.05	**Eddie Plank+ (17)**	L	2.35	289	19	11	133	63	4	1
3.08	**Tim Keefe+ (14)**	R	2.63	336	19	13	146	70	2	0
3.10	**Steve Carlton+ (24)**	L	3.22	369	15	11	194	86	3	0
3.11	Andy Messersmith (12)	R	2.86	362	14	11	173	88	3	2
3.12	**Bert Blyleven (22)**	R	3.31	378	14	12	183	65	3	0
3.14	**Don Sutton+ (23)**	R	3.26	370	14	11	159	60	3	0
3.16	**Old Hoss Radbourn+ (12)**	R	2.68	334	20	13	121	58	2	0
3.16	**Don Drysdale+ (14)**	R	2.95	367	14	11	172	59	3	0
3.22	Fred Toney (12)	R	2.69	329	16	11	80	65	3	1
3.22	Eddie Cicotte (14)	R	2.38	291	16	12	108	65	3	2
3.22	Dean Chance (11)	R	2.92	357	12	11	149	72	3	2
3.23	Dutch Leonard (11)	L	3.25	396	13	12	78	49	2	3
3.26	Silver King (10)	R	3.18	384	18	13	108	86	2	1
3.27	Vida Blue (17)	L	3.27	374	15	11	152	83	3	0
3.30	Mike Cuellar (15)	L	3.14	357	15	11	133	67	3	1
3.33	**Jim Bunning+ (17)**	R	3.27	368	14	11	175	61	2	1
3.33	Sam McDowell (15)	L	3.17	357	12	12	216	116	2	1
3.34	Mel Stottlemyre (11)	R	2.97	350	16	13	119	77	4	0
3.36	George McQuillan (10)	R	2.38	279	13	14	90	61	3	2
3.37	Ron Guidry (14)	L	3.29	384	17	9	175	62	3	0
3.40	**Catfish Hunter+ (15)**	R	3.26	359	16	12	140	66	3	0
3.42	Gary Nolan (10)	R	3.08	355	15	10	142	57	2	0
3.43	Bob Veale (13)	L	3.08	353	13	10	178	89	2	2
3.44	**Phil Niekro (24)**	R	3.35	383	14	12	144	78	2	1
3.45	Joe Horlen (12)	R	3.11	355	12	12	111	58	2	0
3.45	Wilbur Wood (17)	L	3.24	352	12	11	101	52	2	4
3.45	**Ferguson Jenkins (19)**	R	3.34	363	15	12	173	54	3	0

ERA		Lg ERA	W	L	SO	BB	SHO	SV
3.48	**Babe Ruth+ (22)**	**L**	**2.28**	**282**	**21**	**10**	**107**	**97**	**4**	**1**
3.51	Don Gullett (9)	L	3.11	366	16	8	139	75	2	2
3.52	Frank Smith (11)	R	2.59	290	16	12	117	75	3	1
3.53	**Jack Chesbro+ (11)**	**R**	**2.68**	**299**	**19**	**12**	**119**	**65**	**3**	**0**
3.54	Sonny Siebert (12)	R	3.21	357	13	11	146	67	2	2
3.56	Gary Peters (14)	L	3.25	359	13	11	150	74	2	1
3.60	Dave McNally (14)	L	3.24	354	15	10	125	68	3	0
3.68	Harry Coveleski (9)	L	2.39	268	16	11	100	73	3	2
3.75	Earl Moore (14)	R	2.78	291	16	15	134	106	3	1

Shoeless Joe Jackson

The 6th Best Hitter of all-time

Not in the Hall of Fame

1913

Richie Allen

The 14th Best offensive player of all-time

Not in the Hall of Fame

1966

Ryan Braun

The 27th Best Hitter of all-time

All-Time Best Relief Pitchers

Weight given for longevity

1.90	Mariano Rivera (19, 43)	R	2.21	435	5	4	71	17	0	39
2.43	**Hoyt Wilhelm+ (21)**	**R**	**2.52**	**370**	**9**	**7**	**98**	**47**	**0**	**14**
2.77	John Hiller (15)	L	2.83	384	10	9	120	62	1	14
2.79	**Rich Gossage+ (22)**	**R**	**3.01**	**384**	**8**	**7**	**98**	**48**	**0**	**20**
2.82	Dan Quisenberry (12)	R	2.76	386	6	5	38	16	0	25
2.93	**Bruce Sutter+ (12)**	**R**	**2.83**	**381**	**7**	**7**	**89**	**32**	**0**	**31**
2.95	**Rollie Fingers+ (17)**	**R**	**2.90**	**369**	**8**	**8**	**90**	**34**	**0**	**24**
2.98	Sparky Lyle (16)	L	2.88	363	7	6	66	36	0	18
3.06	Don McMahon (18)	R	2.96	363	7	5	78	45	0	12
3.08	Ron Perranoski (13)	L	2.79	356	7	7	63	43	0	16
3.13	**Dennis Eckersley (24)**	**R**	**3.50**	**398**	**9**	**8**	**114**	**35**	**1**	**19**
3.21	Tug McGraw (19)	L	3.14	367	8	7	87	46	0	14

All-Time Best Offensive Single Season Performances

Abs#	Name	Year	Slg ratio	2B	3B	HR	RBI	BB	BA	OBP	Slg %
0.903	Babe Ruth+ (25)	1920	2.28	36	9	54	137	150	0.376	0.532	0.847
0.831	Babe Ruth+ (26)	1921	2.10	44	16	59	171	145	0.378	0.512	0.846
0.806	Babe Ruth+ (28)	1923	1.95	45	13	41	131	170	0.393	0.545	0.764
0.799	Ted Williams+ (22)	1941	1.96	33	3	37	120	147	0.406	0.553	0.735
0.795	Barry Bonds (36)	2001	2.02	32	2	73	137	177	0.328	0.515	0.863
0.793	Ty Cobb+ (24)	1911	1.74	47	24	8	127	44	0.420	0.467	0.621
0.778	Babe Ruth+ (24)	1919	1.89	34	12	29	114	101	0.322	0.456	0.657
0.777	Barry Bonds (37)	2002	1.92	31	2	46	110	198	0.370	0.582	0.799
0.776	Ted Williams+ (23)	1942	1.85	34	5	36	137	145	0.356	0.499	0.648
0.775	Babe Ruth+ (32)	1927	1.96	29	8	60	164	137	0.356	0.486	0.772
0.775	Ted Williams+ (28)	1957	1.68	28	1	38	87	119	0.388	0.526	0.635
0.773	Ted Williams+ (27)	1946	1.85	37	8	38	123	156	0.342	0.497	0.667
0.769	Babe Ruth+ (31)	1926	1.90	30	5	47	153	144	0.372	0.516	0.737
0.768	Barry Bonds (39)	2004	1.90	27	3	45	101	232	0.362	0.609	0.812
0.766	Tip O'Neill (29)	1887	1.85	52	19	14	123	50	0.435	0.490	0.691
0.758	Babe Ruth+ (29)	1924	1.88	39	7	46	121	142	0.378	0.513	0.739
0.755	Dan Brouthers+ (28)	1886	1.75	40	15	11	72	66	0.370	0.445	0.581
0.754	Norm Cash	1961		22	8	41	132	124	0.361	0.487	0.662
0.753	Lou Gehrig+ (24)	1927	1.95	52	18	47	175	109	0.373	0.474	0.765
0.749	Barry Bonds (27)	1992	1.65	36	5	34	103	127	0.311	0.456	0.624
0.747	Ted Williams+ (38)	1957	1.87	28	1	38	87	119	0.388	0.526	0.731
0.746	Jimmie Foxx+ (25)	1933	1.87	37	9	48	163	96	0.356	0.449	0.703
0.744	Jimmie Foxx+ (24)	1932	1.87	33	9	58	169	116	0.364	0.469	0.749
0.739	Fred Dunlap (25)	1884	1.90	39	8	13		29	0.412	0.448	0.621
0.736	Dick Allen (30)	1972	1.70	28	5	37	113	99	0.308	0.420	0.603
0.733	Babe Ruth+ (36)	1931	1.79	31	3	46	163	128	0.373	0.495	0.700

0.733	Mike Schmidt+ (31)	1981	1.75	19	2	31	91	73	0.316	0.435	0.644
0.732	Ty Cobb+ (25)	1912	1.63	30	23	7	83	43	0.409	0.456	0.584
0.724	Stan Musial+ (27)	1948	1.84	46	18	39	131	79	0.376	0.450	0.702
0.723	Willie McCovey+ (31)	1969	1.78	26	2	45	126	121	0.320	0.453	0.656
0.723	Hank Aaron+ (37)	1971	1.83	22	3	47	118	71	0.327	0.410	0.669
0.722	Barry Bonds (38)	2003	1.77	22	1	45	90	148	0.341	0.529	0.749
0.722	Ed Delahanty+ (34)	1902	1.71	43	14	10	93	62	0.376	0.453	0.590
0.722	Jimmie Foxx+ (30)	1938	1.78	33	9	50	175	119	0.349	0.462	0.704
0.721	Mickey Mantle+ (24)	1956	1.78	22	5	52	130	112	0.353	0.464	0.705
0.721	Lou Gehrig+ (31)	1934	1.78	40	6	49	165	109	0.363	0.465	0.706
0.719	Babe Ruth+ (33)	1928	1.79	29	8	54	142	137	0.323	0.463	0.709
0.718	Barry Bonds (28)	1993	1.68	38	4	46	123	126	0.336	0.458	0.677
0.718	Nap Lajoie+ (26)	1901	1.79	48	14	14	125	24	0.426	0.463	0.643
0.717	Ross Barnes (26)	1876	1.84	21	14	1	59	20	0.429	0.462	0.590
0.716	Mark McGwire (34)	1998	1.79	21	0	70	147	162	0.299	0.470	0.753
0.714	Mickey Mantle+ (29)	1961	1.72	16	6	54	128	126	0.317	0.448	0.687
	-										
0.712	Carl Yastrzemski+ (27)	1967	1.74	31	4	44	121	91	0.326	0.418	0.622
0.711	Shoeless Joe Jackson (23)	1911	1.65	45	19	7	83	56	0.408	0.468	0.590
0.709	Ralph Kiner+ (26)	1949	1.71	19	5	54	127	117	0.310	0.432	0.658
0.707	Lou Gehrig+ (28)	1931	1.69	31	15	46	184	117	0.341	0.446	0.662
0.707	Rogers Hornsby+ (26)	1922	1.80	46	14	42	152	65	0.401	0.459	0.722
0.706	Rogers Hornsby+ (29)	1925	1.84	41	10	39	143	83	0.403	0.489	0.756
0.704	Hank Greenberg+ (27)	1938	1.66	23	4	58	146	119	0.315	0.438	0.684
0.703	Willie Mays+ (34)	1965	1.73	21	3	52	112	76	0.317	0.398	0.645
0.702	Jeff Bagwell (26)	1994	1.77	32	2	39	116	65	0.368	0.451	0.750
0.701	Larry Walker (30)	1997	1.72	46	4	49	130	78	0.366	0.452	0.720
0.699	Ed Delahanty+ (28)	1896	1.63	44	17	13	126	62	0.397	0.472	0.631
0.697	Jimmie Foxx+ (31)	1939	1.75	31	10	35	105	89	0.360	0.464	0.694
0.696	George Brett+ (27)	1980	1.71	33	9	24	118	58	0.390	0.454	0.664
0.692	Rogers Hornsby+ (28)	1924	1.79	43	14	25	94	89	0.424	0.507	0.696
0.692	Lou Gehrig+ (33)	1936	1.72	37	7	49	152	130	0.354	0.478	0.696
0.690	Hank Greenberg+ (29)	1940	1.71	50	8	41	150	93	0.340	0.433	0.670
0.689	Willie Mays+ (24)	1955	1.67	18	13	51	127	79	0.319	0.400	0.659
0.688	Willie Mays+ (26)	1957	1.60	26	20	35	97	76	0.333	0.407	0.626
0.688	Joe DiMaggio+ (26)	1941	1.72	43	11	30	125	76	0.357	0.440	0.643

0.688	Frank Thomas	1994	1.72	34	1	38	101	109	0.353	0.487	0.729
0.687	Ralph Kiner+ (24)	1947	1.69	23	4	51	127	98	0.313	0.417	0.639
0.685	Willie Stargell+ (31)	1971	1.72	26	0	48	125	83	0.295	0.398	0.628
0.684	Ralph Kiner+ (28)	1951	1.62	31	6	42	109	137	0.309	0.452	0.627
0.682	Mickey Mantle+ (30)	1962	1.54	15	1	30	89	122	0.321	0.486	0.605
0.681	Mark McGwire (32)	1996	1.71	21	0	52	113	116	0.312	0.467	0.731
0.681	Dick Allen (24)	1966	1.68	25	10	40	110	68	0.317	0.396	0.632
0.680	Kevin Mitchell (27)	1989	1.69	34	6	47	125	87	0.291	0.388	0.635
0.678	Frank Robinson+ (30)	1966	1.69	34	2	49	122	87	0.316	0.410	0.637
0.678	Willie Stargell+ (33)	1973	1.70	43	3	44	119	80	0.299	0.392	0.646
0.677	Willie Mays+ (23)	1954	1.71	33	13	41	110	66	0.345	0.411	0.667
0.676	Hank Aaron+ (29)	1963	1.58	29	4	44	130	78	0.319	0.391	0.586
0.674	Willie Mays+ (33)	1964	1.61	21	9	47	111	82	0.296	0.383	0.607
0.673	Billy Williams+ (34)	1972	1.71	34	6	37	122	62	0.333	0.398	0.606
0.673	Honus Wagner	1900	1.57	45	22	4	100	41	0.381	0.434	0.573
0.672	Ed Delahanty+ (31)	1899	1.59	55	9	9	137	55	0.410	0.464	0.582
0.672	Willie McCovey+ (32)	1970	1.59	39	2	39	126	137	0.289	0.444	0.612
0.671	Babe Ruth+ (35)	1930	1.69	28	9	49	153	136	0.359	0.493	0.732
0.670	Jimmie Foxx+ (27)	1935	1.60	33	7	36	115	114	0.346	0.461	0.636
0.668	Sammy Sosa	2001	1.73	34	5	64	160	116	0.328	0.437	0.737
0.665	Albert Belle (27)	1994	1.68	35	2	36	101	58	0.357	0.438	0.714
0.659	Joe DiMaggio+ (22)	1937	1.69	35	15	46	167	64	0.346	0.412	0.673
0.657	Sam Thompson+ (34)	1894	1.60	32	28	13	147	41	0.415	0.465	0.696
0.657	Jim Thome (31)	2002	1.62	19	2	52	118	122	0.304	0.445	0.677
0.656	Johnny Mize+ (27)	1940	1.62	31	13	43	137	82	0.314	0.404	0.636
0.654	Ed Delahanty+ (25)	1893	1.54	35	18	19	146	47	0.368	0.423	0.583
0.654	Lou Gehrig+ (27)	1930	1.66	42	17	41	174	101	0.379	0.473	0.721
0.651	Babe Ruth+ (34)	1929	1.67	26	6	46	154	72	0.345	0.430	0.697
0.650	Duke Snider+ (26)	1953	1.58	38	4	42	126	82	0.336	0.419	0.627
0.650	Jose Bautista (30)	2011	1.52	24	2	43	103	132	0.302	0.447	0.608
0.648	Mark McGwire (35)	1999	1.61	21	1	65	147	133	0.278	0.424	0.697
0.648	Miguel Cabrera (30)	2013	1.61	26	1	44	137	90	0.348	0.442	0.636
0.647	Barry Bonds (35)	2000	1.57	28	4	49	106	117	0.306	0.440	0.688
0.647	Albert Pujols (29)	2009	1.58	45	1	47	135	115	0.327	0.443	0.659
0.647	Hack Wilson+ (30)	1930	1.67	35	6	56	191	105	0.356	0.454	0.723
0.646	Lou Gehrig+ (25)	1928	1.49	47	13	27	142	95	0.374	0.467	0.648

0.645	Frank Robinson+ (26)	1962	1.59	51	2	39	136	76	0.342	0.421	0.624
0.643	Jim Gentile (27)	1961	1.62	25	2	46	141	96	0.302	0.423	0.646
0.642	Eddie Mathews+ (21)	1953	1.58	31	8	47	135	99	0.302	0.406	0.627
0.641	Fred Lynn (27)	1979	1.60	42	1	39	122	82	0.333	0.423	0.637
0.639	Mike Trout	2012	1.52	27	8	30	83	67	0.326	0.399	0.602
0.639	Derrek Lee (29)	2005	1.58	50	3	46	107	85	0.335	0.418	0.662
0.638	Larry Walker (32)	1999	1.64	26	4	37	115	57	0.379	0.458	0.710
0.638	Frank Robinson+ (24)	1960	1.53	33	6	31	83	82	0.297	0.407	0.595
0.638	Ryan Braun (27)	2011	1.50	38	6	33	111	58	0.332	0.397	0.597
0.637	Rocky Colavito (24)	1958	1.57	26	3	41	113	84	0.303	0.405	0.620
0.637	Albert Pujols (28)	2008	1.57	44	0	37	116	104	0.357	0.462	0.653
0.634	Hank Aaron+ (25)	1959	1.62	46	7	39	123	51	0.355	0.401	0.636
0.633	Kevin Mitchell (32)	1994	1.61	18	1	30	77	59	0.326	0.429	0.681
0.632	Todd Helton (26)	2000	1.60	59	2	42	147	103	0.372	0.463	0.698
0.631	Harry Heilmann+ (32)	1927	1.57	50	9	14	120	72	0.398	0.475	0.616
0.629	Reggie Jackson+ (34)	1980	1.54	22	4	41	111	83	0.300	0.398	0.597
0.628	Johnny Mize+ (26)	1939	1.58	44	14	28	108	92	0.349	0.444	0.626
0.627	Jim Bottomley+ (28)	1928	1.58	42	20	31	136	71	0.325	0.402	0.629
0.627	Albert Pujols (26)	2006	1.55	33	1	49	137	92	0.331	0.431	0.671
0.626	Danny Tartabull (28)	1991	1.54	35	3	31	100	65	0.316	0.397	0.593
0.626	George Brett+ (32)	1985	1.50	38	5	30	112	103	0.335	0.436	0.586
0.625	Tony Perez+ (28)	1970	1.53	28	6	40	129	83	0.317	0.401	0.589
0.625	Jim Rice+ (25)	1978	1.58	25	15	46	139	58	0.315	0.370	0.600
0.623	Shoeless Joe Jackson (32)	1920	1.51	42	20	12	121	56	0.382	0.444	0.590
0.621	Cecil Fielder (26)	1990	1.54	25	1	51	132	90	0.277	0.377	0.592
0.620	Alex Rodriguez (31)	2007	1.52	31	0	54	156	95	0.314	0.422	0.645
0.618	Josh Hamilton (29)	2010	1.57	40	3	32	100	43	0.359	0.411	0.633
0.618	George Foster (28)	1977	1.57	31	2	52	149	61	0.320	0.382	0.631
0.617	Billy Williams+ (32)	1970	1.52	34	4	42	129	72	0.322	0.391	0.587
0.612	Stan Musial+ (29)	1950	1.48	41	7	28	109	87	0.346	0.437	0.596
0.609	Mike Trout	2013	1.49	39	9	27	97	110	0.323	0.432	0.602
0.607	Mike Piazza (28)	1997	1.52	32	1	40	124	69	0.362	0.431	0.639
0.605	Albert Pujols (24)	2004	1.54	51	2	46	123	84	0.331	0.415	0.657
0.605	Gary Sheffield (23)	1992	1.54	34	3	33	100	48	0.330	0.385	0.580
0.603	Chuck Klein+ (26)	1931	1.49	34	10	31	121	59	0.337	0.398	0.584
0.602	Juan Gonzalez (23)	1993	1.57	33	1	46	118	37	0.310	0.368	0.633

		Year	Slg R	2B	3B	HR	RBI	BB	BA	OBP	Slg %
0.602	Alex Rodriguez (26)	2002	1.49	27	2	57	142	87	0.300	0.392	0.623
0.601	Ernie Banks+ (26)	1957	1.48	34	6	43	102	70	0.285	0.360	0.579
0.601	Johnny Bench+ (22)	1970	1.52	35	4	45	148	54	0.293	0.345	0.587
0.596	Robin Yount+ (26)	1982	1.49	46	12	29	114	54	0.331	0.379	0.578
0.594	Miguel Cabrera (29)	2012	1.50	40	0	44	139	66	0.330	0.393	0.606
0.586	Mark McGwire (23)	1987	1.49	28	4	49	118	71	0.289	0.370	0.618
0.584	Lefty O'Doul (32)	1929	1.49	35	6	32	122	76	0.398	0.465	0.622
0.568	Andres Galarraga (32)	1993	1.49	35	4	22	98	24	0.370	0.403	0.602

Absolute Best Pitching Single Seasons

Abs Ratio	Pitcher (Age)	ERA		lg ERA		Year	W	L
0.33	Dutch Leonard (22)	0.96	L	2.91	1914	19	5	
0.35	Greg Maddux+ (28)	1.56	R	4.51	1994	16	6	
0.36	Tim Keefe+ (23)	0.86	R	2.37	1880	6	6	
0.37	Pedro Martinez (28)	1.74	R	4.77	2000	18	6	
0.37	Greg Maddux+ (29)	1.63	R	4.45	1995	19	2	
0.37	Walter Johnson+ (25)	1.15	R	3.06	1913	36	7	
0.38	Bob Gibson+ (32)	1.12	R	2.98	1968	22	9	
0.39	Mordecai Brown+ (29)	1.04	R	2.66	1906	26	6	
0.39	Dwight Gooden (20)	1.53	R	3.89	1985	24	4	
0.41	Jack Taylor (28)	1.30	R	3.17	1902	23	11	
0.41	Kevin Brown (31)	1.89	R	4.61	1996	17	11	
0.41	Walter Johnson+ (24)	1.39	R	3.37	1912	33	12	
0.42	Pete Alexander+ (28)	1.22	R	2.90	1915	31	10	
0.43	Denny Driscoll (26)	1.21	L	2.80	1882	13	9	
0.43	Pedro Martinez (25)	1.90	R	4.39	1997	17	8	
0.44	Carl Hubbell+ (30)	1.66	L	3.81	1933	23	12	
0.44	Roger Clemens (42)	1.87	R	4.29	2005	13	8	
0.44	Old Hoss Radbourn	1.38	R	3.11	1884	59	12	
0.45	Christy Mathewson	1.14	R	2.53	1909	25	6	
0.45	Christy Mathewson+ (2	1.28	R	2.82	1905	31	9	
0.46	Ed Walsh+ (29)	1.27	R	2.77	1910	18	20	
0.46	Walter Johnson+ (30)	1.27	R	2.77	1918	23	13	
0.46	Phil Regan	1.62		3.52	1966	14	1	
0.46	Dean Chance (23)	1.65	R	3.58	1964	20	9	
0.46	Jack Pfiester (29)	1.15	L	2.50	1907	14	9	
0.47	Cy Young+ (34)	1.62	R	3.49	1901	33	10	

0.47	Jack Coombs (27)	1.30	R	2.77	1910	31	9
0.47	Carl Lundgren (27)	1.17	R	2.50	1907	18	7
0.47	Nolan Ryan+ (34)	1.69	R	3.58	1981	11	5
0.47	Ron Guidry (27)	1.74	L	3.69	1978	25	3
0.47	Clayton Kershaw (25)	1.83	L	3.87	2013	16	9
0.48	Sandy Koufax+ (28)	1.74	L	3.58	1964	19	5
0.48	Walter Johnson+ (31)	1.49	R	3.07	1919	20	14
0.49	Addie Joss+ (28)	1.16	R	2.37	1908	24	11
0.49	Sandy Koufax+ (30)	1.73	L	3.52	1966	27	9
0.49	Spud Chandler (35)	1.64	R	3.33	1943	20	4
0.49	Walter Johnson+ (22)	1.36	R	2.77	1910	25	17
0.50	Lefty Grove	2.06		4.12	1931	31	4
0.50	Ed Reulbach (22)	1.42	R	2.82	1905	18	14
0.51	Hal Newhouser+ (24)	1.81	L	3.58	1945	25	9
0.51	Tom Seaver+ (26)	1.76	R	3.47	1971	20	10
0.51	Mort Cooper (29)	1.78	R	3.48	1910	25	14
0.51	Smoky Joe Wood (25)	1.49	R	2.90	1915	15	5
0.52	Eddie Cicotte (29)	1.58	R	3.06	1913	18	11
0.52	Tim Keefe+ (28)	1.58	R	3.03	1885	32	13
0.52	Orel Hershiser	2.03	R	3.89	1985	19	3
0.52	Vida Blue (21)	1.82	L	3.47	1971	24	8
0.52	Rube Waddell+ (28)	1.48	L	2.82	1905	27	10
0.53	Joe Horlen (26)	1.88	R	3.58	1964	13	9
0.53	Lefty Grove	2.54		4.81	1930	28	5
0.53	Cy Young+ (41)	1.26	R	2.37	1908	21	11
0.53	Walter Johnson+ (27)	1.55	R	2.90	1915	27	13
0.54	Luis Tiant (27)	1.60	R	2.98	1968	21	9
0.54	Sandy Koufax+ (27)	1.88	L	3.46	1963	25	5
0.55	Pete Alexander+ (33)	1.91	R	3.46	1920	27	14
0.55	Wilbur Wood (29)	1.91	L	3.47	1971	22	13
0.56	Ed Walsh+ (28)	1.41	R	2.53	1909	15	11
0.56	Mordecai Brown+ (30)	1.39	R	2.50	1907	20	6
0.56	Pete Alexander+ (32)	1.72	R	3.07	1919	16	11
0.57	Walter Johnson+ (23)	1.90	R	3.36	1911	25	13
0.57	Phil Niekro+ (28)	1.87	R	3.30	1967	11	9
0.57	Smoky Joe Wood (22)	1.91	R	3.37	1912	34	5

0.57	Pete Alexander+ (29)	1.55	R	2.72	1916	33	12
0.58	Guy Hecker (28)	1.80	R	3.11	1884	52	20
0.59	Luis Tiant (31)	1.91	R	3.26	1972	15	6
0.59	Gaylord Perry+ (33)	1.92		3.26	1972	24	16
0.59	Tim Keefe+ (31)	1.74	R	2.95	1888	35	12
0.59	Walter Johnson+ (26)	1.72	R	2.91	1914	28	18
0.60	David Cone	2.22	R	3.73	1988	20	3
0.60	Ed Walsh+ (27)	1.42	R	2.37	1908	40	15
0.60	Addie Joss+ (24)	1.59	R	2.66	1904	14	10
0.60	Christy Mathewson	1.43	R	2.37	1908	37	11
0.61	Orel Hershiser	2.26		3.73	1988	23	8
0.61	Sam McDowell (25)	1.81	L	2.98	1965	17	11
0.61	Rube Waddell+ (27)	1.62	L	2.66	1904	25	19
0.61	Smoky Joe Wood (20)	1.69	R	2.77	1910	12	13
0.62	Mordecai Brown+ (31)	1.47	R	2.37	1908	29	9
0.63	Lefty Grove	2.81		4.48	1929	20	6
0.64	Ed Walsh+ (26)	1.60	R	2.50	1907	24	18
0.64	Babe Ruth+ (21)	1.75	L	2.72	1916	23	12
0.65	Addie Joss+ (26)	1.72	R	2.66	1906	21	9
0.66	Monte Ward+ (18)	1.51	R	2.30	1878	22	13
0.66	Denny Mcclain	1.96	R	2.98	1968	31	6
0.67	Mordecai Brown+ (33)	1.86	R	2.77	1909	27	9
0.67	Addie Joss+ (29)	1.71	R	2.53	1909	14	13
0.68	Lefty Grove	2.84		4.18	1932	25	10
0.68	Pete Alexander+ (30)	1.83	R	2.68	1917	30	13
0.68	Christy Mathewson	1.89	R	2.77	1910	27	9
0.69	Roy Face	2.70	R	3.90	1959	18	1
0.70	Walter Johnson+ (20)	1.65	R	2.37	1908	14	14
0.70	Walter Johnson+ (28)	1.90	R	2.72	1916	25	20
0.70	Mordecai Brown+ (27)	1.87	R	2.66	1904	15	10
0.70	Ed Walsh+ (25)	1.88	R	2.66	1906	17	13
0.73	Addie Joss+ (27)	1.83	R	2.50	1907	27	11
0.73	Monte Ward+ (20)	1.74	R	2.37	1880	39	24
0.80	Rube Waddell+ (31)	1.89	L	2.37	1908	19	14
0.84	Lefty Grove	3.20		3.81	1933	24	8

All-Time Defensive Rankings—Catchers

Absolute Fielding		GG	fld %	lg fld %	cs %	lg cs %
1.610	Yadier Molina	6	0.994	0.992	0.45	0.28
1.484	Ivan Rodriguez	13	0.991	0.991	0.46	0.31
1.478	Javy Lopez	0	0.992	0.991	0.31	0.21
1.363	**Roy Campenella**		**0.988**	**0.984**	**0.57**	**0.42**
1.281	**Gabby Hartnett**		**0.984**	**0.978**	**0.56**	**0.44**
1.274	Lance Parrish	3	0.991	0.987	0.33	0.26
1.261	Charles Johnson	4	0.993	0.991	0.39	0.31
1.230	**Johnny Bench**	10	**0.987**	**0.986**	**0.43**	**0.35**
1.226	Joe Mauer		0.995	0.992	0.33	0.27
1.211	Bob Boone	7	0.986	0.987	0.4	0.33
1.181	Jim Sundberg	6	0.993	0.985	0.41	0.35
1.163	Elston Howard	2	0.993	0.989	0.44	0.38
1.156	Thurman Munson		0.982	0.984	0.44	0.38
1.153	**Bill Dickey**		**0.988**	**0.982**	**0.47**	**0.41**
1.124	**Raymond Schalk**		**0.981**	**0.972**	**0.49**	**0.44**
1.099	**Gary Carter**	3	**0.991**	**0.986**	**0.35**	**0.32**
1.091	**Yogi Berra**		**0.988**	**0.986**	**0.49**	**0.45**
1.081	**Joe Torre**		**0.99**	**0.988**	**0.41**	**0.38**
1.075	**Richard Ferrell**		**0.984**	**0.982**	**0.44**	**0.41**
1.057	**Buck Ewing**		**0.931**	**0.905**	**0.38**	**0.37**
1.043	**Ernie Lombardi**		**0.979**	**0.98**	**0.47**	**0.45**
1.041	Walker Cooper		0.977	0.982	0.45	0.43
1.001	Ted Simmons		0.987	0.986	0.34	0.34
0.981	**Roger Bresnahan**		**0.971**	**0.968**	**0.44**	**0.45**
0.979	Bill Freehan	5	0.993	0.988	0.37	0.38
0.972	**Carlton Fisk**		**0.987**	**0.986**	**0.34**	**0.35**
0.937	Sandy Alomar Jr		0.99	0.991	0.3	0.32

0.934	Jorge Posada		0.992	0.991	0.28	0.3
0.933	**Mickey Cochrane**		**0.985**	**0.98**	**0.39**	**0.42**
0.927	Smokey Burgess		0.988	0.986	0.37	0.4
0.913	B J Surhoff		0.988	0.984	0.3	0.33
0.887	Mike Napoli		0.99	0.992	0.24	0.27
0.881	Mickey Tettleton		0.991	0.989	0.29	0.33
0.856	Brian McCann		0.991	0.992	0.24	0.28
0.847	Bob Uecker		0.981	0.98	0.33	0.39
0.824	Tony Pena	4	0.991	0.987	0.32	0.39
0.795	Victor Martinez		0.993	0.991	0.23	0.29
0.740	Mike Piazza		0.989	0.991	0.23	0.31
0.730	Bill Schroeder		0.992	0.988	0.24	0.33

All-Time Defensive Rankings—First Base

Abs#		GG	Fldg %	Range	Lg Fldg%	Lg Range	Slg %
1.11	Albert Pujols	2	0.994	10.36	0.993	9.36	0.585
1.03	Wes Parker	6	0.996	10.1	0.991	9.88	0.457
1.02	Keith Hernandez	11	0.994	10.2	0.992	9.98	0.499
1.02	Mark Teixeira	5	0.997	9.53	0.994	9.36	0.516
1.02	**Stan Musial**		**0.992**	**9.87**	**0.99**	**9.69**	**0.604**
1.01	Don Mattingly	9	0.996	9.71	0.992	9.65	0.482
1.01	**Hank Greenberg**		**0.991**	**9.92**	**0.99**	**9.86**	**0.639**
1.00	Bill White	7	0.992	9.89	0.99	9.87	0.506
1.00	George Scott	8	0.99	9.8	0.991	9.77	0.488
1.00	Steve Garvey	4	0.996	9.95	0.992	9.99	0.467
1.00	**Dan Brouthers**		**0.971**	**10.42**	**0.971**	**10.44**	**0.601**
1.00	**Willie McCovey**		**0.987**	**9.9**	**0.991**	**9.89**	**0.611**
0.98	Mark McGwire	1	0.993	9.35	0.992	9.52	0.598
0.96	**Jimmie Foxx**		**0.992**	**9.6**	**0.99**	**10.01**	**0.645**
0.95	**Johnny Mize**		**0.992**	**9.53**	**0.99**	**10.02**	**0.596**
0.95	**Lou Gehrig**		**0.991**	**9.64**	**0.99**	**10.19**	**0.65**

All-Time Defensive Rankings—Second Base

Abs Fldg	Abs Slg %		GG	Fldg %	Range	Lg Fldg	Lg Rang
1.13	0.565	**Nap Lajoie**		0.963	5.78	0.949	5.21
1.09	0.392	**Bill Mazeroski**	8	0.983	5.72	0.976	5.3
1.06	0.491	Bobby Grich	4	0.984	5.7	0.979	5.4
1.05	0.415	Frank White	8	0.984	5.56	0.98	5.33
1.04	0.511	**Robert Doerr**		0.98	5.74	0.971	5.56
1.03	0.421	**Red Schoendist**		0.983	5.61	0.975	5.47
1.03	0.387	**Nellie Fox**	3	0.984	5.55	0.977	5.41
1.03	0.503	**Ryne Sandberg**	9	0.989	5.31	0.981	5.21
1.03	0.497	Chase Utley		0.981	5.01	0.983	4.87
1.02	0.482	Robinson Cano	2	0.986	4.94	0.985	4.83
1.02	0.562	**Eddie Collins**		0.97	5.34	0.958	5.31
1.02	0.477	**Frankie Frisch**		0.974	5.89	0.965	5.84
1.01	0.542	**Jackie Robinson**		0.983	5.59	0.975	5.6
0.99	0.507	**Rod Carew**		0.973	5.23	0.977	5.25
0.99	0.576	**Joe Morgan**	5	0.981	5.31	0.977	5.38
0.99	0.523	**Charlie Gehringer**		0.976	5.64	0.968	5.74
0.99	0.533	**Flash Gordon**		0.97	5.47	0.971	5.54
0.99	0.486	**Roberto Alomar**	1	0.984	4.97	0.981	5.06
0.96	0.502	Alfonso Soriano		0.971	4.78	0.981	4.92
0.92	0.608	**Rogers Hornsby**		0.965	5.36	0.964	5.82
0.92	0.509	**Toni Lazzeri**		0.967	5.35	0.968	5.81

All-Time Defensive Rankings—Shortstop

Abs Fldg		GG	Fldg %	Range	Lg Fldg%	Lg Range
1.16	Troy Tulowitzki	2	5.00	0.985	0.973	4.36
1.13	**Hugh Jennings**		**6.16**	**0.922**	**0.900**	**5.57**
1.13	**Cal Ripken**	2	**4.73**	**0.979**	**0.966**	**4.25**
1.13	Rey Sanchez		5.14	0.981	0.970	4.61
1.11	Tony Fernandez	4	4.83	0.980	0.969	4.39
1.08	Mark Belanger	8	5.24	0.977	0.964	4.92
1.07	Rick Burleson		5.25	0.971	0.964	4.92
1.07	Gene Alley	2	5.31	0.971	0.965	4.99
1.07	**Ozzie Smith+**	13	**5.03**	**0.978**	**0.966**	**4.77**
1.06	Tim Foli		5.24	0.973	0.964	4.97
1.06	Roy Mcmillan	3	5.24	0.972	0.961	4.98
1.06	**George Davis**		**5.85**	**0.940**	**0.923**	**5.60**
1.06	**John Ward**		**5.04**	**0.887**	**0.880**	**4.80**
1.06	**David Bancroft**		**5.97**	**0.944**	**0.941**	**5.67**
1.05	**Joe Tinker**		**5.52**	**0.938**	**0.926**	**5.32**
1.05	**Rodrick Wallace**		**5.72**	**0.938**	**0.926**	**5.52**
1.05	**Rabbit Maranville**		**5.80**	**0.952**	**0.940**	**5.60**
1.05	**Joe Sewell**		**5.37**	**0.951**	**0.944**	**5.16**
1.05	**Robin Yount**	1	**5.13**	**0.964**	**0.964**	**4.90**
1.05	Omar Vizquel	11	4.62	0.985	0.972	4.47
1.04	**Luis Aparicio**	9	**5.05**	**0.972**	**0.963**	**4.88**
1.04	Luke Appling		5.27	0.948	0.952	5.05
1.03	Rey Ordonez	3	4.60	0.976	0.969	4.51
1.02	**Honus Wager**		**5.30**	**0.947**	**0.936**	**5.24**
1.02	**Barry Larkin+**	3	**4.62**	**0.975**	**0.968**	**4.57**
1.02	Don Kessinger	2	5.05	0.965	0.964	4.98

1.01	Orlando Cabrera	2	4.51	0.977	0.971	4.48
1.01	**Travis Jackson**		**5.67**	**0.952**	**0.949**	**5.63**
1.01	JJ Hardy	2	4.39	0.982	0.975	4.38
1.01	Chris Speier		5.00	0.970	0.964	4.99
1.01	Alan Trammell	4	4.71	0.977	0.967	4.72
1.01	**Ernie Banks**		**5.00**	**0.969**	**0.962**	**5.00**
1.01	Alex Rodriguez	2	4.62	0.977	0.972	4.62
1.00	Dave Concepcion	5	4.98	0.971	0.965	4.99
1.00	**Joe Cronin**		**5.16**	**0.951**	**0.946**	**5.17**
0.99	Maury Wills	2	4.59	0.962	0.962	4.62
0.99	Zoilo Versalles	2	4.71	0.956	0.963	4.74
0.98	**Arky Vaughn**		**5.24**	**0.951**	**0.949**	**5.38**
0.97	Larry Bowa (	2	4.78	0.980	0.965	4.99
0.97	**Lou Boudreau**		**4.87**	**0.973**	**0.954**	**5.12**
0.97	**Pee Wee Reese**		**4.86**	**0.962**	**0.958**	**5.04**
0.97	Edgar Renteria	2	4.33	0.970	0.971	4.48
0.96	Jimmy Rollins	4	4.21	0.983	0.973	4.43
0.96	**Phil Rizzuto**		**4.79**	**0.968**	**0.959**	**5.04**
0.90	Derek Jeter	5	4.08	0.976	0.972	4.53

There has been a lot of initial negative reaction to the fact that Ozzie Smith is # 9 on this list of defensive short stops. Some people have suggested that possibly since Ozzie played on turf it is skewing the #'s? All I can say is that these are the raw facts relative their individual era's.

All-Time Defensive Rankings—Third Base

Abs Fldg		GG	Fldg %	Range	Lg Fldg%	Lg Range
1.111053	Darrel Evans		0.946	3.24	0.948	2.91
1.1045	**Mike Schmidt**	**10**	**0.955**	**3.15**	**0.949**	**2.87**
1.090727	**Jimmie Collins**		**0.929**	**3.61**	**0.907**	**3.39**
1.08688	Scott Rolen	8	0.968	2.86	0.954	2.67
1.078702	**Ron Santo**	**5**	**0.954**	**3.13**	**0.948**	**2.92**
1.078379	Eric Chavez	6	0.97	2.85	0.953	2.69
1.07	Matt Williams	4	0.963	2.85	0.95	2.7
1.055159	**Brooks Robinson**	**16**	**0.971**	**3.2**	**0.953**	**3.09**
1.054054	**Pie Traynor**		**0.947**	**3.12**	**0.947**	**2.96**
1.053197	Craig Nettles	2	0.961	3.13	0.952	3
1.051633	Evan Longoria	2	0.965	2.74	0.956	2.63
1.041434	**George Brett**	**1**	**0.951**	**3.11**	**0.953**	**2.98**
1.032548	**Paul Molitar**		**0.95**	**2.98**	**0.952**	**2.88**
1.030437	**Home Run Baker**		**0.943**	**3.43**	**0.937**	**3.35**
1.025566	Ken Boyer	5	0.952	3.06	0.95	2.99
1.016149	Ron Cey		0.961	2.9	0.949	2.89
1.015245	**Wad Boggs**	**2**	**0.962**	**2.76**	**0.951**	**2.75**
1.009659	**Eddie Mathews**		**0.956**	**3.02**	**0.95**	**3.01**
1.004745	**Fred Lindstrom**		**0.959**	**2.93**	**0.948**	**2.95**
0.989289	Bobby Bonilla		0.931	2.74	0.948	2.72
0.965872	**George Kell**		**0.969**	**3.1**	**0.954**	**3.26**
0.964215	Edgar Martinez		0.946	2.66	0.949	2.75
0.954326	Dick Allen		0.927	2.84	0.948	2.91
0.932736	Richie Hebner		0.946	2.72	0.948	2.91
0.928043	**Deacon White**		**0.853**	**3.11**	**0.861**	**3.32**
0.91756	Aramis Ramirez		0.951	2.43	0.954	2.64
0.914166	Chipper Jones		0.954	2.42	0.953	2.65
0.910485	**Harmon Killebrew**		**0.94**	**2.88**	**0.953**	**3.12**
0.901488	Bill Madlock		0.948	2.59	0.949	2.87

All-Time Defensive Rankings—Outfielders

Abs Fldg		Fldg %	Range	Lg Fldg%	Lg Range	Slg%
1.32552	**Richie Ashburn**	**0.983**	**3.02**	**0.978**	**2.29**	**0.457**
1.290338	Gary Maddox	0.983	2.93	0.979	2.28	0.462
1.284851	Curt Flood	0.987	2.63	0.976	2.07	0.429
1.279418	Paul Blair	0.988	2.83	0.98	2.23	0.44
1.250469	**Willie Mays**	**0.981**	**2.69**	**0.977**	**2.16**	**0.621**
1.247888	**Tris Speaker**	**0.97**	**2.68**	**0.96**	**2.17**	**0.604**
1.223972	Jim Edmonds	0.988	2.74	0.983	2.25	0.52
1.221305	Andruw Jones	0.99	2.68	0.983	2.21	0.488
1.2081	**Max Carey**	**0.966**	**2.77**	**0.963**	**2.3**	**0.51**
1.205246	Devon White	0.986	2.77	0.981	2.31	0.454
1.184179	Charlie Keller	0.98	2.91	0.975	2.47	0.609
1.167117	**Kirby Puckett**	**0.989**	**2.79**	**0.981**	**2.41**	**0.491**
1.16333	**Ed Delahanty**	**0.951**	**2.37**	**0.927**	**2.09**	**0.612**
1.158166	Cesar Cedeno	0.985	2.59	0.979	2.25	0.539
1.15581	**Lloyd Waner**	**0.983**	**2.76**	**0.974**	**2.41**	**0.408**
1.142725	**Larry Doby**	**0.983**	**2.72**	**0.979**	**2.39**	**0.541**
1.141692	Gorman Thomas	0.984	2.8	0.981	2.46	0.51
1.137314	Torii Hunter	0.992	2.6	0.986	2.3	0.464
1.133669	**Joe Dimagio**	**0.978**	**2.8**	**0.974**	**2.48**	**0.607**
1.119722	Fred Lynn	0.988	2.71	0.98	2.44	0.527
1.119342	**Fred Clarke**	**0.952**	**2.3**	**0.945**	**2.07**	**0.554**
1.110562	**Edd Roush**	**0.972**	**2.58**	**0.965**	**2.34**	**0.498**
1.109876	**Billy Hamilton**	**0.926**	**2.29**	**0.923**	**2.07**	**0.649**
1.106142	**Ken Griffey Jr**	**0.985**	**2.55**	**0.983**	**2.31**	**0.543**
1.086629	**Earl Averill**	**0.97**	**2.57**	**0.968**	**2.37**	**0.552**
1.086047	Reggie Smith	0.976	2.41	0.98	2.21	0.558

1.082596	Eric Davis	0.984	2.45	0.981	2.27	0.552
1.080937	**Ty Cobb**	**0.961**	**2.3**	**0.96**	**2.13**	**0.65**
1.079488	**Earle Combs**	**0.974**	**2.54**	**0.967**	**2.37**	**0.494**
1.07244	Ryan Braun	0.991	1.97	0.984	1.85	0.57
1.063841	**Mickey Mantle**	**0.982**	**2.41**	**0.98**	**2.27**	**0.633**
1.060963	**Hugh Duffy**	**0.943**	**2.16**	**0.923**	**2.08**	**0.592**
1.051455	**Andre Dawson**	**0.983**	**2.39**	**0.98**	**2.28**	**0.506**
1.0514	**Ricky Henderson**	**0.979**	**2.51**	**0.982**	**2.38**	**0.57**
1.048323	Cy Williams	0.973	2.42	0.964	2.33	0.518
1.031585	**Al Simmons**	**0.982**	**2.41**	**0.968**	**2.37**	**0.54**
1.029244	**Duke Snider**	**0.985**	**2.33**	**0.978**	**2.28**	**0.577**
1.028477	**Joe Kelly**	**0.955**	**2.1**	**0.933**	**2.09**	**0.586**
1.028179	Ellis Burks	0.983	2.36	0.981	2.3	0.521
1.025155	Dale Murphy	0.983	2.32	0.98	2.27	0.522
1.025141	**Roberto Clemente**	**0.973**	**2.18**	**0.976**	**2.12**	**0.51**
1.023632	Ken Williams	0.958	2.4	0.964	2.33	0.581
1.01978	**Al Kaline**	**0.986**	**2.24**	**0.98**	**2.21**	**0.533**
1.019208	Ichiro Suzuki	0.992	2.33	0.986	2.3	0.383
1.00939	**Monte Irvin**	**0.983**	**2.36**	**0.978**	**2.35**	**0.521**
1.00879	**Hank Aaron**	**0.98**	**2.15**	**0.976**	**2.14**	**0.607**
1.003417	Bobby Bonds	0.977	2.26	0.978	2.25	0.581
1.001948	George Foster	0.984	2.22	0.979	2.227	0.517
0.991718	Bob Johnson	0.968	2.38	0.972	2.39	0.571
0.986541	**Zach Wheat**	**0.966**	**2.24**	**0.962**	**2.28**	**0.518**
0.98589	Pete Rose	0.991	2.08	0.977	2.14	0.472
0.98295	Sammy Sosa	0.973	2.21	0.981	2.23	0.539
0.981799	**Jesse Burkett**	**0.917**	**2.06**	**0.934**	**2.06**	**0.559**
0.967938	**Kiki Cuyler**	**0.972**	**2.34**	**0.971**	**2.42**	**0.509**
0.967074	Barry Bonds	0.984	2.15	0.981	2.23	0.655
0.962	Dusty Baker	0.985	2.18	0.979	2.28	0.491
0.95925	**Goose Goslin**	**0.96**	**2.29**	**0.967**	**2.37**	**0.52**
0.957082	**Sam Rice**	**0.965**	**2.23**	**0.965**	**2.33**	**0.483**
0.953189	**Tony Gwynn**	**0.987**	**2.12**	**0.98**	**2.24**	**0.488**
0.952087	**Tom McCarthy**	**0.897**	**1.92**	**0.909**	**1.99**	**0.449**
0.950961	Dave Parker	0.965	2.19	0.979	2.27	0.502
0.950741	**Carl Yastemski**	**0.981**	**2.08**	**0.98**	**2.19**	**0.537**
0.949451	**Frank Robinson**	**0.984**	**2.01**	**0.978**	**2.13**	**0.595**

0.944785	**Joe Medwick**	**0.98**	**2.23**	**0.976**	**2.37**	**0.525**
0.943945	Bobby Murcer	0.981	2.15	0.98	2.28	0.513
0.942012	Shoeless Joe Jackson	0.962	1.97	0.958	2.1	0.649
0.940293	Vladimir Guerrero	0.963	2.15	0.983	2.24	0.534
0.937489	Larry Walker	0.986	2.08	0.981	2.23	0.572
0.931589	Dwight Evans	0.987	2.25	0.981	2.43	0.528
0.931077	**Paul Waner**	**0.975**	**2.23**	**0.973**	**2.4**	**0.51**
0.925141	Jack Clark	0.978	2.13	0.979	2.3	0.545
0.921659	Rocky Colavito	0.98	2	0.98	2.17	0.542
0.917084	**Heinie Manush**	**0.979**	**2.14**	**0.968**	**2.36**	**0.479**
0.913167	Rico Carty	0.97	1.9	0.975	2.07	0.52
0.909415	**Dave Winfield**	**0.982**	**2.16**	**0.98**	**2.38**	**0.519**
0.905925	**Reggie Jackson**	**0.967**	**2.13**	**0.98**	**2.32**	**0.558**
0.904569	Rusty Staub	0.969	1.97	0.977	2.16	0.489
0.900712	**Chick Hafey**	**0.971**	**2.2**	**0.972**	**2.44**	**0.528**
0.898694	Jose Canseco	0.971	2.17	0.981	2.39	0.539
0.895498	**James O'Rourke**	**0.892**	**1.71**	**0.878**	**1.94**	**0.506**
0.892055	**Elmer Flick**	**0.947**	**1.77**	**0.949**	**1.98**	**0.594**
0.884796	**Chuck Klein**	**0.962**	**2.15**	**0.974**	**2.4**	**0.563**
0.882675	**Babe Ruth**	**0.968**	**2.07**	**0.966**	**2.35**	**0.743**
0.880469	**Harry Hooper**	**0.966**	**1.89**	**0.96**	**2.16**	**0.504**
0.876656	**Jim Rice**	**0.98**	**2.15**	**0.981**	**2.45**	**0.522**
0.876482	**Lou Brock**	**0.959**	**1.9**	**0.976**	**2.13**	**0.527**
0.874019	**Sam Crawford**	**0.965**	**1.69**	**0.952**	**1.96**	**0.578**
0.87231	**Billy Williams**	**0.973**	**1.82**	**0.976**	**2.08**	**0.547**
0.871274	Don Baylor	0.977	2.08	0.98	2.38	0.486
0.86869	Darryl Strawberry	0.977	1.98	0.981	2.27	0.559
0.843992	**Ralph Kiner**	**0.974**	**2**	**0.978**	**2.36**	**0.605**
0.841846	Gary Sheffield	0.977	1.87	0.982	2.21	0.537
0.83244	**Willie Keeler**	**0.96**	**1.65**	**0.942**	**2.02**	**0.512**
0.831484	**Enos Slaughter**	**0.98**	**1.95**	**0.978**	**2.35**	**0.503**
0.827239	**Ted Williams**	**0.974**	**1.95**	**0.977**	**2.35**	**0.69**
0.814132	**Ross Youngs**	**0.953**	**1.96**	**0.964**	**2.38**	**0.513**
0.795836	**Harry Heilmann**	**0.962**	**1.87**	**0.966**	**2.34**	**0.554**
0.790876	Manny Ramirez	0.978	1.84	0.985	2.31	0.567
0.772086	**King Kelly**	**0.82**	**1.57**	**0.873**	**1.91**	**0.537**
0.089393	**Sam Thompson**	**0.934**	**1.74**	**9.09**	**2**	**0.557**

All-Time Best Absolute Player Rankings—Catchers

c	0.586	**Johnny Bench**	17	1.27	10	29	2	29	103	5	67	0.267	0.342	0.476
c	0.555	**Roy Campanella**	10	1.29		24	2	32	114	3	71	0.276	0.360	0.500
c	0.554	**Joe Torre**	18	1.28	1	25	4	18	87	2	57	0.297	0.365	0.452
c	0.525	**Gabby Hartnett**	20	1.23		32	5	19	96	2	57	0.297	0.370	0.489
c	0.520	**Buck Ewing**	18	1.29		31	22	9	109		48	0.303	0.351	0.456
c	0.519	**Carlton Fisk**	24	1.20	1	27	3	24	86	8	55	0.269	0.341	0.457
c	0.517	**Roger Bresnahan**	17	1.07		24	8	3	59	24	80	0.279	0.386	0.377
c	0.516	Ivan Rodriguez	21	**1.11**	13	36	3	20	85	8	33	0.296	0.334	0.464
c	0.512	**Bill Dickey**	17	**1.25**		31	7	18	109	3	61	0.313	0.382	0.486
c	0.508	**Yogin Berra**	19	**1.25**		25	4	27	109	2	54	0.285	0.348	0.482
c	0.505	Javy Lopez	15	**1.17**		29	2	28	93	1	38	0.287	0.337	0.491
c	0.498	Ted Simmons	21	**1.15**		32	3	16	92	1	56	0.285	0.348	0.437
c	0.491	Walker Cooper	18	**1.23**		26	4	19	89	2	34	0.285	0.332	0.464
c	0.487	**Gordon Cochrane**	13	**1.20**		36	7	13	91	7	94	0.320	0.419	0.478
c	0.487	**Ernie Lombardi**	17	**1.21**		24	2	17	87	1	38	0.306	0.358	0.460
c	0.483	Smoky Burgess	18	**1.16**		22	3	12	64	1	46	0.295	0.362	0.446
c	0.479	Jorge Posada	17	**1.07**		23	2	27	80	3	104	0.241	0.369	0.449
c	0.476	**Cary Carter**	19	**1.14**	3	26	2	23	86	3	60	0.262	0.335	0.439
c	0.470	Mike Piazza	16	**1.30**		29	1	36	113	1	64	0.308	0.377	0.545
c	0.462	Bill Freehan	15	**1.11**	5	22	3	18	69	2	57	0.262	0.340	0.412
c	0.461	Joe Mauer	10	**1.13**		39	3	14	87	6	85	0.323	0.405	0.468
c	0.457	Mickey Tettleton	14	**1.13**		23	2	27	80	3	104	0.241	0.369	0.449
c	0.450	Thurman Munson	11	**1.09**	3	26	4	13	80	5	50	0.292	0.346	0.410
c	0.449	Elston Howard	14	**1.12**	2	22	5	17	77	1	38	0.274	0.322	0.427
c	0.435	Mike Napoli	8	**1.22**		28	1	32	88	5	73	0.259	0.357	0.502
c	0.430	**Richard Ferrell**	18	**0.94**		28	4	2	63	2	80	0.281	0.378	0.363
c	0.423	Bob Boone	19	**0.90**	7	22	2	8	59	3	47	0.254	0.315	0.346
c	0.422	Yadier Molina	10	**0.98**	6	30	0	12	73	5	44	0.284	0.339	0.404
c	0.420	BJ Surhoff	19	**1.00**		31	3	13	81	10	45	0.282	0.332	0.413
c	0.405	**Ray Schalk**	18	**0.85**		18	5	1	55	16	59	0.253	0.340	0.316

c	0.405	Brian McCann	9	**1.15**		33	0	26	97	3	61	0.277	0.350	0.473
c	0.391	Victor Martinez	11	**1.12**		39	0	19	102	0	63	0.303	0.369	0.464
c	0.389	Tony Pena	18	**0.92**	4	24	2	9	58	7	37	0.260	0.309	0.364
c	0.389	Sandy Alomar Jr	20	**0.99**	1	29	1	13	69	3	25	0.273	0.309	0.406

All-Time Best Absolute Player—First Base

1b	0.677	**Jimmie Foxx+**	**20**	**1.56**		**32**	**9**	**37**	**134**	**6**	**102**	**0.325**	**0.428**	**0.609**
1b	0.650	**Lou Gehrig+**	**17**	**1.58**		**40**	**12**	**37**	**149**	**8**	**113**	**0.340**	**0.447**	**0.632**
1b	0.634	**Stan Musial+**	**22**	**1.47**		**39**	**9**	**25**	**104**	**4**	**86**	**0.331**	**0.417**	**0.559**
1b	0.614	**Mel Ott**	**22**	**1.38**		**29**	**4**	**30**	**110**	**5**	**101**	**0.304**	**0.414**	**0.533**
1b	0.607	**Hank Greenberg)**	**13**	**1.55**		**44**	**8**	**38**	**148**	**7**	**99**	**0.313**	**0.412**	**0.605**
1b	0.604	**Willie McCovey**	**22**	**1.37**		22	3	33	97	2	84	0.270	0.374	0.515
1b	0.637	**Dan Brouthers**	**19**	**1.48**		**45**	**20**	**10**	**125**	**25**	**81**	**0.342**	**0.423**	**0.519**
1b	0.599	**Willie Stargell**	**21**	**1.41**		**29**	**4**	**33**	**106**	**1**	**64**	**0.282**	**0.360**	**0.529**
1b	0.598	Mark McGwire	16	**1.44**	1	22	1	50	122	1	114	0.263	0.394	0.588
1b	0.596	**Johnny Mize**	**15**	**1.46**		**32**	**7**	**31**	**115**	**2**	**74**	**0.312**	**0.397**	**0.562**
1b	0.592	**Roger Conner**	**18**	**1.37**		**36**	**19**	**11**	**107**	**13**	**81**	**0.316**	**0.397**	**0.486**
1b	0.589	Jim Thome	22	**1.33**		29	2	39	108	1	111	0.276	0.402	0.554
1b	0.584	Albert Pujols	13	**1.44**	2	43	1	41	124	8	88	0.321	0.410	0.599
1b	0.579	**Frank Chance**	**17**	**1.17**		**25**	**10**	**3**	**75**	**51**	**70**	**0.296**	**0.394**	**0.394**
1b	0.558	**Frank Thomas**	**19**	**1.33**		**35**	**1**	**36**	**119**	**2**	**116**	**0.301**	**0.419**	**0.555**
1b	0.573	**Cap Anson**	**22**	**1.28**		**37**	**9**	**6**	**133**	**11**	**63**	**0.334**	**0.394**	**0.447**
1b	0.554	Jeff Bagwell	15	**1.29**	1	37	2	34	115	15	106	0.297	0.408	0.540
1b	0.550	Norm Cash	17	**1.30**		19	3	29	86	3	81	0.271	0.374	0.488
1b	0.548	Frank Howard	16	**1.33**		21	3	33	96	1	67	0.273	0.352	0.499
1b	0.547	Lance Berkman	15	**1.28**		36	3	32	106	7	104	0.293	0.406	0.537
1b	0.545	Rafael Palmeiro	20	**1.26**	3	33	2	33	105	6	77	0.288	0.371	0.515
1b	0.540	David Ortiz	17	**1.31**		43	1	35	118	1	89	0.287	0.381	0.549
1b	0.540	Orlando Cepeda	17	**1.33**		32	2	29	104	11	45	0.297	0.350	0.499
1b	0.539	**Jacob Beckley**	**20**	**1.23**		**32**	**17**	**6**	**107**	**21**	**42**	**0.308**	**0.361**	**0.436**
1b	0.537	Todd Helton	17	**1.29**	3	43	3	27	101	3	96	0.316	0.414	0.539
1b	0.534	Dolph Camilli	12	**1.29**		28	9	26	103	7	103	0.277	0.388	0.492
1b	0.533	**Hack Wilson**	**12**	**1.37**		**32**	**8**	**29**	**128**	**6**	**81**	**0.307**	**0.395**	**0.545**
1b	0.532	**Eddie Murray**	**21**	**1.21**	3	**30**	**2**	**27**	**103**	**6**	**71**	**0.287**	**0.359**	**0.476**
1b	0.532	Gil Hodges	18	**1.26**	3	23	4	29	100	5	74	0.273	0.359	0.487
1b	0.529	**Tony Perez**	**23**	**1.23**		**29**	**5**	**22**	**96**	**3**	**54**	**0.279**	**0.341**	**0.463**

1b	0.529	Boog Powell	17	**1.24**		21	1	27	94	2	79	0.266	0.361	0.462
1b	0.527	Miguel Cabrera	11	**1.37**		40	1	36	123	4	78	0.321	0.399	0.568
1b	0.526	Fred McGriff	19	**1.24**		29	2	32	102	5	86	0.284	0.377	0.509
1b	0.525	Hal Trosky	11	**1.35**		40	7	27	122	3	66	0.302	0.371	0.522
1b	0.524	Keith Hernandez	17	**1.13**	11	33	5	13	83	8	83	0.296	0.384	0.436
1b	0.523	Pedro Guerrero	15	**1.24**		28	3	23	95	10	64	0.300	0.370	0.480
1b	0.519	**George Sisler**	**15**	1.24		**34**	**13**	**8**	**93**	**30**	**37**	**0.340**	**0.379**	**0.468**
1b	0.517	Jason Giambi	19	**1.24**		29	1	32	104	1	98	0.278	0.400	0.519
1b	0.516	Dave Kingman	16	**1.26**		20	2	37	101	7	51	0.236	0.302	0.478
1b	0.515	Ted Kluszewski	15	**1.28**		27	3	26	97	2	46	0.298	0.353	0.498
1b	0.515	Mark Teixeira	11	**1.27**	5	38	2	37	119	2	81	0.278	0.368	0.525
1b	0.511	John Mayberry	15	**1.17**		21	2	26	88	2	88	0.253	0.360	0.439
1b	0.511	Ryan Howard	10	**1.32**		30	3	43	132	2	81	0.271	0.361	0.545
1b	0.510	Roy Sievers	17	**1.22**		25	4	27	98	1	72	0.267	0.354	0.475
1b	0.510	Joey Votto	7	**1.33**		41	2	29	96	9	103	0.314	0.419	0.541
1b	0.509	Will Clark	15	**1.22**	1	36	4	23	99	5	77	0.303	0.384	0.497
1b	0.507	Ryan Klesko	16	**1.19**		32	3	26	92	8	76	0.279	0.370	0.500
1b	0.505	Bill White	13	**1.20**	7	27	6	20	84	10	58	0.286	0.351	0.455
1b	0.502	**James Bottemley**	**16**	1.25		**38**	**12**	**18**	**116**	**5**	**54**	**0.310**	**0.369**	**0.500**
1b	0.500	Dave Orr	8	**1.47**		41	22	8	128		20	0.342	0.366	0.502
1b	0.495	Bob Watson	19	**1.19**		27	4	16	87	2	58	0.295	0.364	0.447
1b	0.495	Derrek Lee	15	**1.18**	3	36	3	28	90	9	73	0.281	0.365	0.495
1b	0.493	Adrian Gonzalez	10	**1.21**	3	38	1	29	103	1	70	0.294	0.367	0.501
1b	0.493	Kent Hrbek	14	**1.23**		29	2	27	101	3	78	0.282	0.367	0.481
1b	0.491	Andres Galarraga	19	**1.23**	2	32	2	29	102	9	42	0.288	0.347	0.499
1b	0.491	Cecil Cooper	17	**1.22**	2	35	4	21	96	8	38	0.298	0.337	0.466
1b	0.490	Steve Garvey	19	**1.17**	4	31	3	19	91	6	33	0.294	0.329	0.446
1b	0.490	Lee May	18	**1.23**		27	2	28	97	3	38	0.267	0.313	0.459
1b	0.489	Mo Vaughn	12	**1.26**		29	1	35	114	3	78	0.293	0.383	0.523
1b	0.487	George Scott	14	**1.17**	8	24	5	22	84	5	56	0.268	0.333	0.435
1b	0.483	**Bill Terry**	**14**	1.27		**35**	**11**	**14**	**101**	**5**	**51**	**0.341**	**0.393**	**0.506**
1b	0.482	John Olerud	17	**1.13**	3	36	1	18	89	1	92	0.295	0.398	0.465
1b	0.481	Dick Stuart	10	**1.28**		23	4	33	108	0	44	0.264	0.316	0.489
1b	0.481	Don Mattingly	14	**1.20**	9	40	2	20	100	1	53	0.307	0.358	0.471
1b	0.480	Jim Gentile	9	**1.27**		20	1	31	95	1	82	0.260	0.368	0.486
1b	0.477	Paul Konerko	17	**1.17**		29	1	31	99	1	65	0.281	0.356	0.491
1b	0.474	Cecil Fielder	13	**1.20**		22	1	35	111	0	76	0.255	0.345	0.482
1b	0.473	Tony Clark	15	**1.15**		24	1	26	86	1	55	0.262	0.339	0.485
1b	0.473	Travis Hafner	12	**1.20**		34	2	29	100	2	82	0.273	0.376	0.498
1b	0.473	Prince Fielder	9	**1.28**		33	1	35	107	2	89	0.286	0.389	0.527

1b	0.470	Mike Sweeney	16	**1.15**		36	1	24	101	6	58	0.297	0.366	0.486
1b	0.466	Tino Martinez	16	**1.13**		29	2	27	102	2	62	0.271	0.344	0.471
1b	0.465	Mark Grace	16	**1.08**	4	37	3	12	83	5	78	0.303	0.383	0.442
1b	0.461	Bill Buckner	22	**1.07**		32	3	11	78	12	29	0.289	0.321	0.408
1b	0.458	Kevin Youkilis	10	**1.15**		39	3	23	94	4	82	0.281	0.382	0.478
1b	0.457	Ripper Collins	9	**1.25**		31	10	20	98	3	53	0.296	0.360	0.492
1b	0.456	Zeke Bonura	7	**1.23**		41	5	21	124	3	71	0.307	0.380	0.487
1b	0.455	Chris Davis	6	**1.26**		33	1	35	98	3	49	0.266	0.327	0.512
1b	0.451	Bill Skowron	14	**1.19**		24	5	21	87	2	37	0.282	0.332	0.459
1b	0.450	Justin Morneau	11	**1.16**		36	2	27	107	1	64	0.277	0.347	0.482
1b	**0.448**	**George Kelly**	**16**	**1.08**		**35**	**5**	**7**	**79**	**5**	**56**	**0.306**	**0.367**	**0.414**
1b	0.447	Joe Pepitone	12	**1.17**		18	4	25	84	5	35	0.258	0.301	0.432
1b	0.436	Corey Hart	9	**1.18**		36	6	26	87	14	46	0.276	0.334	0.491
1b	0.432	Wes Parker	9	**1.02**	6	24	4	8	59	8	67	0.267	0.351	0.375
1b	0.424	Lyle Overbay	13	**1.04**		38	1	16	71	2	67	0.267	0.348	0.434
1b	0.418	Vic Power	12	**1.06**	7	29	5	13	66	4	28	0.284	0.315	0.411

All-Time Best Absolute Player—Second Base

2b	0.638	**Rogers Hornsby**	23	1.51		39	12	22	114	10	74	0.358	0.434	0.577
2b	0.623	**Nap Lajoie**	21	1.37		43	11	5	104	25	34	0.338	0.380	0.466
2b	0.605	**Joe Morgan**	22	1.14	5	27	6	16	69	42	114	0.271	0.392	0.427
2b	0.590	**Eddie Collins**	25	1.19		25	11	3	75	42	86	0.333	0.424	0.429
2b	0.538	**Ryne Sandberg**	16	1.15	9	30	6	21	79	26	57	0.285	0.344	0.452
2b	0.523	**Charlie Gehringer**	19	1.22		40	10	13	100	13	83	0.320	0.404	0.480
2b	0.516	Bobby Grich	17	**1.11**	4	26	4	18	70	8	88	0.266	0.371	0.424
2b	0.514	**Jackie Robinson**	10	1.22		32	6	16	86	23	87	0.311	0.409	0.474
2b	0.507	**Rod Carew**	19	1.14		29	7	6	67	23	67	0.328	0.393	0.429
2b	0.506	**Flash Gordon**	11	1.23		27	5	26	101	9	79	0.268	0.357	0.466
2b	0.502	Alfonso Soriano	15	**1.21**		40	3	34	96	24	42	0.272	0.321	0.504
2b	0.486	**Bid Mcphee**	18	1.04		23	14	4	81		74	0.272	0.355	0.373
2b	0.486	**Roberto Alomar**	17	1.08	1	34	5	14	77	32	70	0.300	0.371	0.443
2b	0.485	**Robert Doerr**	14	1.22		33	8	19	108	5	70	0.288	0.362	0.461
2b	0.484	**John Evers**	18	0.99		20	6	1	49	29	71	0.270	0.356	0.334
2b	0.484	**Tony Lazerri**	14	1.17		31	11	17	111	14	81	0.292	0.380	0.467
2b	0.481	Craig Bigio	20	**1.05**	4	38	3	17	67	24	66	0.281	0.363	0.433
2b	0.481	Jeff Kent	17	**1.19**		39	3	27	107	7	56	0.290	0.356	0.500
2b	0.477	**Frank Frisch**	19	1.09		33	10	7	87	29	51	0.316	0.369	0.432
2b	0.473	Chase Utley	11	**1.20**		36	5	27	99	16	67	0.287	0.373	0.498
2b	0.447	**Billy Herman**	15	1.06		41	7	4	71	6	62	0.304	0.367	0.407
2b	0.445	Davey Johnson	13	**1.09**	3	27	2	15	69	4	63	0.261	0.340	0.404
2b	0.445	Willie Randolph	18	**0.91**		23	5	4	51	20	91	0.276	0.373	0.351
2b	0.434	Robinson Cano	9	**1.22**	2	44	3	24	97	4	41	0.309	0.355	0.504
2b	0.426	Dustin Pedroia	8	**1.10**		46	2	16	79	19	67	0.302	0.370	0.454
2b	0.421	Dan Uggla	8	**1.11**		30	2	30	90	3	79	0.246	0.340	0.458
2b	0.421	**Red Schoendist**	19	1.01		31	6	6	57	7	44	0.289	0.337	0.387
2b	0.415	Frank White	18	**1.00**	8	28	4	11	62	12	29	0.255	0.293	0.383
2b	0.413	Bret Boone	14	**1.05**	4	33	3	23	93	9	50	0.266	0.325	0.442
2b	0.411	**Bill Mazorowski**	17	0.97	8	22	5	10	64	2	33	0.260	0.299	0.367

2b	0.387	**Nellie Fox**	**19**	**0.94**	**3**	**24**	**8**	**2**	**54**	**5**	**49**	**0.288**	**0.348**	**0.363**
2b	0.383	Placido Polanco	16	**0.95**	3	29	3	9	61	7	36	0.297	0.343	0.397
2b	0.382	Mark Grudzielanek	15	**0.93**	1	35	3	8	58	12	33	0.289	0.332	0.393
2b	0.381	Manny Trillo	17	**0.90**	3	22	3	6	52	5	41	0.263	0.316	0.345
2b	0.340	Bobby Richardson	12	**0.87**	5	22	4	4	45	8	30	0.266	0.299	0.335

All-Time Best Absolute Player Rankings—Shortstop

ss	0.663	**Honus Wagner+**	**21**	**1.38**		37	15	6	100	42	56	0.328	0.391	0.467
ss	0.583	Alex Rodriguez (20,)	20	**1.33**	2	33	2	41	124	20	78	0.299	0.384	0.558
ss	0.548	Bill Dahlen	21	**1.09**		27	11	6	82	36	71	0.272	0.358	0.382
ss	0.539	**Joe Cronin**	**20**	**1.21**		**39**	**9**	**13**	**109**	**7**	**81**	**0.301**	**0.390**	**0.468**
ss	0.523	**Ernie Banks+ (19)**	**19**	**1.31**	**1**	**26**	**6**	**33**	**105**	**3**	**49**	**0.274**	**0.330**	**0.500**
ss	0.514	**Barry Larkin**	**19**	**1.08**	**3**	**33**	**6**	**15**	**71**	**28**	**70**	**0.295**	**0.371**	**0.444**
ss	0.512	Vern Stephens (15)	15	**1.23**		29	4	23	111	2	65	0.286	0.355	0.460
ss	0.509	Alan Trammel	20	**1.06**	4	29	4	13	71	17	60	0.285	0.352	0.415
ss	0.507	**Cal Ripken**	**21**	**1.11**	**2**	**33**	**2**	**23**	**91**	**2**	**61**	**0.276**	**0.340**	**0.447**
ss	0.497	**Robin Yount**	**20**	**1.12**	**1**	**33**	**7**	**14**	**80**	**15**	**55**	**0.285**	**0.342**	**0.430**
ss	0.494	Troy Tulowitzki (8, 28)	8	**1.24**	2	35	4	29	103	10	67	0.295	0.367	0.509
ss	0.489	**Arky Vaughn**	**14**	**1.18**		**32**	**11**	**9**	**83**	**11**	**84**	**0.318**	**0.406**	**0.453**
ss	0.489	Hanley Ramirez (9, 29)	9	**1.23**		40	4	26	86	37	67	0.302	0.373	0.506
ss	0.483	**Roderick Wallace**	**25**	**1.03**		**27**	**10**	**2**	**76**	**14**	**53**	**0.268**	**0.332**	**0.358**
ss	0.480	Julian Franco	23	**1.03**		26	3	11	77	18	59	0.298	0.365	0.417
ss	0.480	**Joe Tinker**	**15**	**1.07**		**24**	**10**	**3**	**70**	**30**	**37**	**0.262**	**0.308**	**0.353**
ss	0.476	**Lou Boudreou**	**15**	**1.11**		**38**	**6**	**7**	**78**	**5**	**78**	**0.295**	**0.380**	**0.415**
ss	0.474	**Luke Appling**	**18**	**1.03**		**29**	**7**	**3**	**75**	**12**	**87**	**0.310**	**0.399**	**0.398**
ss	0.469	Nomar Garciaparra	14	**1.23**		42	6	26	106	11	46	0.313	0.361	0.521
ss	0.465	Tony Fernandez	17	**1.00**	4	31	7	7	63	18	52	0.288	0.347	0.399
ss	0.463	**Hugh Jennings**	**17**	**1.09**		**29**	**11**	**2**	**106**	**45**	**44**	**0.312**	**0.391**	**0.406**
ss	0.461	**Pee Wee Reese**	**16**	**0.98**		**25**	**6**	**9**	**66**	**17**	**90**	**0.269**	**0.366**	**0.377**
ss	0.459	Derek Jeter (19, 39)	19	**1.06**	5	33	4	16	79	22	65	0.312	0.381	0.446
ss	0.448	**Ozzie Smith**	**19**	**0.83**	**##**	**25**	**4**	**2**	**50**	**37**	**67**	**0.262**	**0.337**	**0.328**
ss	0.441	Bert Campanaris	19	**0.91**		22	6	5	45	45	43	0.259	0.311	0.342
ss	0.440	**Luis Aparicio**	**18**	**0.91**	**9**	**25**	**6**	**5**	**49**	**32**	**46**	**0.262**	**0.311**	**0.343**
ss	0.439	**Travis Jackson**	**15**	**1.09**		**28**	**8**	**13**	**91**	**7**	**40**	**0.291**	**0.337**	**0.433**
ss	0.437	Jimmy Rollins	14	**1.02**	4	38	9	17	69	35	57	0.269	0.327	0.426
ss	0.437	Omar Visquel	24	**0.85**	##	25	4	4	52	22	56	0.272	0.336	0.352

ss	0.435	Miguel Tejada (16, 39)	16	**1.09**		35	2	23	97	6	41	0.285	0.336	0.456
ss	0.425	Dave Conception	19	**0.93**	5	25	3	7	62	21	48	0.267	0.322	0.357
ss	0.425	**David Bancroft**	**16**	0.94		**27**	**7**	**3**	**50**	**12**	**70**	**0.279**	**0.355**	**0.358**
ss	0.424	**Rabbit Maranville**	**23**	0.90		**23**	**11**	**2**	**54**	**18**	**51**	**0.258**	**0.318**	**0.340**
ss	0.419	Maury Wills	14	**0.89**	2	15	6	2	38	49	46	0.281	0.330	0.331
ss	0.418	Edgar Renteria	16	**0.95**	2	33	2	11	69	22	54	0.286	0.343	0.398
ss	0.415	**Joe Sewell**	**14**	1.04		**37**	**6**	**4**	**90**	**6**	**72**	**0.312**	**0.391**	**0.413**
ss	0.408	Chris Speier	19	**0.91**		22	4	8	52	3	61	0.246	0.327	0.349
ss	**0.406**	**John Ward**	**17**	0.99		**20**	**9**	**2**	**77**		**37**	**0.275**	**0.314**	**0.341**
ss	0.398	Orlando Cabrera	15	**0.93**	2	37	3	10	70	18	42	0.272	0.317	0.390
ss	0.397	**Phil Rizzuto**	**13**	0.93		**23**	**6**	**4**	**55**	**15**	**63**	**0.273**	**0.351**	**0.355**
ss	0.392	Zoilo Versalles	12	**0.98**	2	27	7	11	55	11	37	0.242	0.290	0.367
ss	0.383	Mark Belanger	18	**0.75**	8	14	3	2	31	13	46	0.228	0.300	0.280
ss	0.377	Larry Bowa	16	**0.84**	2	19	7	1	38	23	34	0.260	0.300	0.320

All-Time Best Absolute Player Rankings—Third Base

3b	0.625	**Mike Schmidt**	18	**1.38**	10	27	4	37	107	12	102	0.267	0.380	0.527
3b	0.610	Dick Allen	15	**1.44**		30	7	33	104	12	83	0.292	0.378	0.534
3b	0.575	**Harmon Killebrew**	22	**1.34**		19	2	38	105	1	104	0.256	0.376	0.509
3b	0.571	**Eddie Mathews**	17	**1.33**		24	5	35	98	5	98	0.271	0.376	0.509
3b	0.564	Darrel Evans	21	**1.13**		20	2	25	82	6	97	0.248	0.361	0.431
3b	0.560	**George Brett**	21	1.27	1	40	8	19	96	12	66	0.305	0.369	0.487
3b	0.553	**Ron Santo**	15	1.24	5	26	5	25	96	3	80	0.277	0.362	0.464
3b	0.531	Edgar Martinez	18	**1.25**		41	1	24	99	4	101	0.312	0.418	0.515
3b	0.528	**Paul Molitar**	21	**1.13**		37	7	14	79	30	66	0.306	0.369	0.448
3b	0.523	**Home Run Baker**	13	**1.29**		32	11	10	102	24	49	0.307	0.363	0.442
3b	0.522	Craig Nettles	22	**1.11**	2	20	2	23	79	2	65	0.248	0.329	0.421
3b	0.518	Al Rosen	10	**1.28**		26	3	30	111	6	91	0.285	0.384	0.495
3b	0.514	Chipper Jones	19	**1.26**		36	2	30	105	10	98	0.303	0.401	0.529
3b	0.510	Scott Rolen	17	**1.17**	8	41	3	25	102	9	71	0.281	0.364	0.490
3b	0.507	Bob Elliott	15	**1.17**		31	8	14	98	5	79	0.289	0.375	0.440
3b	0.506	Ken Boyer	15	**1.21**	5	25	5	22	91	8	57	0.287	0.349	0.462
3b	0.503	David Wright	10	**1.22**		41	3	26	103	22	79	0.301	0.382	0.506
3b	0.501	Matt Williams	17	**1.20**	4	29	3	33	106	5	41	0.268	0.317	0.489
3b	0.500	Eric Chavez	16	**1.14**	6	32	2	27	92	5	65	0.268	0.342	0.476
3b	0.499	Robin Ventura	16	**1.08**	6	26	1	23	92	2	84	0.267	0.362	0.444
3b	0.498	Bob Horner	10	**1.29**		27	1	35	109	2	59	0.277	0.340	0.499
3b	0.497	Ron Cey	17	**1.16**		26	2	25	89	2	79	0.261	0.354	0.445
3b	0.495	Jim Ray Hart	12	**1.27**		21	4	24	83	2	55	0.278	0.345	0.467
3b	0.490	**Jimmy Collings**	14	**1.18**		33	11	6	92	18	40	0.294	0.343	0.409
3b	0.487	Doug DeCinces	15	**1.16**		31	3	23	86	6	61	0.259	0.329	0.445
3b	0.486	Bobby Bonilla	16	**1.16**		31	5	22	90	3	70	0.279	0.358	0.472
3b	0.483	Lave Cross	21	**1.08**		29	10	3	98	22	33	0.292	0.329	0.383
3b	**0.481**	**Wade Boggs**	18	**1.11**	2	38	4	8	67	2	94	0.328	0.415	0.443
3b	**0.480**	**Brooks Robinson**	23	**1.06**	16	27	4	15	76	2	48	0.267	0.322	0.401
3b	0.471	Troy Glaus	13	**1.16**		31	1	34	100	6	90	0.254	0.358	0.489

3b	0.471	Evan Longoria	6	**1.26**	2	41	2	33	111	8	76	0.275	0.357	0.512
3b	0.469	**Pie Traynor**	**17**	**1.10**		**31**	**14**	**5**	**106**	**13**	**39**	**0.320**	**0.362**	**0.435**
3b	0.468	Ken Caminiti	15	**1.10**	3	32	2	22	90	8	67	0.272	0.347	0.447
3b	0.467	Buddy Bell	18	**1.06**	6	29	4	14	74	4	56	0.279	0.341	0.406
3b	0.463	Gary Gaetti	20	**1.09**	4	29	3	23	87	6	41	0.255	0.308	0.434
3b	0.462	Adrian Beltre	16	**1.14**	4	35	2	27	93	8	45	0.282	0.334	0.478
3b	0.461	Bill Madlock	15	**1.14**		31	3	15	77	16	54	0.305	0.365	0.442
3b	0.459	Russell Branyan	14	**1.15**		22	1	30	71	2	62	0.232	0.329	0.485
3b	0.457	Richie Hebner	18	**1.16**		23	5	17	76	3	58	0.276	0.352	0.438
3b	0.456	Larry Parrish	15	**1.12**		31	3	22	85	3	45	0.263	0.318	0.439
3b	0.453	**George Kell**	**15**	1.09		**35**	**5**	**7**	**79**	**5**	**56**	**0.306**	**0.367**	**0.414**
3b	0.451	Vinny Castilla	16	**1.14**		30	2	28	97	3	37	0.276	0.321	0.476
3b	0.449	Aramis Ramirez	16	**1.20**		37	2	30	107	2	49	0.285	0.345	0.501
3b	0.448	Dean Palmer	14	**1.14**		28	2	33	101	6	60	0.251	0.324	0.472
3b	0.442	**Deacon White**	**15**	**1.17**		**28**	**10**	**2**	**103**		**32**	**0.312**	**0.346**	**0.393**
3b	0.436	Tim Wallach	17	**1.06**	3	32	3	19	82	4	48	0.257	0.316	0.416
3b	0.435	Edwin Encarnacion	9	**1.16**		33	1	29	91	7	65	0.265	0.348	0.479
3b	0.432	Ryan Zimmerman	9	**1.16**		39	2	26	96	5	65	0.286	0.352	0.477
3b	0.428	**Fred Lindstom**	**13**	1.12		**34**	**9**	**12**	**88**	**9**	**38**	**0.311**	**0.351**	**0.449**
3b	0.428	Eric Hinske	12	**1.04**		28	2	16	61	7	53	0.249	0.332	0.430
3b	0.423	Travis Fryman	13	**1.07**	1	33	4	21	98	7	57	0.274	0.336	0.443

All-Time Best Absolute Player Rankings—Outfielders

0.741	**Babe Ruth**	22	**1.82**		33	9	46	144	8	133	**0.342**	**0.474**	**0.690**
0.701	Barry Bonds	22	**1.48**	8	33	4	41	108	28	139	0.298	0.444	0.607
0.690	**Ted Williams**	19	**1.65**		37	5	37	130	2	143	**0.344**	**0.482**	**0.634**
0.685	**Willie Mays**	22	**1.47**	12	28	8	36	103	18	79	**0.302**	**0.384**	**0.557**
0.683	**Ty Cobb**	24	**1.45**		39	16	6	103	48	67	**0.366**	**0.433**	**0.512**
0.640	**Mickey Mantle**	18	**1.46**	1	23	5	36	102	10	117	**0.298**	**0.421**	**0.557**
0.637	**Hank Aaron**	23	**1.47**	3	31	5	37	113	12	69	**0.305**	**0.374**	**0.555**
0.635	**Tris Speaker**	22	**1.40**		46	13	7	89	25	80	**0.345**	**0.428**	**0.500**
0.625	**Frank Robinson**	21	**1.43**	1	30	4	34	105	12	82	**0.294**	**0.389**	**0.537**
0.617	**Billy Hamilton**	14	**1.18**		25	10	4	75	93	121	**0.344**	**0.455**	**0.432**
0.616	Shoeless Joe Jackson	13	**1.54**		37	20	7	95	25	63	0.356	0.423	0.517
0.612	**Ed Delahanty**	16	**1.39**		46	16	9	129	40	65	**0.346**	**0.411**	**0.505**
0.605	**Joe DiMaggio**	13	**1.51**		36	12	34	143	3	74	**0.325**	**0.398**	**0.579**
0.598	**Ricky Henerson**	25	**1.04**	1	27	3	16	59	74	115	**0.279**	**0.401**	**0.419**
0.598	Ken Griffey Jr	22	**1.30**	10	32	2	38	111	11	80	0.284	0.370	0.538
0.592	**Hugh Duffy**	17	**1.26**		30	11	10	121	54	62	**0.326**	**0.386**	**0.451**
0.586	**Joseph Kelly**	17	**1.27**		31	17	6	104	39	80	**0.317**	**0.402**	**0.451**
0.586	**Reggie Jackson**	21	**1.29**		27	3	32	98	13	79	**0.262**	**0.356**	**0.490**
0.582	**Fred Clarke**	21	**1.23**		26	16	5	73	37	63	**0.312**	**0.386**	**0.429**
0.579	Charlie Keller	13	**1.39**		23	10	26	105	6	109	0.286	0.410	0.518
0.577	**Duke Snider**	18	**1.39**		27	6	31	101	7	73	**0.295**	**0.380**	**0.540**
0.572	Larry Walker	17	**1.37**	7	38	5	31	107	19	74	0.313	0.400	0.565
0.567	**Al Simmons**	20	**1.36**		39	11	22	134	6	45	**0.334**	**0.380**	**0.535**
0.566	Cesar Cedeno (17)	17	**1.16**	5	35	5	16	79	44	54	0.285	0.347	0.443
0.564	**Carl Yastremski**	23	**1.23**	7	32	3	22	90	8	90	**0.285**	**0.379**	**0.462**
0.562	**Max Carey**	20	**1.05**		27	10	5	52	48	68	**0.285**	**0.361**	**0.386**
0.560	Tim Raines	23	**1.06**		28	7	11	63	52	86	0.294	0.385	0.425
0.560	**Al Kaline+ (22)**	22	**1.26**	1	28	4	23	90	8	73	**0.297**	**0.376**	**0.480**
0.559	**Jesse Burkett**	16	**1.24**		25	14	6	75	30	81	**0.338**	**0.415**	**0.446**
0.558	Reggie Smith (17)	17	**1.31**	1	30	5	26	89	11	73	0.287	0.366	0.489

0.554	Dwight Evans (20)	20	**1.23**	8	30	5	24	86	5	86	0.272	0.370	0.470
0.554	Fred Lynn (17)	17	**1.26**	4	32	4	25	91	6	71	0.283	0.360	0.484
0.552	Eric Davis (17)	17	**1.19**	3	24	3	28	93	35	74	0.269	0.359	0.482
0.552	Bobby Bonds (14)	14	**1.26**	3	26	6	29	90	40	80	0.268	0.353	0.471
0.552	Ken Williams (14)	14	**1.40**		33	9	23	106	18	66	0.319	0.393	0.530
0.550	Jim Wynn (15)	15	**1.18**		24	3	25	81	19	103	0.250	0.366	0.436
0.549	**Sam Crawford**	19	1.35		29	20	6	98	24	49	0.309	0.362	0.452
0.546	**Ralph Kiner+ (10)**	10	1.43		24	4	41	112	2	111	0.279	0.398	0.548
0.546	Jim Edmonds (17)	17	**1.25**	8	35	2	32	97	5	80	0.284	0.376	0.527
0.545	Jack Clark (18)	18	**1.24**		27	3	28	96	6	103	0.267	0.379	0.476
0.544	**Dave Windfield**	22	1.22	7	29	5	25	100	12	66	0.283	0.353	0.475
0.542	Bob Johnson (13)	13	**1.33**		34	8	25	112	8	93	0.296	0.393	0.506
0.540	**Larry Doby**	13	1.26		26	5	27	103	5	92	0.283	0.386	0.490
0.539	Manny Ramirez (19, 41)	19	**1.39**		38	1	39	129	3	94	0.312	0.411	0.585
0.539	Sammy Sosa (18)	18	**1.29**		26	3	42	115	16	64	0.273	0.344	0.534
0.539	Jeff Heath (14)	14	**1.35**		33	12	23	104	7	69	0.293	0.370	0.509
0.536	**Elmer Flick**	13	1.32		29	18	5	83	36	65	0.313	0.389	0.445
0.536	Gary Sheffield (22)	22	**1.24**		29	2	32	105	16	93	0.292	0.393	0.514
0.536	**Roberto Clemente**	18	1.27	12	29	11	16	87	6	41	0.317	0.359	0.475
0.536	**Paul Waner**	20	1.22		38	12	7	83	7	69	0.333	0.404	0.473
0.535	**Chuck Klein+ (17)**	17	1.39		37	7	28	111	7	56	0.320	0.379	0.543
0.534	Hank Sauer (15)	15	**1.30**		23	2	33	101	1	65	0.266	0.347	0.496
0.534	Vladimir Guerrero (16)	16	**1.31**		36	3	34	113	14	56	0.318	0.379	0.553
0.532	Albert Belle (12)	12	**1.38**		41	2	40	130	9	72	0.295	0.369	0.564
0.531	Darryl Strawberry (17)	17	**1.26**		26	4	34	102	23	84	0.259	0.357	0.505
0.531	**Andre Dawson**	21	1.23	8	31	6	27	98	19	36	0.279	0.323	0.482
0.530	Kirk Gibson (17)	17	**1.18**		26	5	25	86	28	71	0.268	0.352	0.463
0.529	Juan Gonzalez (17)	17	**1.36**		37	2	42	135	2	44	0.295	0.343	0.561
0.529	**Sam Thompson**	15	1.41		39	18	14	150		52	0.331	0.384	0.505
0.528	Bill Nicholson (16)	16	**1.23**		26	6	23	92	3	77	0.268	0.365	0.465
0.527	Tip O'Neill (10)	10	1.35		34	14	8	117		65	0.326	0.392	0.458
0.526	**Harry Heilmann**	17	1.37		41	11	14	116	9	65	0.342	0.410	0.520
0.525	**Joe Medwick**	17	1.33		44	9	17	113	3	36	0.324	0.362	0.505
0.525	Bobby Abreu (17)	17	**1.14**	1	39	4	20	93	28	100	0.292	0.396	0.477
0.525	**Earl Averill**	13	1.34		39	12	23	113	7	75	0.318	0.395	0.534
0.524	Greg Luzinski (15)	15	**1.26**		31	2	27	100	3	75	0.276	0.363	0.478
0.523	**Edd Roush**	18	1.20		28	15	6	81	22	40	0.323	0.369	0.446
0.522	Carlos Delgado (17)	17	**1.29**		38	1	38	120	1	88	0.280	0.383	0.546
0.522	Rick Monday (19)	19	**1.18**		20	5	20	63	8	75	0.264	0.361	0.443
0.522	**Lefty O'Doul (11)**	11	1.35		29	7	19	91	6	56	0.349	0.413	0.532

0.522	Dale Murphy (18)	18	**1.21**	5	26	3	30	94	12	73	0.265	0.346	0.469
0.521	Ellis Burks (18)	18	**1.24**	1	33	5	29	98	15	64	0.291	0.363	0.510
0.520	Rico Carty (15)	15	**1.25**		27	2	20	87	2	63	0.299	0.369	0.464
0.520	**Pete Browning (13)**	**13**	**1.33**		**40**	**12**	**6**	**90**		**64**	**0.341**	**0.403**	**0.467**
0.520	**Bill Williams**	**18**	**1.32**		**28**	**6**	**28**	**96**	**6**	**68**	**0.290**	**0.361**	**0.492**
0.520	**Goose Goslin**	**18**	**1.25**		**35**	**12**	**18**	**114**	**12**	**67**	**0.316**	**0.387**	**0.500**
0.520	Tony Oliva (15)	15	**1.29**	1	32	5	21	92	8	43	0.304	0.353	0.476
0.519	Babe Herman (13)	13	**1.34**		42	11	19	104	10	54	0.324	0.383	0.532
0.519	Brian Giles (15)	15	**1.19**		36	5	25	95	10	104	0.291	0.400	0.502
0.518	Cy Williams (19)	19	**1.26**		25	6	20	81	9	56	0.292	0.365	0.470
0.518	**Zach Wheat**	**19**	**1.25**		**32**	**12**	**9**	**84**	**14**	**44**	**0.317**	**0.367**	**0.450**
0.518	Tommy Henrich (11)	11	**1.28**		34	9	23	100	5	90	0.282	0.382	0.491
0.517	Bob Allison (13)	13	**1.25**		23	6	27	84	9	84	0.255	0.358	0.471
0.517	George Foster (18)	18	**1.26**		25	4	29	102	4	55	0.274	0.338	0.480
0.516	Bernie Williams (16)	16	**1.14**	4	35	4	22	98	11	83	0.297	0.381	0.477
0.515	Rocky Colavito (14)	14	**1.28**		25	2	33	102	2	84	0.266	0.359	0.489
0.514	Carlos Beltran (16, 36)	16	**1.18**	3	35	6	28	104	24	73	0.283	0.359	0.496
0.513	Rusty Staub (23)	23	**1.15**		27	3	16	80	3	69	0.279	0.362	0.431
0.513	Oscar Gamble (17)	17	**1.20**		19	3	20	68	5	62	0.265	0.356	0.454
0.513	Bobby Murcer (17)	17	**1.18**	1	24	4	21	89	11	73	0.277	0.357	0.445
0.513	Ryan Braun (7, 29)	7	**1.38**		41	5	36	117	22	57	0.312	0.374	0.564
0.512	**Tony Gwynn+ (20)**	**20**	**1.14**	**5**	**36**	**6**	**9**	**76**	**21**	**52**	**0.338**	**0.388**	**0.459**
0.512	Andruw Jones (17)	17	**1.16**	10	28	3	32	95	11	66	0.254	0.337	0.486
0.512	Jose Canseco (17)	17	**1.27**		29	1	40	121	17	78	0.266	0.353	0.515
0.511	Ken Singleton (15)	15	**1.15**		25	2	19	83	2	98	0.282	0.388	0.436
0.510	Reggie Sanders (17)	17	**1.16**		31	5	28	90	28	61	0.267	0.343	0.487
0.510	**King Kelly**	**16**	**1.29**		**40**	**11**	**8**	**106**		**61**	**0.308**	**0.368**	**0.438**
0.510	Gary Matthews (16)	16	**1.15**		25	4	19	78	15	75	0.281	0.364	0.439
0.509	Minnie Minoso (17)	17	**1.19**		30	7	16	90	18	72	0.298	0.389	0.459
0.509	Gorman Thomas (13)	13	**1.18**		24	1	30	88	6	79	0.225	0.324	0.448
0.509	**Kiki Cuyler**	**18**	**1.19**		**34**	**14**	**11**	**92**	**28**	**58**	**0.321**	**0.386**	**0.474**
0.508	Moises Alou (17)	17	**1.24**		35	3	28	107	9	61	0.303	0.369	0.516
0.508	Kevin Mitchell (13)	13	**1.30**		30	3	31	101	4	65	0.284	0.360	0.520
0.508	Vic Wertz (17)	17	**1.21**		25	4	23	102	1	72	0.277	0.364	0.469
0.507	Jay Buhner (15)	15	**1.21**	1	26	2	34	106	1	87	0.254	0.359	0.494
0.507	**Sam Rice**	**20**	**1.12**		**34**	**12**	**2**	**73**	**24**	**48**	**0.322**	**0.374**	**0.427**
0.507	Jimmy Ryan (18)	18	**1.23**		36	13	9	88		65	0.308	0.375	0.444
0.506	Harold Baines (22)	22	**1.16**		28	3	22	93	2	61	0.289	0.356	0.465
0.506	Joe Adcock (17)	17	**1.25**		24	3	28	93	2	49	0.277	0.337	0.485
0.506	Brian Downing	20	**1.11**		25	2	19	74	3	83	0.267	0.370	0.425

0.504	Ron Gant (16)	16	**1.14**		27	4	28	89	21	68	0.256	0.336	0.468
0.503	Danny Tartabull (14)	14	**1.25**		33	3	30	107	4	88	0.273	0.368	0.496
0.502	Dave Parker (19)	19	**1.23**	3	35	5	22	98	10	45	0.290	0.339	0.471
0.502	**Chick Hafey**	**13**	1.32		**43**	**8**	**21**	**105**	**9**	**47**	**0.317**	**0.372**	**0.526**
0.501	**Lou Brock**	**19**	1.09		**30**	**9**	**9**	**56**	**58**	**47**	**0.293**	**0.343**	**0.410**
0.501	Matt Holliday (10, 33)	10	**1.28**		42	3	28	109	11	67	0.311	0.387	0.531
0.499	Sid Gordon (13)	13	**1.23**		24	5	22	88	2	80	0.283	0.377	0.466
0.499	Wally Berger (11)	11	**1.31**		36	7	29	108	4	52	0.300	0.359	0.522
0.498	Roger Maris (12)	12	**1.26**	1	22	5	30	94	2	72	0.260	0.345	0.476
0.497	Ron Fairly	21	**1.09**		20	2	14	69	2	70	0.266	0.360	0.408
0.497	Willie Horton (18)	18	**1.23**		23	3	26	93	2	50	0.273	0.332	0.457
0.496	Paul O'Neill (17)	17	**1.16**		36	2	22	100	11	70	0.288	0.363	0.470
0.496	Ben Oglivie (16)	16	**1.18**		26	3	22	83	8	52	0.273	0.336	0.450
0.496	**Jim Rice**	**16**	1.30		**29**	**6**	**30**	**113**	**4**	**52**	**0.298**	**0.352**	**0.502**
0.495	Pete Rose	24	**1.09**	2	34	6	7	60	9	71	0.303	0.375	0.409
0.495	Carlos Gonzalez	6	**1.31**	3	35	7	29	98	25	53	0.300	0.357	0.530
0.495	Vada Pinson	18	**1.18**	1	32	8	17	77	20	38	0.286	0.327	0.442
0.495	David Justice (14)	14	**1.22**		28	2	31	102	5	91	0.279	0.378	0.500
0.494	Ray Lankford (14)	14	**1.15**		34	5	23	83	25	79	0.272	0.364	0.477
0.494	Larry Hisle (14)	14	**1.20**		26	4	22	91	17	63	0.273	0.347	0.452
0.493	Adam Dunn (13, 33)	13	**1.19**		27	1	38	96	5	108	0.238	0.366	0.495
0.492	Chili Davis (19)	19	**1.13**		28	2	23	91	9	79	0.274	0.360	0.451
0.491	Dusty Baker (19)	19	**1.14**	1	25	2	19	80	11	61	0.278	0.347	0.432
0.490	Johnny Callison (16)	16	**1.17**		28	8	19	72	6	56	0.264	0.331	0.441
0.490	Ken Griffey (19)	19	**1.12**		28	6	12	66	15	56	0.296	0.359	0.431
0.490	Shawn Green (15)	15	**1.17**	1	37	3	27	89	13	62	0.283	0.355	0.494
0.489	**Kirby Puckett**	**12**	1.21	6	**38**	**5**	**19**	**99**	**12**	**41**	**0.318**	**0.360**	**0.477**
0.488	Magglio Ordonez (15)	15	**1.19**		37	2	26	108	8	57	0.309	0.369	0.502
0.487	Torii Hunter (17, 37)	17	**1.11**	9	34	3	24	95	15	47	0.279	0.335	0.466
0.486	**Willie Keeler**	**19**	1.19		**18**	**11**	**3**	**62**	**38**	**40**	**0.341**	**0.388**	**0.415**
0.486	Jesse Barfield (12)	12	**1.21**	2	25	3	27	81	7	63	0.256	0.335	0.466
0.485	Gary Maddox	15	**1.08**	8	31	6	11	70	23	30	0.285	0.320	0.413
0.485	Luis Gonzalez (19)	19	**1.15**		37	4	22	90	8	72	0.283	0.367	0.479
0.483	Andrew McCutchen	5	**1.21**	1	36	7	23	84	28	80	0.296	0.380	0.489
0.482	Bobby Veach (14)	14	**1.22**		35	13	6	104	17	51	0.310	0.370	0.442
0.482	Richie Zisk (13)	13	**1.23**		27	3	23	88	1	59	0.287	0.353	0.466
0.481	**James O'Rourke**	**19**	1.26		**38**	**12**	**5**	**98**		**42**	**0.310**	**0.352**	**0.422**
0.481	Matt Stairs (19)	19	**1.14**		25	1	23	77	3	61	0.262	0.356	0.477
0.480	**Richie Ashburn**	**15**	0.98		**23**	**8**	**2**	**43**	**17**	**89**	**0.308**	**0.396**	**0.382**
0.480	Tim Salmon (14)	14	**1.19**		33	2	29	98	5	94	0.282	0.385	0.498

0.479	Curtis Granderson	10	**1.18**		27	11	30	83	17	70	0.261	0.340	0.488
0.479	Joe Carter (16)	16	**1.16**		32	4	29	107	17	39	0.259	0.306	0.464
0.479	**Heinie Manush**	**17**	**1.20**		**40**	**13**	**9**	**95**	**9**	**41**	**0.330**	**0.377**	**0.479**
0.479	**Harry Hooper**	**17**	**1.08**		**27**	**11**	**5**	**57**	**26**	**80**	**0.281**	**0.368**	**0.387**
0.479	Al Oliver (18)	18	**1.20**		36	5	15	91	6	37	0.303	0.344	0.451
0.479	Andy Pafko (17)	17	**1.18**		23	5	19	85	3	49	0.285	0.350	0.449
0.478	J.D. Drew (14)	14	**1.16**		28	5	25	82	9	89	0.278	0.384	0.489
0.478	Jose Bautista (10, 32)	10	**1.18**		28	2	31	85	7	86	0.254	0.361	0.487
0.478	Ruben Sierra (20)	20	**1.10**		32	4	23	98	11	45	0.268	0.315	0.450
0.478	**Enos Slaughter**	**19**	**1.18**		28	10	12	89	5	69	0.300	0.382	0.453
0.477	Bob Meusel (11)	11	**1.24**		42	11	18	123	16	43	0.309	0.356	0.497
0.477	George Hendrick (18)	18	**1.17**		27	2	21	88	5	45	0.278	0.329	0.446
0.476	Devon White	17	**1.03**	7	32	6	17	71	29	45	0.263	0.319	0.419
0.475	Bill Robinson (16)	16	**1.17**		25	3	18	71	8	29	0.258	0.300	0.438
0.475	Chet Lemon (16)	16	**1.15**		32	5	18	72	5	61	0.273	0.355	0.442
0.475	Mike Cameron (17)	17	**1.05**		32	5	23	80	25	72	0.249	0.338	0.444
0.473	Josh Hamilton (7, 32)	7	**1.30**		37	4	33	115	9	57	0.295	0.354	0.530
0.471	Del Ennis (14)	14	**1.22**		30	6	25	109	4	51	0.284	0.340	0.472
0.471	Sixto Lezcano (12)	12	**1.15**		23	4	19	74	5	72	0.271	0.360	0.440
0.471	Rob Deer (11)	11	**1.13**		21	2	32	84	6	81	0.220	0.324	0.442
0.470	Dante Bichette (14)	14	**1.22**		38	3	26	108	14	34	0.299	0.336	0.499
0.469	**Earle Coombs**	**12**	**1.16**		**34**	**17**	**6**	**70**	**11**	**75**	**0.325**	**0.397**	**0.462**
0.469	**Monte Irvin**	**8**	**1.22**		**21**	**7**	**21**	**94**	**6**	**74**	**0.293**	**0.383**	**0.475**
0.468	Felipe Alou (17)	17	**1.15**		28	4	16	66	8	33	0.286	0.328	0.433
0.465	Dixie Walker (18)	18	**1.09**		32	8	9	87	5	69	0.306	0.383	0.437
0.465	Matt Kemp (8, 28)	8	**1.20**	2	30	5	26	94	27	52	0.293	0.350	0.493
0.465	Richie Sexson (12)	12	**1.19**		31	2	36	112	2	70	0.261	0.344	0.507
0.465	Tony Conigliaro (8)	8	**1.28**		26	4	31	95	4	53	0.264	0.327	0.476
0.463	**Ross Youngs**	**10**	**1.17**		**32**	**12**	**6**	**79**	**20**	**74**	**0.322**	**0.399**	**0.441**
0.462	Paul Blair	17	**1.02**	8	23	5	11	52	14	37	0.250	0.302	0.382
0.462	Don Baylor (19)	19	**1.14**		26	2	24	90	20	57	0.260	0.342	0.436
0.462	Willie Wilson	19	**0.97**	1	21	11	3	44	50	32	0.285	0.326	0.376
0.462	Raul Ibanez (18, 41)	18	**1.12**		33	4	23	92	4	53	0.276	0.338	0.471
0.461	Steve Finley (19)	19	**1.07**	5	28	8	19	73	20	53	0.271	0.332	0.442
0.460	Johnny Damon (18)	18	**1.03**		34	7	15	74	27	65	0.284	0.352	0.433
0.460	Raul Mondesi (13)	13	**1.14**	2	34	5	29	91	24	50	0.273	0.331	0.485
0.451	Vernon Wells (15, 34)	15	**1.10**	3	35	3	25	90	10	44	0.270	0.319	0.459
0.450	Curt Flood	15	**1.03**	7	25	4	8	59	8	41	0.293	0.342	0.389
0.450	Nelson Cruz (9, 32)	9	**1.20**		34	2	32	99	13	50	0.268	0.327	0.495
0.448	Justin Upton (7, 25)	7	**1.16**		32	6	25	80	16	70	0.275	0.356	0.473

0.446	Willie Davis	18	**1.05**	3	26	9	12	70	27	28	0.279	0.311	0.412
0.445	Brian Jordan (15)	15	**1.08**		30	4	20	91	13	39	0.282	0.333	0.455
0.444	Jermaine Dye (14)	14	**1.15**	1	33	2	30	99	4	55	0.274	0.338	0.488
0.439	Shane Victorino (10, 32)	10	**1.05**	4	30	9	14	64	30	49	0.277	0.342	0.432
0.438	Willie Mcgee	18	**0.99**	3	26	7	6	63	26	33	0.295	0.333	0.396
0.435	Garret Anderson (17)	17	**1.09**		38	3	21	99	6	31	0.293	0.324	0.461
0.428	**Lloyd Waner**	**18**	**1.01**		**23**	**10**	**2**	**49**	**5**	**34**	**0.316**	**0.353**	**0.393**
0.427	**Tom McCarthy**	**13**	**1.05**		**24**	**7**	**6**	**93**		**68**	**0.292**	**0.364**	**0.375**
0.425	Richard Hidalgo (9)	9	**1.15**		35	3	28	92	8	59	0.269	0.345	0.490
0.425	Geoff Jenkins (11)	11	**0.95**		31	11	5	98	42	60	0.295	0.362	0.405
0.424	Carlos Quentin (8, 30)	8	**1.19**		35	1	31	98	3	58	0.255	0.350	0.492
0.418	Tommy Davis	18	**1.02**		22	3	12	85	11	31	0.294	0.329	0.405
0.413	Bobby Thomson (15)	15	**1.01**		24	7	24	93	3	51	0.270	0.332	0.462
0.364	Ichiro Suzuki	13	**0.92**	10	28	4	11	62	12	29	0.255	0.293	0.383

Absolute Adjusted Slugging Rankings— Total Offense only

No adjustment for defense or total years played

Total bases plus walks and stolen bases

Rank	Abs Adj slg	Player	2B	3B	HR	RBI	SB	BB	BA	SLG
1	1.98	Babe Ruth+ (22)	33	9	46	144	8	133	0.342	0.690
2	1.84	Ted Williams+ (19)	37	5	37	130	2	143	0.344	0.634
3	1.75	Barry Bonds (22)	33	4	41	108	28	139	0.298	0.607
4	1.73	Ty Cobb+ (24)	39	16	6	103	48	67	0.366	0.512
5	1.73	Lou Gehrig+ (17)	40	12	37	149	8	113	0.340	0.632
6	1.73	Billy Hamilton	25	10	4	75	93	121	0.344	0.432
7	1.73	Shoeless Joe Jackson	37	20	7	95	25	63	0.356	0.517
8	1.72	Jimmie Foxx+ (20)	32	9	37	134	6	102	0.325	0.609
9	1.70	Hank Greenberg	44	8	38	148	7	99	0.313	0.605
10	1.69	Mickey Mantle	23	5	36	102	10	117	0.298	0.557
11	1.66	Willie Mays+ (22)	28	8	36	103	18	79	0.302	0.557
12	1.65	Honus Wagner+ (21)	37	15	6	100	42	56	0.328	0.467
13	1.63	Ed Delahanty+ (16)	46	16	9	129	40	65	0.346	0.505
14	1.63	Dick Allen (15)	30	7	33	104	12	83	0.292	0.534
15	1.62	Charlie Keller (13)	23	10	26	105	6	109	0.286	0.518
16	1.62	Rogers Hornsby+ (23)	39	12	22	114	10	74	0.358	0.577
17	1.62	Hank Aaron+ (23)	31	5	37	113	12	69	0.305	0.555
18	1.62	Joe DiMaggio+ (13)	36	12	34	143	3	74	0.325	0.579
19	1.61	Ralph Kiner+ (10)	24	4	41	112	2	111	0.279	0.548
20	1.61	Tris Speaker	46	13	7	89	25	80	0.345	0.500
21	1.61	Stan Musial+ (22)	39	9	25	104	4	86	0.331	0.559
22	1.60	Dan Brouthers+ (19)	45	20	10	125		81	0.342	0.519

23	1.60	Mark McGwire (16)	22	1	50	122	1	114	0.263	0.588
24	1.59	Johnny Mize+ (15)	32	7	31	115	2	74	0.312	0.562
25	1.59	Frank Robinson+ (21)	30	4	34	105	12	82	0.294	0.537
26	1.59	Mike Schmidt+ (18)	27	4	37	107	12	102	0.267	0.527
27	1.58	Elmer Flick	29	18	5	83	36	65	0.313	0.445
28	1.58	Roger Conner	36	19	11	107	13	81	0.316	0.486
29	1.58	Hugh Duffy	30	11	10	121	54	62	0.326	0.451
30	1.56	Joe Kelly	31	17	6	104	39	80	0.317	0.451
31	1.56	Albert Pujols (13, 33)	43	1	41	124	8	88	0.321	0.599
32	1.56	Mel Ott+ (22)	29	4	30	110	5	101	0.304	0.533
33	1.55	Bobby Bonds (14)	26	6	29	90	40	80	0.268	0.471
34	1.55	Ken Williams (14)	33	9	23	106	18	66	0.319	0.530
35	1.54	Frank Chance	25	10	3	75	51	70	0.296	0.394
36	1.54	Sam Crawford	29	20	6	98	24	49	0.309	0.452
37	1.54	Duke Snider	27	6	31	101	7	73	0.295	0.540
38	1.54	Harmon Killebrew+ (22)	19	2	38	105	1	104	0.256	0.509
39	1.54	Joe Morgan	27	6	16	69	42	114	0.271	0.427
40	1.53	Willie McCovey+ (22)	22	3	33	97	2	84	0.270	0.515
41	1.53	Larry Walker (17)	38	5	31	107	19	74	0.313	0.565
42	1.52	Eddie Mathews	24	5	35	98	5	98	0.271	0.509
43	1.52	Bob Johnson (13)	34	8	25	112	8	93	0.296	0.506
44	1.52	Willie Stargell+ (21)	29	4	33	106	1	64	0.282	0.529
45	1.52	Ricky Henderson	27	3	16	59	74	115	0.279	0.419
46	1.52	Ryan Braun (7, 29)	41	5	36	117	22	57	0.312	0.564
47	1.51	Manny Ramirez (19, 41)	38	1	39	129	3	94	0.312	0.585
48	1.51	Jeff Heath (14)	33	12	23	104	7	69	0.293	0.509
49	1.51	Joey Votto (7, 29)	41	2	29	96	9	103	0.314	0.541
50	1.51	Nap Lajoie+ (21)	43	11	5	104	25	34	0.338	0.466
51	1.50	Chuck Klein+ (17)	37	7	28	111	7	56	0.320	0.543
52	1.50	Dolph Camilli (12)	28	9	26	103	7	103	0.277	0.492
53	1.50	Eddie Collins	25	11	3	75	42	86	0.333	0.429
54	1.50	Hack Wilson+ (12)	32	8	29	128	6	81	0.307	0.545
55	1.50	Jim Thome (22)	29	2	39	108	1	111	0.276	0.554
56	1.49	Albert Belle (12)	41	2	40	130	9	72	0.295	0.564
57	1.49	Darryl Strawberry (17)	26	4	34	102	23	84	0.259	0.505
58	1.49	Jesse Burkett	25	14	6	75	30	81	0.338	0.446

59	1.49	**Reggie Jackson**	27	3	32	98	13	79	0.262	0.490
60	1.49	Reggie Smith (17)	30	5	26	89	11	73	0.287	0.489
61	1.49	**Frank Thomas+ (19)**	35	1	36	119	2	116	0.301	0.555
62	1.49	**Sam Thompson**	39	18	14	150		52	0.331	0.505
63	1.48	Dave Orr (8)	41	22	8	128		20	0.342	0.502
64	1.48	Miguel Cabrera (11, 30)	40	1	36	123	4	78	0.321	0.568
65	1.48	Alex Rodriguez (20, 37)	33	2	41	124	20	78	0.299	0.558
66	1.48	**Tip O'Neill (10)**	34	14	8	117		65	0.326	0.458
67	1.48	Jeff Bagwell (15)	37	2	34	115	15	106	0.297	0.540
68	1.48	**Fred Clarke**	26	16	5	73	37	63	0.312	0.429
69	1.48	**Harry Heilmann**	41	11	14	116	9	65	0.342	0.520
70	1.47	Hal Trosky (11)	40	7	27	122	3	66	0.302	0.522
71	1.47	**Earl Averill**	39	12	23	113	7	75	0.318	0.534
72	1.47	Eric Davis (17)	24	3	28	93	35	74	0.269	0.482
73	1.47	**Home Run Baker**	32	11	10	102	24	49	0.307	0.442
74	1.47	Norm Cash (17)	19	3	29	86	3	81	0.271	0.488
75	1.47	Carlos Gonzalez	35	7	29	98	25	53	0.300	0.530
76	1.47	Jim Wynn (15)	24	3	25	81	19	103	0.250	0.436
77	1.47	**Lefty O'Doul (11)**	29	7	19	91	6	56	0.349	0.532
78	1.46	Frank Howard (16)	21	3	33	96	1	67	0.273	0.499
79	1.46	**Pete Browning**	40	12	6	90		64	0.341	0.467
80	1.46	**Billy Williams**	28	6	28	96	6	68	0.290	0.492
81	1.46	Lance Berkman (15, 37)	36	3	32	106	7	104	0.293	0.537
82	1.46	Babe Herman (13)	42	11	19	104	10	54	0.324	0.532
83	1.45	Al Rosen (10)	26	3	30	111	6	91	0.285	0.495
84	1.45	Tommy Henrich (11)	34	9	23	100	5	90	0.282	0.491
85	1.45	Bob Allison (13)	23	6	27	84	9	84	0.255	0.471
86	1.45	Jack Clark (18)	27	3	28	96	6	103	0.267	0.476
87	1.45	Hanley Ramirez (9, 29)	40	4	26	86	37	67	0.302	0.506
88	1.45	Ken Griffey (22)	32	2	38	111	11	80	0.284	0.538
89	1.44	Rocky Colavito (14)	25	2	33	102	2	84	0.266	0.489
90	1.44	**Jackie Robinson**	32	6	16	86	23	87	0.311	0.474
91	1.44	**Larry Doby**	26	5	27	103	5	92	0.283	0.490
92	1.44	Chipper Jones (19)	36	2	30	105	10	98	0.303	0.529
93	1.44	**George Davis**	31	11	5	98	42	60	0.295	0.405
94	1.44	David Ortiz (17, 37)	43	1	35	118	1	89	0.287	0.549

95	**1.44**	**Al Simmons**	**39**	**11**	**22**	**134**	**6**	**45**	**0.334**	**0.535**
96	**1.44**	Orlando Cepeda+ (17)	32	2	29	104	11	45	0.297	0.499
97	**1.44**	Cesar Cedeno (17)	35	5	16	79	44	54	0.285	0.443
98	**1.44**	Sammy Sosa (18)	26	3	42	115	16	64	0.273	0.534
99	**1.44**	Jose Canseco (17)	29	1	40	121	17	78	0.266	0.515
100	**1.44**	Ryan Howard (10, 33)	30	3	43	132	2	81	0.271	0.545
101	**1.43**	**Carl Yastremski**	**32**	**3**	**22**	**90**	**8**	**90**	**0.285**	**0.462**
102	**1.43**	Gary Sheffield (22)	29	2	32	105	16	93	0.292	0.514
103	**1.43**	Andrew McCutchen (5, 26)	36	7	23	84	28	80	0.296	0.489
104	**1.43**	**King Kelly**	**40**	**11**	**8**	**106**		**61**	**0.308**	**0.438**
105	**1.43**	Todd Helton (17, 39)	43	3	27	101	3	96	0.316	0.539
106	**1.43**	Kevin Mitchell (13)	30	3	31	101	4	65	0.284	0.520
107	**1.42**	Hank Sauer (15)	23	2	33	101	1	65	0.266	0.496
108	**1.42**	Vladimir Guerrero (16)	36	3	34	113	14	56	0.318·	0.553
109	**1.42**	Tim Raines	28	7	11	63	52	86	0.294	0.425
110	**1.42**	Jim Gentile (9)	20	1	31	95	1	·82	0.260	0.486
111	**1.42**	**George Brett**	**40**	**8**	**19**	**96**	**12**	**66**	**0.305**	**0.487**
112	**1.42**	**Johnny Bench**	**29**	**2**	**29**	**103**	**5**	**67**	**0.267**	**0.476**
113	**1.42**	**Al Kaline+ (22)**	**28**	**4**	**23**	**90**	**8**	**73**	**0.297**	**0.480**
114	**1.42**	**Flash Gordon**	**27**	**5**	**26**	**101**	**9**	**79**	**0.268**	**0.466**
115	**1.42**	Gil Hodges (18)	23	4	29	100	5	74	0.273	0.487
116	**1.42**	**Roy Campanella+ (10)**	**24**	**2**	**32**	**114**	**3**	**71**	**0.276**	**0.500**
117	**1.42**	Edgar Martinez (18)	41	1	24	99	4	101	0.312	0.515
118	**1.41**	Kirk Gibson (17)	26	5	25	86	28	71	0.268	0.463
119	**1.41**	David Wright (10, 30)	41	3	26	103	22	79	0.301	0.506
120	**1.41**	Juan Gonzalez (17)	37	2	42	135	2	44	0.295	0.561
121	**1.41**	Danny Tartabull (14)	33	3	30	107	4	88	0.273	0.496
122	**1.41**	**Cap Anson**	**37**	**9**	**6**	**133**		**63**	**0.334**	**0.447**
123	**1.41**	Boog Powell (17)	21	1	27	94	2	79	0.266	0.462
124	**1.41**	**Chick Hafey**	**43**	**8**	**21**	**105**	**9**	**47**	**0.317**	**0.526**
125	**1.41**	Bill Nicholson (16)	26	6	23	92	3	77	0.268	0.465
126	**1.41**	**Joe Torre+ (18)**	**25**	**4**	**18**	**87**	**2**	**57**	**0.297**	**0.452**
127	**1.41**	Dwight Evans (20)	30	5	24	86	5	86	0.272	0.470
128	**1.41**	Fred Lynn (17)	32	4	25	91	6	71	0.283	0.484
129	**1.41**	**Lou Brock**	**30**	**9**	**9**	**56**	**58**	**47**	**0.293**	**0.410**
130	**1.41**	**Ron Santo**	**26**	**5**	**25**	**96**	**3**	**80**	**0.277**	**0.464**

131	**1.41**	Matt Holliday (10, 33)	42	3	28	109	11	67	0.311	0.531
132	**1.40**	Sid Gordon (13)	24	5	22	88	2	80	0.283	0.466
133	**1.40**	Fred McGriff (19)	29	2	32	102	5	86	0.284	0.509
134	**1.40**	Josh Hamilton (7, 32)	37	4	33	115	9	57	0.295	0.530
135	**1.40**	**Joe Medwick**	**44**	**9**	**17**	**113**	**3**	**36**	**0.324**	**0.505**
136	**1.40**	Bobby Abreu (17)	39	4	20	93	28	100	0.292	0.477
137	**1.40**	Prince Fielder (9, 29)	33	1	35	107	2	89	0.286	0.527
138	**1.40**	Wally Berger (11)	36	7	29	108	4	52	0.300	0.522
139	**1.40**	Roger Maris (12)	22	5	30	94	2	72	0.260	0.476
140	**1.40**	Bob Horner (10)	27	1	35	109	2	59	0.277	0.499
141	**1.40**	Evan Longoria (6, 27)	41	2	33	111	8	76	0.275	0.512
142	**1.40**	Greg Luzinski (15)	31	2	27	100	3	75	0.276	0.478
143	**1.40**	**Ernie Banks+ (19)**	**26**	**6**	**33**	**105**	**3**	**49**	**0.274**	**0.500**
144	**1.39**	Pedro Guerrero (15)	28	3	23	95	10	64	0.300	0.480
145	**1.39**	Mike Piazza (16)	29	1	36	113	1	64	0.308	0.545
146	**1.39**	**Charlie Gehringer**	**40**	**10**	**13**	**100**	**13**	**83**	**0.320**	**0.480**
147	**1.39**	Carlos Delgado (17)	38	1	38	120	1	88	0.280	0.546
148	**1.39**	Rick Monday (19)	20	5	20	63	8	75	0.264	0.443
149	**1.39**	Dale Murphy (18)	26	3	30	94	12	73	0.265	0.469
150	**1.39**	Bill Dahlen	27	11	6	82	36	71	0.272	0.382
151	**1.39**	**Jim Rice**	**29**	**6**	**30**	**113**	**4**	**52**	**0.298**	**0.502**
152	**1.39**	Jim Ray Hart (12)	21	4	24	83	2	55	0.278	0.467
153	**1.39**	Ellis Burks (18)	33	5	29	98	15	64	0.291	0.510
154	**1.39**	David Justice (14)	28	2	31	102	5	91	0.279	0.500
155	**1.39**	**Monte Irvin**	**21**	**7**	**21**	**94**	**6**	**74**	**0.293**	**0.475**
156	**1.39**	Rico Carty (15)	27	2	20	87	2	63	0.299	0.464
157	**1.39**	**Buck Ewing**	**31**	**22**	**9**	**109**		**48**	**0.303**	**0.456**
158	**1.39**	**Goose Goslin**	**35**	**12**	**18**	**114**	**12**	**67**	**0.316**	**0.500**
159	**1.39**	Ray Lankford (14)	34	5	23	83	25	79	0.272	0.477
160	**1.39**	Tony Oliva (15)	32	5	21	92	8	43	0.304	0.476
161	**1.39**	Jim Edmonds (17)	35	2	32	97	5	80	0.284	0.527
162	**1.39**	Larry Hisle (14)	26	4	22	91	17	63	0.273	0.452
163	**1.38**	Adam Dunn (13, 33)	27	1	38	96	5	108	0.238	0.495
164	**1.38**	**George Sisler+ (15)**	**34**	**13**	**8**	**93**	**30**	**37**	**0.340**	**0.468**
165	**1.38**	Rafael Palmeiro (20)	33	2	33	105	6	77	0.288	0.515
166	**1.38**	Brian Giles (15)	36	5	25	95	10	104	0.291	0.502

167	1.38	Kent Hrbek (14)	29	2	27	101	3	78	0.282	0.481
168	1.38	**Dave Winfield**	**29**	**5**	**25**	**100**	**12**	**66**	**0.283**	**0.475**
169	1.38	Cy Williams (19)	25	6	20	81	9	56	0.292	0.470
170	1.38	**Zack Wheat**	**32**	**12**	**9**	**84**	**14**	**44**	**0.317**	**0.450**
171	1.38	**Roger Bresnahan**	**24**	**8**	**3**	**59**	**24**	**80**	**0.279**	**0.377**
172	1.38	Jason Giambi (19, 42)	29	1	32	104	1	98	0.278	0.519
173	1.38	George Foster (18)	25	4	29	102	4	55	0.274	0.480
174	1.38	Matt Kemp (8, 28)	30	5	26	94	27	52	0.293	0.493
175	1.38	Tony Conigliaro (8)	26	4	31	95	4	53	0.264	0.476
176	1.38	Mark Teixeira (11, 33)	38	2	37	119	2	81	0.278	0.525
177	1.38	Dave Kingman (16)	20	2	37	101	7	51	0.236	0.478
178	1.37	**Arky Vaughn**	**32**	**11**	**9**	**83**	**11**	**84**	**0.318**	**0.453**
179	1.37	Ted Kluszewski (15)	27	3	26	97	2	46	0.298	0.498
180	1.37	Mo Vaughn (12)	29	1	35	114	3	78	0.293	0.523
181	1.37	Carlos Beltran (16, 36)	35	6	28	104	24	73	0.283	0.496
182	1.37	**Joe Cronin**	**39**	**9**	**13**	**109**	**7**	**81**	**0.301**	**0.468**
183	1.37	Oscar Gamble (17)	19	3	20	68	5	62	0.265	0.454
184	1.37	**Jacob Beckley**	**32**	**17**	**6**	**107**	**21**	**42**	**0.308**	**0.436**
185	1.37	Bobby Murcer (17)	24	4	21	89	11	73	0.277	0.445
186	1.37	**Mickey Cochrane**	**36**	**7**	**13**	**91**	**7**	**94**	**0.320**	**0.478**
187	1.37	**Ross Youngs**	**32**	**12**	**6**	**79**	**20**	**74**	**0.322**	**0.441**
188	1.37	**Bill Dickey**	**31**	**7**	**18**	**109**	**3**	**61**	**0.313**	**0.486**
189	1.36	Vern Stephens (15)	29	4	23	111	2	65	0.286	0.460
190	1.36	**Willie Keeler**	**18**	**11**	**3**	**62**	**38**	**40**	**0.341**	**0.415**
191	1.36	John Mayberry (15)	21	2	26	88	2	88	0.253	0.439
192	1.36	Jesse Barfield (12)	25	3	27	81	7	63	0.256	0.466
193	1.36	Darrel Evans	20	2	25	82	6	97	0.248	0.431
194	1.36	Ken Singleton (15)	25	2	19	83	2	98	0.282	0.436
195	1.36	**Robert Doerr**	**33**	**8**	**19**	**108**	**5**	**70**	**0.288**	**0.461**
196	1.36	Gorman Thomas (13)	24	1	30	88	6	79	0.225	0.448
197	1.36	Reggie Sanders (17)	31	5	28	90	28	61	0.267	0.487
198	1.36	**Roberto Clemente+ (18)**	**29**	**11**	**16**	**87**	**6**	**41**	**0.317**	**0.475**
199	1.36	**Max Carey**	**27**	**10**	**5**	**52**	**48**	**68**	**0.285**	**0.386**
200	1.36	**Paul Waner**	**38**	**12**	**7**	**83**	**7**	**69**	**0.333**	**0.473**
201	1.36	Roy Sievers (17)	25	4	27	98	1	72	0.267	0.475
202	1.36	Gary Matthews (16)	25	4	19	78	15	75	0.281	0.439

203	1.36	Mike Napoli (8, 31)	28	1	32	88	5	73	0.259	0.502
204	1.36	Minnie Minoso (17)	30	7	16	90	18	72	0.298	0.459
205	1.36	**Toni Lazerri**	**31**	**11**	**17**	**111**	**14**	**81**	**0.292**	**0.467**
206	1.36	**Kiki Cuyler**	**34**	**14**	**11**	**92**	**28**	**58**	**0.321**	**0.474**
207	1.36	Will Clark (15)	36	4	23	99	5	77	0.303	0.497
208	1.36	**Bill Terry+ (14)**	**35**	**11**	**14**	**101**	**5**	**51**	**0.341**	**0.506**
209	1.36	Moises Alou (17)	35	3	28	107	9	61	0.303	0.516
210	1.35	Vic Wertz (17)	25	4	23	102	1	72	0.277	0.469
211	1.35	**Yogi Berra**	**25**	**4**	**27**	**109**	**2**	**54**	**0.285**	**0.482**
212	1.35	Jay Buhner (15)	26	2	34	106	1	87	0.254	0.494
213	1.35	Ripper Collins (9)	31	10	20	98	3	53	0.296	0.492
214	1.35	Bob Elliott (15)	31	8	14	98	5	79	0.289	0.440
215	1.35	**Rod Carew**	**29**	**7**	**6**	**67**	**23**	**67**	**0.328**	**0.429**
216	1.35	Ryan Klesko (16)	32	3	26	92	8	76	0.279	0.500
217	1.35	Bobby Veach (14)	35	13	6	104	17	51	0.310	0.442
218	1.35	Richie Zisk (13)	27	3	23	88	1	59	0.287	0.466
219	1.35	Zeke Bonura (7)	41	5	21	124	3	71	0.307	0.487
220	1.35	Jimmy Ryan (18)	36	13	9	88		65	0.308	0.444
221	1.35	**Eddie Murray**	**30**	**2**	**27**	**103**	**6**	**71**	**0.287**	**0.476**
222	1.35	Dick Stuart (10)	23	4	33	108	0	44	0.264	0.489
223	1.35	Mickey Tettleton (14)	23	2	27	80	3	104	0.241	0.449
224	1.35	**James O'Rourke**	**38**	**12**	**5**	**98**		**42**	**0.310**	**0.422**
225	1.35	Ken Boyer (15)	25	5	22	91	8	57	0.287	0.462
226	1.35	Bill White (13)	27	6	20	84	10	58	0.286	0.455
227	1.35	Chris Davis	33	1	35	98	3	49	0.266	0.512
228	1.35	Joe Adcock (17)	24	3	28	93	2	49	0.277	0.485
229	1.35	**Andre Dawson**	**31**	**6**	**27**	**98**	**19**	**36**	**0.279**	**0.482**
230	1.35	Tim Salmon (14)	33	2	29	98	5	94	0.282	0.498
231	1.35	Ron Gant (16)	27	4	28	89	21	68	0.256	0.468
232	1.34	Curtis Granderson (10, 32)	27	11	30	83	17	70	0.261	0.488
233	1.34	**Harry Hooper**	**27**	**11**	**5**	**57**	**26**	**80**	**0.281**	**0.387**
234	1.34	**Tony Perez**	**29**	**5**	**22**	**96**	**3**	**54**	**0.279**	**0.463**
235	1.34	J.D. Drew (14)	28	5	25	82	9	89	0.278	0.489
236	1.34	Jose Bautista (10, 32)	28	2	31	85	7	86	0.254	0.487
237	1.34	**Enos Slaughter**	**28**	**10**	**12**	**89**	**5**	**69**	**0.300**	**0.453**
238	1.34	**Ryne Sandberg**	**30**	**6**	**21**	**79**	**26**	**57**	**0.285**	**0.452**

239	1.34	Bob Meusel (11)	42	11	18	123	16	43	0.309	0.497
240	1.34	**Paul Molitar**	37	7	14	79	30	66	0.306	0.448
241	1.34	Alfonso Soriano (15, 37)	40	3	34	96	24	42	0.272	0.504
242	1.34	Dave Parker (19)	35	5	22	98	10	45	0.290	0.471
243	1.34	**James Bottomley**	38	12	18	116	5	54	0.310	0.500
244	1.34	**Tom McCarthy**	24	7	6	93	36	68	0.292	0.375
245	1.33	Nelson Cruz (9, 32)	34	2	32	99	13	50	0.268	0.495
246	1.33	**Gabby Hartnet**	32	5	19	96	2	57	0.297	0.489
247	1.33	Keith Hernandez (17)	33	5	13	83	8	83	0.296	0.436
248	1.33	Cecil Fielder (13)	22	1	35	111	0	76	0.255	0.482
249	1.33	**Edd Roush**	28	15	6	81	22	40	0.323	0.446
250	1.33	Travis Hafner (12, 36)	34	2	29	100	2	82	0.273	0.498
251	1.33	Justin Upton (7, 25)	32	6	25	80	16	70	0.275	0.473
252	1.33	Chase Utley (11, 34)	36	5	27	99	16	67	0.287	0.498
253	1.33	Willie Horton (18)	23	3	26	93	2	50	0.273	0.457
254	1.32	Ron Cey (17)	26	2	25	89	2	79	0.261	0.445
255	1.32	Paul O'Neill (17)	36	2	22	100	11	70	0.288	0.470
256	1.32	Troy Glaus (13)	31	1	34	100	6	90	0.254	0.489
257	1.32	Del Ennis (14)	30	6	25	109	4	51	0.284	0.472
258	1.32	Ben Oglivie (16)	26	3	22	83	8	52	0.273	0.450
259	1.32	Sixto Lezcano (12)	23	4	19	74	5	72	0.271	0.440
260	1.32	Rob Deer (11)	21	2	32	84	6	81	0.220	0.442
261	1.32	Bob Watson (19)	27	4	16	87	2	58	0.295	0.447
262	1.32	Derrek Lee (15)	36	3	28	90	9	73	0.281	0.495
263	1.32	Vada Pinson (19)	32	8	17	77	20	38	0.286	0.442
264	1.32	Dante Bichette (14)	38	3	26	108	14	34	0.299	0.499
265	1.32	**Carlton Fisk**	27	3	24	86	8	55	0.269	0.457
266	1.32	Adrian Gonzalez (10, 31)	38	1	29	103	1	70	0.294	0.501
267	1.32	Nomar Garciaparra (14)	42	6	26	106	11	46	0.313	0.521
268	1.32	**Earle Combs**	34	17	6	70	11	75	0.325	0.462
269	1.31	Chili Davis (19)	28	2	23	91	9	79	0.274	0.451
270	1.31	Bernie Williams (16)	35	4	22	98	11	83	0.297	0.477
271	1.31	Bobby Grich	26	4	18	70	8	88	0.266	0.424
272	1.31	**Jimmy Collins**	33	11	6	92	18	40	0.294	0.409
273	1.31	Andres Galarraga (19)	32	2	29	102	9	42	0.288	0.499
274	1.31	Dusty Baker (19)	25	2	19	80	11	61	0.278	0.432

275	1.31	Cecil Cooper (17)	35	4	21	96	8	38	0.298	0.466
276	1.31	Walker Cooper (18)	26	4	19	89	2	34	0.285	0.464
277	1.31	**Kirby Puckett**	**38**	**5**	**19**	**99**	**12**	**41**	**0.318**	**0.477**
278	1.31	Johnny Callison (16)	28	8	19	72	6	56	0.264	0.441
279	1.31	Ken Griffey (19)	28	6	12	66	15	56	0.296	0.431
280	1.31	Shawn Green (15)	37	3	27	89	13	62	0.283	0.494
281	1.31	Lee May (18)	27	2	28	97	3	38	0.267	0.459
282	1.30	**Barry Larkin**	**33**	**6**	**15**	**71**	**28**	**70**	**0.295**	**0.444**
283	1.30	Richie Sexson (12)	31	2	36	112	2	70	0.261	0.507
284	1.30	Rusty Staub (23)	27	3	16	80	3	69	0.279	0.431
285	1.30	Magglio Ordonez (15)	37	2	26	108	8	57	0.309	0.502
286	1.30	**Tony Gwynn+ (20)**	**36**	**6**	**9**	**76**	**21**	**52**	**0.338**	**0.459**
287	1.30	George Scott (14)	24	5	22	84	5	56	0.268	0.435
288	1.30	Andruw Jones (17)	28	3	32	95	11	66	0.254	0.486
289	1.30	**Ernie Lombardi**	**24**	**2**	**17**	**87**	**1**	**38**	**0.306**	**0.460**
290	1.30	Doug DeCinces (15)	31	3	23	86	6	61	0.259	0.445
291	1.30	Don Baylor (19)	26	2	24	90	20	57	0.260	0.436
292	1.30	Bobby Bonilla (16)	31	5	22	90	3	70	0.279	0.472
293	1.30	**Roberto Alomar**	**34**	**5**	**14**	**77**	**32**	**70**	**0.300**	**0.443**
294	1.29	Joe Mauer (10, 30)	39	3	14	87	6	85	0.323	0.468
295	1.29	Scott Rolen (17)	41	3	25	102	9	71	0.281	0.490
296	1.29	Bill Madlock (15)	31	3	15	77	16	54	0.305	0.442
297	1.29	Luis Gonzalez (19)	37	4	22	90	8	72	0.283	0.479
298	1.29	**John Evers**	**20**	**6**	**1**	**49**	**29**	**71**	**0.270**	**0.334**
299	1.29	Corey Hart (9, 31)	36	6	26	87	14	46	0.276	0.491
300	1.29	Raul Mondesi (13)	34	5	29	91	24	50	0.273	0.485
301	1.29	Russell Branyan (14)	22	1	30	71	2	62	0.232	0.485
302	1.29	Edwin Encarnacion	33	1	29	91	7	65	0.265	0.479
303	1.29	Smoky Burgess (18)	22	3	12	64	1	46	0.295	0.446
304	1.29	**Sam Rice**	**34**	**12**	**2**	**73**	**24**	**48**	**0.322**	**0.427**
305	1.29	Robinson Cano (9, 30)	44	3	24	97	4	41	0.309	0.504
306	1.29	John Olerud (17)	36	1	18	89	1	92	0.295	0.465
307	1.28	Don Mattingly (14)	40	2	20	100	1	53	0.307	0.471
308	1.28	Kevin Youkilis (10, 34)	39	3	23	94	4	82	0.281	0.478
309	1.28	Harold Baines (22)	28	3	22	93	2	61	0.289	0.465
310	1.28	Richie Hebner (18)	23	5	17	76	3	58	0.276	0.438

311	1.28	Brian Downing	25	2	19	74	3	83	0.267	0.425
312	**1.28**	**Wade Boggs**	**38**	**4**	**8**	**67**	**2**	**94**	**0.328**	**0.443**
313	1.28	Jeff Kent (17)	39	3	27	107	7	56	0.290	0.500
314	1.28	Matt Stairs (19)	25	1	23	77	3	61	0.262	0.477
315	**1.28**	**Joe Tinker**	**24**	**10**	**3**	**70**	**30**	**37**	**0.262**	**0.353**
316	1.28	Ryan Zimmerman (9, 28)	39	2	26	96	5	65	0.286	0.477
317	1.28	Joe Carter (16)	32	4	29	107	17	39	0.259	0.464
318	**1.28**	**Heinie Manush**	**40**	**13**	**9**	**95**	**9**	**41**	**0.330**	**0.479**
319	1.28	Al Oliver (18)	36	5	15	91	6	37	0.303	0.451
320	1.28	Jorge Posada (17)	23	2	27	80	3	104	0.241	0.449
321	1.28	Andy Pafko (17)	23	5	19	85	3	49	0.285	0.449
322	**1.27**	**Frank Frisch**	**33**	**10**	**7**	**87**	**29**	**51**	**0.316**	**0.432**
323	1.27	Matt Williams (17)	29	3	33	106	5	41	0.268	0.489
324	1.27	George Hendrick (18)	27	2	21	88	5	45	0.278	0.446
325	1.27	Paul Konerko (17, 37)	29	1	31	99	1	65	0.281	0.491
326	**1.27**	**Lou Boudreau**	**38**	**6**	**7**	**78**	**5**	**78**	**0.295**	**0.415**
327	**1.27**	**Gary Carter**	**26**	**2**	**23**	**86**	**3**	**60**	**0.262**	**0.439**
328	1.27	Eric Chavez (16, 35)	32	2	27	92	5	65	0.268	0.476
329	1.27	Bill Robinson (16)	25	3	18	71	8	29	0.258	0.438
330	1.27	Chet Lemon (16)	32	5	18	72	5	61	0.273	0.442
331	1.27	Mike Cameron (17)	32	5	23	80	25	72	0.249	0.444
332	1.27	Bill Skowron (14)	24	5	21	87	2	37	0.282	0.459
333	**1.27**	**Luke Appling**	**29**	**7**	**3**	**75**	**12**	**87**	**0.310**	**0.398**
334	1.26	Ted Simmons (21)	32	3	16	92	1	56	0.285	0.437
335	1.26	Craig Nettles	20	2	23	79	2	65	0.248	0.421
336	1.26	Ron Fairly	20	2	14	69	2	70	0.266	0.408
337	**1.26**	**Robin Yount**	**33**	**7**	**14**	**80**	**15**	**55**	**0.285**	**0.430**
338	1.26	Brian McCann (9, 29)	33	0	26	97	3	61	0.277	0.473
339	1.26	Justin Morneau (11, 32)	36	2	27	107	1	64	0.277	0.482
340	1.26	Dustin Pedroia (8, 29)	46	2	16	79	19	67	0.302	0.454
341	1.26	Tony Clark (15)	24	1	26	86	1	55	0.262	0.485
342	1.26	Aramis Ramirez (16, 35)	37	2	30	107	2	49	0.285	0.501
343	1.26	Richard Hidalgo (9)	35	3	28	92	8	59	0.269	0.490
344	1.26	Dean Palmer (14)	28	2	33	101	6	60	0.251	0.472
345	1.26	Pete Rose	34	6	7	60	9	71	0.303	0.409
346	1.26	Carlos Quentin (8, 30)	35	1	31	98	3	58	0.255	0.492

347	1.26	Joe Pepitone (12)	18	4	25	84	5	35	0.258	0.432
348	1.25	Mike Sweeney (16)	36	1	24	101	6	58	0.297	0.486
349	1.25	Davey Johnson	27	2	15	69	4	63	0.261	0.404
350	1.25	Dan Uggla (8, 33)	30	2	30	90	3	79	0.246	0.458
351	1.25	Felipe Alou (17)	28	4	16	66	8	33	0.286	0.433
352	1.25	Ken Caminiti (15)	32	2	22	90	8	67	0.272	0.447
353	1.25	Steve Garvey (19)	31	3	19	91	6	33	0.294	0.446
354	1.25	Jermaine Dye (14)	33	2	30	99	4	55	0.274	0.488
355	1.24	Robin Ventura (16)	26	1	23	92	2	84	0.267	0.444
356	1.24	Tino Martinez (16)	29	2	27	102	2	62	0.271	0.471
357	1.24	**Deacon White**	**28**	**10**	**2**	**103**		**32**	**0.312**	**0.393**
358	1.24	Mark Grace (16)	37	3	12	83	5	78	0.303	0.442
359	1.24	Dixie Walker (18)	32	8	9	87	5	69	0.306	0.437
360	1.24	Torii Hunter (17, 37)	34	3	24	95	15	47	0.279	0.466
361	1.23	**Hugh Jennings**	**29**	**11**	**2**	**106**	**45**	**44**	**0.312**	**0.406**
362	1.23	Gary Maddox	31	6	11	70	23	30	0.285	0.413
363	1.23	Adrian Beltre (16, 34)	35	2	27	93	8	45	0.282	0.478
364	1.23	Willie Wilson	21	11	3	44	50	32	0.285	0.376
365	1.23	Raul Ibanez (18, 41)	33	4	23	92	4	53	0.276	0.471
366	1.23	Bill Freehan	22	3	18	69	2	57	0.262	0.412
367	1.23	Shane Victorino (10, 32)	30	9	14	64	30	49	0.277	0.432
368	1.23	Alan Trammel	29	4	13	71	17	60	0.285	0.415
369	1.23	Steve Finley (19)	28	8	19	73	20	53	0.271	0.442
370	1.23	**Pee Wee Reese**	**25**	**6**	**9**	**66**	**17**	**90**	**0.269**	**0.377**
371	1.23	Lave Cross	29	10	3	98	22	33	0.292	0.383
372	1.23	Johnny Damon (18)	34	7	15	74	27	65	0.284	0.433
373	1.23	**Cal Ripken**	**33**	**2**	**23**	**91**	**2**	**61**	**0.276**	**0.447**
374	1.23	Jimmy Rollins	38	9	17	69	35	57	0.269	0.426
375	1.23	**Roderick Wallace**	**27**	**10**	**2**	**76**	**14**	**53**	**0.268**	**0.358**
376	1.22	Javy Lopez (15)	29	2	28	93	1	38	0.287	0.491
377	1.22	Derek Jeter (19, 39)	33	4	16	79	22	65	0.312	0.446
378	1.22	Craig Bigio	38	3	17	67	24	66	0.281	0.433
379	1.22	**Richie Ashburn**	**23**	**8**	**2**	**43**	**17**	**89**	**0.308**	**0.382**
380	1.22	Julian Franco	26	3	11	77	18	59	0.298	0.417
381	1.22	Victor Martinez (11, 34)	39	0	19	102	0	63	0.303	0.464
382	1.22	Wes Parker	24	4	8	59	8	67	0.267	0.375

383	1.22	Larry Parrish (15)	31	3	22	85	3	45	0.263	0.439
384	1.21	Ruben Sierra (20)	32	4	23	98	11	45	0.268	0.450
385	1.21	**Bid McPhee**	**23**	**14**	**4**	**81**		**74**	**0.272**	**0.373**
386	1.21	Devon White	32	6	17	71	29	45	0.263	0.419
387	1.21	**George Kell**	**35**	**5**	**7**	**79**	**5**	**56**	**0.306**	**0.414**
388	1.20	Thurman Munson	26	4	13	80	5	50	0.292	0.410
389	1.20	**Frederick Lindstrom**	**34**	**9**	**12**	**88**	**9**	**38**	**0.311**	**0.449**
390	1.20	Eric Hinske (12, 35)	28	2	16	61	7	53	0.249	0.430
391	1.20	Vernon Wells (15, 34)	35	3	25	90	10	44	0.270	0.459
392	1.20	Vinny Castilla (16)	30	2	28	97	3	37	0.276	0.476
393	1.20	Elston Howard	22	5	17	77	1	38	0.274	0.427
394	1.20	**George Kelly**	**35**	**5**	**7**	**79**	**5**	**56**	**0.306**	**0.414**
395	1.19	Ivan Rodriguez (21)	36	3	20	85	8	33	0.296	0.464
396	1.19	Geoff Jenkins (11)	31	11	5	98	42	60	0.295	0.405
397	1.19	**Billy Herman**	**41**	**7**	**4**	**71**	**6**	**62**	**0.304**	**0.407**
398	1.19	**Pie Traynor**	**31**	**14**	**5**	**106**	**13**	**39**	**0.320**	**0.435**
399	1.19	Lyle Overbay (13, 36)	38	1	16	71	2	67	0.267	0.434
400	1.19	Willie Davis	26	9	12	70	27	28	0.279	0.412
401	1.19	Travis Fryman (13)	33	4	21	98	7	57	0.274	0.443
402	1.19	Willie Randolph	23	5	4	51	20	91	0.276	0.351
403	1.19	Brian Jordan (15)	30	4	20	91	13	39	0.282	0.455
404	1.19	Buddy Bell	29	4	14	74	4	56	0.279	0.406
405	1.18	Bert Campanaris	22	6	5	45	45	43	0.259	0.342
406	1.18	Maury Wills	15	6	2	38	49	46	0.281	0.331
407	1.18	Gary Gaetti	29	3	23	87	6	41	0.255	0.434
408	1.17	Paul Blair	23	5	11	52	14	37	0.250	0.382
409	1.17	**Travis Jackson**	**28**	**8**	**13**	**91**	**7**	**40**	**0.291**	**0.433**
410	1.17	Bill Buckner	32	3	11	78	12	29	0.289	0.408
411	1.17	Willie Mcgee	26	7	6	63	26	33	0.295	0.396
412	1.17	**Joe Sewell**	**37**	**6**	**4**	**90**	**6**	**72**	**0.312**	**0.413**
413	1.16	Tim Wallach	32	3	19	82	4	48	0.257	0.416
414	1.16	Miguel Tejada (16, 39)	35	2	23	97	6	41	0.285	0.456
415	1.16	**Brooks Robinson**	**27**	**4**	**15**	**76**	**2**	**48**	**0.267**	**0.401**
416	1.16	Tony Fernandez	31	7	7	63	18	52	0.288	0.399
417	1.16	Garret Anderson (17)	38	3	21	99	6	31	0.293	0.461
418	1.16	Bret Boone (14)	33	3	23	93	9	50	0.266	0.442

419	1.15	**Richard Ferrell**	**28**	**4**	**2**	**63**	**2**	**80**	**0.281**	**0.363**
420	1.14	Troy Tulowitzki (8, 28)	35	4	29	103	10	67	0.295	0.509
421	1.14	Curt Flood	25	4	8	59	8	41	0.293	0.389
422	1.13	Dave Conception	25	3	7	62	21	48	0.267	0.357
423	1.13	**David Bancroft**	**27**	**7**	**3**	**50**	**12**	**70**	**0.279**	**0.358**
424	1.12	**Red Schoendist**	**31**	**6**	**6**	**57**	**7**	**44**	**0.289**	**0.387**
425	1.12	BJ Surhoff	31	3	13	81	10	45	0.282	0.413
426	1.12	**Luis Aparicio**	**25**	**6**	**5**	**49**	**32**	**46**	**0.262**	**0.343**
427	1.12	Vic Power	29	5	13	66	4	28	0.284	0.411
428	1.12	**Ozzie Smith**	**25**	**4**	**2**	**50**	**37**	**67**	**0.262**	**0.328**
429	1.12	Tommy Davis	22	3	12	85	11	31	0.294	0.405
430	1.12	**Phil Rizzuto**	**23**	**6**	**4**	**55**	**15**	**63**	**0.273**	**0.355**
431	1.11	Edgar Renteria	33	2	11	69	22	54	0.286	0.398
432	1.11	Frank White	28	4	11	62	12	29	0.255	0.383
433	1.10	Bobby Thomson (15)	24	7	24	93	3	51	0.270	0.462
434	1.10	Zoilo Versalles	27	7	11	55	11	37	0.242	0.367
435	1.09	Chris Speier	22	4	8	52	3	61	0.246	0.349
436	1.09	**Lloyd Waner**	**23**	**10**	**2**	**49**	**5**	**34**	**0.316**	**0.393**
437	1.08	**John Ward**	**20**	**9**	**2**	**77**		**37**	**0.275**	**0.341**
438	1.08	**Ray Schalk**	**18**	**5**	**1**	**55**	**16**	**59**	**0.253**	**0.316**
439	1.08	Yadier Molina	30	0	12	73	5	44	0.284	0.404
440	1.08	**Rabit Maranville**	**23**	**11**	**2**	**54**	**18**	**51**	**0.258**	**0.340**
441	1.06	Orlando Cabrera	37	3	10	70	18	42	0.272	0.390
442	1.04	**Bill Mazeroski**	**22**	**5**	**10**	**64**	**2**	**33**	**0.260**	**0.367**
443	1.04	Sandy Alomar Jr	29	1	13	69	3	25	0.273	0.406
444	1.04	Tony Pena	24	2	9	58	7	37	0.260	0.364
445	1.04	Omar Visquel	25	4	4	52	22	56	0.272	0.352
446	1.03	**Nellie Fox**	**24**	**8**	**2**	**54**	**5**	**49**	**0.288**	**0.363**
447	1.03	Bob Boone	22	2	8	59	3	47	0.254	0.346
448	1.02	Ichiro Suzuki	28	4	11	62	12	29	0.255	0.383
449	1.02	Placido Polanco	29	3	9	61	7	36	0.297	0.397
450	1.02	Mark Grudzielanek	35	3	8	58	12	33	0.289	0.393
451	1.01	Manny Trillo	22	3	6	52	5	41	0.263	0.345
452	1.01	Larry Bowa	19	7	1	38	23	34	0.260	0.320
453	0.95	Bobby Richardson	22	4	4	45	8	30	0.266	0.335
454	0.95	Mark Belanger	14	3	2	31	13	46	0.228	0.280

Absolute Single Season Home Run Totals Pro Rated For Era

Absolute Projected			year	ab	ab/hr	league		All-Time ave
141	Babe Ruth+ (25)	54	1920	458	8.48	133.6	0.06	51.18
107	Babe Ruth+ (32)	60	1927	540	9.00	91.6	0.10	51.18
105	Babe Ruth+ (26)	59	1921	540	9.15	90.9	0.10	51.18
83	Ned Williamson	27	1884	417	15.44	158	0.10	51.18
73	Charley Jones	9	1879	355	39.44	416	0.09	51.18
66	Rogers Hornsby+ (26)	42	1922	623	14.83	80.9	0.18	51.18
61	Lou Gehrig+ (31)	49	1934	579	11.82	63.9	0.18	51.18
59	Honus Wagner	10	1908	568	56.80	302.1	0.19	51.18
55	Ty Cobb	9	1909	573	63.67	311.2	0.20	51.18
54	Ralph Kiner+ (24)	51	1947	565	11.08	53.9	0.21	51.18
46	Paul Hines	4	1878	257	64.25	593	0.11	51.18
46	Ed Delahanty	19	1893	595	31.32	123.6	0.25	51.18
45	Mark McGwire (34)	70	1998	509	7.27	33	0.22	51.18
43	Barry Bonds (36)	73	2001	476	6.52	30.45	0.21	51.18
43	Dan Brouthers	14	1884	398	28.43	158.6	0.18	51.18
43	Sammy Sosa (29)	66	1998	643	9.74	33	0.30	51.18
42	Roger Maris (26)	61	1961	590	9.67	35.5	0.27	51.18
42	Hank Aaron+ (37)	47	1971	495	10.53	45.6	0.23	51.18
41	Willie Mays+ (34)	52	1965	558	10.73	40.8	0.26	51.18
41	Frank Baker	12	1913	564	47.00	172.8	0.27	51.18
40	Fred Dunlap	13	1884	449	34.54	158	0.22	51.18
38	Mark McGwire (35)	65	1999	521	8.02	30.23	0.27	51.18
38	Harmon Killebrew	49	1964	577	11.78	40	0.29	51.18
38	Sammy Sosa (32)	64	2001	577	9.02	30.45	0.30	51.18
37	Willie Mays+ (24)	51	1955	580	11.37	37.6	0.30	51.18

37	Chris Davis (27)	53	2013	584	11.02	35.62	0.31	51.18
36	Tris Speaker	10	1912	580	58.00	185.6	0.31	51.18
32	Mark McGwire (32)	52	1996	423	8.13	31.6	0.26	51.18
31	Brady Anderson (32)	50	1996	579	11.58	31.6	0.37	51.18

Absolute Best Power Hitters of All Time

Home Runs per At Bat Relative to Era

Ratio	Player (yrs)	Hr/Ab		Lg Ave
0.137	Babe Ruth+ (22)	11.76	L	85.7
0.178	Jimmie Foxx+ (20)	15.23	R	85.7
0.226	Ted Williams+ (19)	14.79	L	65.42
0.245	Hank Greenberg+ (13)	15.69	R	64.08
0.253	Lou Gehrig+ (17)	16.23	L	64.08
0.274	Johnny Mize+ (15)	17.95	L	65.43
0.297	Mark McGwire (16)	10.61	R	35.76
0.322	Frank Baker	62.33		193.58
0.333	Dave Kingman (16)	15.11	R	45.43
0.335	Mike Schmidt+ (18)	15.24	R	45.47
0.344	Harmon Killebrew+ (22)	14.22	R	41.28
0.349	Ralph Kiner+ (10)	14.11	R	40.43
0.363	Jose Canseco (17)	15.27	R	42.06
0.366	Mickey Mantle+ (18)	15.12	B	41.28
0.381	Willie McCovey+ (22)	15.73	L	41.28
0.395	Ryan Howard (10, 33)	13.96	L	35.3
0.397	Hank Aaron+ (23)	16.38	R	41.28
0.404	Barry Bonds (22)	12.92	L	31.97
0.405	Sammy Sosa (18)	14.47	R	35.76
0.412	Eddie Mathews+ (17)	16.67	L	40.43
0.421	Rocky Colavito (14)	17.39	R	41.28
0.430	Jim Thome (22)	13.76	L	31.97
0.459	Adam Dunn (13, 33)	14.67	L	31.97
0.464	Manny Ramirez (19, 41)	14.85	R	31.97
0.465	Albert Pujols (13, 33)	14.86	R	31.97
0.470	Alex Rodriguez (20, 37)	15.01	R	31.97
0.473	Juan Gonzalez (17)	15.11	R	31.97
0.497	Ryan Braun (7, 29)	17.55	R	35.3

Absolute Batting Average Adjusted Relative To Era

Abs BA	Ratio	Player (Yrs)	Actual	Bats	Decade Lg Ave
0.376	1.43	Ty Cobb+ (24)	0.366	L	256
0.366	1.39	Shoeless Joe Jackson (13)	0.356	L	256
0.358	1.36	Dan Brouthers+ (19)	0.342	L	251
0.358	1.36	Dave Orr (8)	0.342	R	251
0.358	1.36	Pete Browning (13)	0.342	R	251
0.354	1.35	Tris Speaker+ (22)	0.345	L	256
0.350	1.33	Ted Williams+ (19)	0.344	L	259
0.349	1.33	Nap Lajoie+ (21)	0.338	R	255
0.343	1.31	Tony Gwynn+ (20)	0.338	L	259
0.338	1.28	Albert Pujols (13, 33)	0.321	R	250
0.337	1.28	Miguel Cabrera (11, 30)	0.321	R	250
0.337	1.28	Rod Carew+ (19)	0.328	L	256
0.336	1.28	Roberto Clemente+ (18)	0.317	R	248
0.335	1.27	Stan Musial+ (22)	0.331	L	260
0.333	1.27	Wade Boggs+ (18)	0.328	L	259
0.331	1.26	Rogers Hornsby+ (23)	0.359	R	285
0.329	1.25	Lefty O'Doul (11)	0.349	L	279
0.328	1.25	Joe DiMaggio+ (13)	0.325	R	260
0.327	1.24	Ed Delahanty+ (16)	0.346	R	278
0.326	1.24	Billy Hamilton+ (14)	0.344	L	278
0.323	1.23	Willie Keeler+ (19)	0.341	L	278
0.323	1.23	Tony Oliva (15)	0.304	L	248
0.322	1.22	Bill Terry+ (14)	0.341	L	279
0.321	1.22	Lou Gehrig+ (17)	0.340	L	279
0.320	1.22	Willie Mays+ (22)	0.302	R	248

0.316	1.20	Ichiro Suzuki (13, 39)	0.319	L	265
0.316	1.20	Babe Ruth+ (22)	0.342	L	285
0.315	1.20	Harry Heilmann+ (17)	0.342	R	285
0.314	1.19	George Sisler+ (15)	0.340	L	285
0.314	1.19	Sam Thompson+ (15)	0.331	L	278

Absolute Best Hitter Per Slugging Percentage Relative to Era

(Does not include walks or stolen bases)

Rank	Ratio	Player (Yrs)	Slg %	Lg Ave
1	1.74	Babe Ruth+ (22)	0.69	0.397
2	1.73	Ted Williams+ (19)	0.634	0.367
3	1.65	Hank Greenberg+ (13)	0.605	0.367
4	1.58	Lou Gehrig+ (17)	0.632	0.399
5	1.54	Dan Brouthers+ (19)	0.519	0.336
6	1.53	Shoeless Joe Jackson	0.517	0.337
7	1.53	Johnny Mize+ (15)	0.562	0.367
8	1.53	Jimmie Foxx+ (20)	0.609	0.399
9	1.52	Ty Cobb+ (24)	0.512	0.337
10	1.49	Dave Orr (8)	0.502	0.336
11	1.49	Willie Mays+ (22)	0.558	0.374
12	1.49	Mickey Mantle+ (18)	0.557	0.374
13	1.48	Tris Speaker+ (22)	0.5	0.337
14	1.48	Hank Aaron+ (23)	0.555	0.374
15	1.48	Joe DiMaggio+ (13)	0.579	0.391
16	1.45	Rogers Hornsby+ (23)	0.577	0.397
17	1.44	Mark McGwire (16)	0.588	0.409
18	1.44	Frank Robinson+ (21)	0.537	0.374
19	1.43	Barry Bonds (22)	0.607	0.423
20	1.43	Stan Musial+ (22)	0.559	0.391
21	1.42	Miguel Cabrera (11, 30)	0.568	0.4
22	1.42	Dick Allen (15)	0.534	0.376
23	1.42	Honus Wagner+ (21)	0.467	0.329
24	1.42	Nap Lajoie+ (21)	0.466	0.329

25	1.42	Albert Pujols (13, 33)	0.599	0.423
26	1.41	Charlie Keller (13)	0.518	0.367
27	1.41	Ryan Braun (7, 29)	0.564	0.4
28	1.41	Willie Stargell+ (21)	0.529	0.376
29	1.40	Mike Schmidt+ (18)	0.527	0.376
30	1.40	Ralph Kiner+ (10)	0.548	0.391
31	1.39	Jeff Heath (14)	0.509	0.367
32	1.38	Manny Ramirez (19, 41)	0.585	0.423
33	1.38	Larry Walker (17)	0.565	0.409
34	1.38	Duke Snider+ (18)	0.54	0.391
35	1.38	Albert Belle (12)	0.564	0.409
36	1.38	Bob Johnson (13)	0.506	0.367
37	1.38	Willie McCovey+ (22)	0.515	0.374
38	1.37	Hack Wilson+ (12)	0.545	0.399
39	1.36	Ryan Howard (10, 33)	0.545	0.4
40	1.36	Chuck Klein+ (17)	0.543	0.399
41	1.36	Harmon Killebrew+ (22)	0.509	0.374
42	1.36	Sam Thompson+ (15)	0.505	0.372
43	1.36	Ed Delahanty+ (16)	0.505	0.372
44	1.36	Frank Thomas+ (19)	0.555	0.409
45	1.35	Jim Thome (22)	0.554	0.409
46	1.35	Joey Votto (7, 29)	0.541	0.4
47	1.35	Vladimir Guerrero (16)	0.553	0.409
48	1.34	Al Simmons+ (20)	0.535	0.399
49	1.34	Ken Williams (14)	0.53	0.396
50	1.34	Tommy Henrich (11)	0.491	0.367
51	1.34	Earl Averill+ (13)	0.534	0.399
52	1.34	Mel Ott+ (22)	0.533	0.399
53	1.34	Ernie Banks+ (19)	0.5	0.374
54	1.33	Orlando Cepeda+ (17)	0.499	0.374
55	1.34	Jim Rice+ (16)	0.502	0.376
56	1.33	Frank Howard (16)	0.499	0.374
57	1.33	Babe Herman (13)	0.532	0.399
58	1.33	Lefty O'Doul (11)	0.532	0.399
59	1.33	Mike Piazza (16)	0.545	0.409
60	1.33	Jose Canseco (17)	0.515	0.387

61	1.33	Chick Hafey+ (13)	0.526	0.396
62	1.33	Juan Gonzalez (17)	0.561	0.423
63	1.33	Josh Hamilton (7, 32)	0.53	0.4
64	1.32	Jeff Bagwell (15)	0.54	0.409
65	1.32	Alex Rodriguez (20, 37)	0.558	0.423
66	1.32	Todd Helton (17, 39)	0.539	0.409
67	1.32	Fred McGriff (19)	0.509	0.387
68	1.32	Billy Williams+ (18)	0.492	0.374
69	1.32	Ken Griffey (22)	0.538	0.409
70	1.32	Harry Heilmann+ (17)	0.521	0.396
71	1.31	Home Run Baker+ (13)	0.442	0.337
72	1.31	Dick Stuart (10)	0.489	0.374
73	1.31	Wally Berger (11)	0.522	0.399
74	1.31	Hal Trosky (11)	0.522	0.399
75	1.31	Rocky Colavito (14)	0.489	0.374
76	1.30	Darryl Strawberry (17)	0.505	0.387
77	1.30	Norm Cash (17)	0.488	0.374
78	1.31	Sammy Sosa (18)	0.534	0.409
79	1.30	Reggie Jackson+ (21)	0.49	0.376
80	1.30	Eddie Mathews+ (17)	0.509	0.391
81	1.30	Reggie Smith (17)	0.489	0.376
82	1.30	Jim Gentile (9)	0.486	0.374
83	1.30	David Ortiz (17, 37)	0.549	0.423
84	1.29	David Justice (14)	0.5	0.387
85	1.29	Ryan Klesko (16)	0.5	0.387
86	1.29	Carlos Delgado (17)	0.546	0.423
87	1.29	Bob Horner (10)	0.499	0.387
88	1.28	Evan Longoria (6, 27)	0.512	0.4
89	1.28	Roy Campanella+ (10)	0.5	0.391
90	1.27	Roger Maris (12)	0.476	0.374
91	1.27	Ted Kluszewski (15)	0.498	0.391
92	1.27	Nomar Garciaparra (14)	0.521	0.409
93	1.27	Troy Tulowitzki (8, 28)	0.509	0.4
94	1.27	Tony Conigliaro (8)	0.476	0.374
95	1.27	Kevin Mitchell (13)	0.52	0.409
96	1.27	Joe Medwick+ (17)	0.505	0.397

97	1.27	Roberto Clemente+ (18)	0.475	0.374
98	1.27	Hank Sauer (15)	0.496	0.391
99	1.27	Bill Terry+ (14)	0.506	0.399
100	1.27	Lance Berkman (15, 37)	0.537	0.424
101	1.27	David Wright (10, 30)	0.506	0.4
102	1.27	Al Rosen (10)	0.495	0.391
103	1.27	Johnny Bench+ (17)	0.476	0.376
104	1.27	Hanley Ramirez (9, 29)	0.506	0.4
105	1.26	Jim Bottomley+ (16)	0.5	0.396
106	1.26	Robinson Cano (9, 30)	0.505	0.4
107	1.26	Moises Alou (17)	0.516	0.409
108	1.26	Edgar Martinez (18)	0.516	0.409
109	1.26	George Brett+ (21)	0.487	0.387
110	1.26	Rafael Palmeiro (20)	0.515	0.409
111	1.26	Gary Sheffield (22)	0.514	0.409
112	1.26	Mike Napoli (8, 31)	0.502	0.4
113	1.26	Bob Meusel (11)	0.497	0.396
114	1.25	Matt Holliday (10, 33)	0.532	0.424
115	1.25	Larry Doby+ (13)	0.49	0.391
116	1.25	Adrian Gonzalez (10, 31)	0.501	0.4
117	1.25	Goose Goslin+ (18)	0.5	0.399
118	1.25	Bobby Bonds (14)	0.471	0.376
119	1.25	Dave Parker (19)	0.471	0.376
120	1.25	Chipper Jones (19)	0.529	0.423
121	1.25	Ellis Burks (18)	0.51	0.409
122	1.25	Jim Edmonds (17)	0.527	0.423
123	1.25	Gil Hodges (18)	0.487	0.391
124	1.25	Prince Fielder (9, 29)	0.528	0.424
125	1.25	Chase Utley (11, 34)	0.498	0.4
126	1.24	Ron Santo+ (15)	0.464	0.374
127	1.24	Rico Carty (15)	0.464	0.374
128	1.24	Richie Sexson (12)	0.507	0.409
129	1.24	Mark Teixeira (11, 33)	0.525	0.424
130	1.24	Nelson Cruz (9, 32)	0.495	0.4
131	1.24	Carl Yastrzemski+ (23)	0.462	0.374
132	1.24	Matt Kemp (8, 28)	0.494	0.4

133	1.23	Mo Vaughn (12)	0.523	0.424
134	1.23	Yogi Berra+ (19)	0.482	0.391
135	1.23	Ripper Collins (9)	0.492	0.399
136	1.23	Dolph Camilli (12)	0.492	0.399
137	1.23	Eddie Murray+ (21)	0.476	0.387
138	1.23	Boog Powell (17)	0.462	0.376
139	1.23	Gabby Hartnett+ (20)	0.489	0.399
140	1.22	Jason Giambi (19, 42)	0.519	0.424
141	1.22	Andrew McCutchen	0.489	0.4
142	1.22	Zeke Bonura (7)	0.487	0.399
143	1.22	Jeff Kent (17)	0.5	0.409
144	1.22	Curtis Granderson	0.488	0.4
145	1.22	Dante Bichette (14)	0.499	0.409
146	1.22	Andres Galarraga (19)	0.499	0.409
147	1.22	Willie Horton (18)	0.457	0.376
148	1.22	Will Clark (15)	0.497	0.409
149	1.21	Danny Tartabull (14)	0.496	0.409
150	1.21	Hugh Duffy+ (17)	0.451	0.372
151	1.21	Jay Buhner (15)	0.494	0.409
152	1.20	Cecil Cooper (17)	0.466	0.387
153	1.20	Matt Williams (17)	0.489	0.409
154	1.19	Jermaine Dye (14)	0.488	0.409
155	1.19	Alfonso Soriano (15, 37)	0.504	0.423
156	1.19	Gorman Thomas (13)	0.448	0.376
157	1.18	Brian Giles (15)	0.502	0.424
158	1.18	Magglio Ordonez (15)	0.502	0.424
159	1.18	Aramis Ramirez (16, 35)	0.501	0.424
160	1.18	Tim Salmon (14)	0.499	0.424
161	1.17	Travis Hafner (12, 36)	0.498	0.424
162	1.18	Bill Madlock (15)	0.442	0.376
163	1.17	Carlos Beltran (16, 36)	0.496	0.424
164	1.17	Adam Dunn (13, 33)	0.495	0.424
165	1.17	Derrek Lee (15)	0.495	0.424
166	1.17	Shawn Green (15)	0.495	0.424
167	1.16	Carlos Quentin (8, 30)	0.492	0.424
168	1.16	Javy Lopez (15)	0.491	0.424

169	1.16	Paul Konerko (17, 37)	0.491	0.424
170	1.16	Corey Hart (9, 31)	0.491	0.424
171	1.16	Scott Rolen (17)	0.49	0.424
172	1.16	Geoff Jenkins (11)	0.49	0.424
173	1.16	Richard Hidalgo (9)	0.49	0.424
174	1.16	J.D. Drew (14)	0.49	0.424
175	1.16	Troy Glaus (13)	0.49	0.424
176	1.15	Reggie Sanders (17)	0.487	0.424
177	1.15	Jose Bautista (10, 32)	0.487	0.424

All-Time Career Slugging Percentage Leaders

—Actual

1	Babe Ruth+ (22)	0.6897
2	Ted Williams+ (19)	0.6338
3	Lou Gehrig+ (17)	0.6324
4	Jimmie Foxx+ (20)	0.6093
5	Barry Bonds (22)	0.6069
6	Hank Greenberg+ (13)	0.605
7	Albert Pujols (13, 33)	0.5988
8	Mark McGwire (16)	0.5882
9	Manny Ramirez (19)	0.5854
10	Joe DiMaggio+ (13)	0.5788
11	Rogers Hornsby+ (23)	0.5765
12	Miguel Cabrera (11, 30)	0.5677
13	Larry Walker (17)	0.5652
14	Ryan Braun (7, 29)	0.564
15	Albert Belle (12)	0.5638
16	Johnny Mize+ (15)	0.562
17	Juan Gonzalez (17)	0.5607
18	Stan Musial+ (22)	0.5591
19	Alex Rodriguez (20, 37)	0.5582
20	Willie Mays+ (22)	0.5575
21	Mickey Mantle+ (18)	0.5568
22	Frank Thomas+ (19)	0.5549
23	Hank Aaron+ (23)	0.5545
24	Jim Thome (22)	0.5541
25	Vladimir Guerrero (16)	0.5525
26	David Ortiz (17, 37)	0.5487

27	Ralph Kiner+ (10)	0.5479
28	Carlos Delgado (17)	0.5459
29	Ryan Howard (10, 33)	0.5454
30	Mike Piazza (16)	0.5452
31	Hack Wilson+ (12)	0.5447
32	Chuck Klein+ (17)	0.543
33	Joey Votto (7, 29)	0.5412
34	Jeff Bagwell (15)	0.5403
35	Duke Snider+ (18)	0.5397
36	Todd Helton (17, 39)	0.5391
37	Ken Griffey (22)	0.5378
38	Frank Robinson+ (21)	0.537
39	Lance Berkman (15, 37)	0.5369
40	Al Simmons+ (20)	0.5349
41	Sammy Sosa (18)	0.5338
42	Dick Allen (15)	0.5336
	Earl Averill+ (13)	0.5336
44	Mel Ott+ (22)	0.5331
45	Babe Herman (13)	0.5319
	Lefty O'Doul (11)	0.5319
47	Matt Holliday (10, 33)	0.5315
48	Ken Williams (14)	0.5304
49	Josh Hamilton (7, 32)	0.5296
50	Chipper Jones (19)	0.5293
51	Willie Stargell+ (21)	0.5286
52	Prince Fielder (9, 29)	0.5275
53	Mike Schmidt+ (18)	0.5273
54	Jim Edmonds (17)	0.5271
55	Chick Hafey+ (13)	0.5261
56	Mark Teixeira (11, 33)	0.5253
57	Mo Vaughn (12)	0.5231
58	Wally Berger (11)	0.5216
	Hal Trosky (11)	0.5216
60	Nomar Garciaparra (14)	0.5206
61	Harry Heilmann+ (17)	0.5205
62	Kevin Mitchell (13)	0.5198
63	Dan Brouthers+ (19)	0.5191

64	Jason Giambi (19, 42)	0.5185
65	Charlie Keller (13)	0.5177
66	Shoeless Joe Jackson (13)	0.5174
67	Moises Alou (17)	0.5157
68	Edgar Martinez (18)	0.5155
69	Willie McCovey+ (22)	0.5147
70	Jose Canseco (17)	0.5145
	Rafael Palmeiro (20)	0.5145
72	Gary Sheffield (22)	0.5139
73	Evan Longoria (6, 27)	0.5124
74	Ty Cobb+ (24)	0.512
75	Ellis Burks (18)	0.5104
76	Eddie Mathews+ (17)	0.5094
77	Fred McGriff (19)	0.5091
	Troy Tulowitzki	0.5091
79	Jeff Heath (14)	0.5088
80	Harmon Killebrew+ (22)	0.5085
81	Richie Sexson (12)	0.5069
82	David Wright (10, 30)	0.5064
83	Bob Johnson (13)	0.5059
	Bill Terry+ (14)	0.5059
85	Hanley Ramirez (9, 29)	0.5057
86	Darryl Strawberry (17)	0.5054
87	Sam Thompson+ (15)	0.5053
88	Ed Delahanty+ (16)	0.5051
89	Robinson Cano (9, 30)	0.5045
	Joe Medwick+ (17)	0.5045
91	Alfonso Soriano (15, 37)	0.5039
92	Brian Giles (15)	0.5024
	Magglio Ordonez (15)	0.5024
94	Mike Napoli (8, 31)	0.5022
95	Jim Rice+ (16)	0.502
96	Dave Orr (8)	0.5017
97	Adrian Gonzalez (10, 31)	0.5013
98	Aramis Ramirez (16, 35)	0.5012
99	David Justice (14)	0.5003
	Ryan Klesko (16)	0.5003

All-Time Career Home Run Leaders

1	Barry Bonds (22)	762	L
2	Hank Aaron+ (23)	755	R
3	Babe Ruth+ (22)	714	L
4	Willie Mays+ (22)	660	R
5	Alex Rodriguez (20, 37)	654	R
6	Ken Griffey (22)	630	L
7	Jim Thome (22)	612	L
8	Sammy Sosa (18)	609	R
9	Frank Robinson+ (21)	586	R
10	Mark McGwire (16)	583	R
11	Harmon Killebrew+ (22)	573	R
12	Rafael Palmeiro (20)	569	L
13	Reggie Jackson+ (21)	563	L
14	Manny Ramirez (19)	555	R
15	Mike Schmidt+ (18)	548	R
16	Mickey Mantle+ (18)	536	B
17	Jimmie Foxx+ (20)	534	R
18	Willie McCovey+ (22)	521	L
	Frank Thomas+ (19)	521	R
	Ted Williams+ (19)	521	L
21	Ernie Banks+ (19)	512	R
	Eddie Mathews+ (17)	512	L
23	Mel Ott+ (22)	511	L
24	Gary Sheffield (22)	509	R
25	Eddie Murray+ (21)	504	B
26	Lou Gehrig+ (17)	493	L
	Fred McGriff (19)	493	L
28	Albert Pujols (13, 33)	492	R
29	Stan Musial+ (22)	475	L

	Willie Stargell+ (21)	475	L
31	Carlos Delgado (17)	473	L
32	Chipper Jones (19)	468	B
33	Dave Winfield+ (22)	465	R
34	Jose Canseco (17)	462	R
35	Carl Yastrzemski+ (23)	452	L
36	Jeff Bagwell (15)	449	R
	Vladimir Guerrero (16)	449	R
38	Dave Kingman (16)	442	R
39	Adam Dunn (13, 33)	440	L
40	Andre Dawson+ (21)	438	R
	Jason Giambi (19, 42)	438	L
42	Juan Gonzalez (17)	434	R
	Andruw Jones (17)	434	R
	Paul Konerko (17, 37)	434	R
45	David Ortiz (17, 37)	431	L
	Cal Ripken+ (21)	431	R
47	Mike Piazza (16)	427	R
48	Billy Williams+ (18)	426	L
49	Darrell Evans (21)	414	L
50	Duke Snider+ (18)	407	L
51	Alfonso Soriano	406	R
52	Andres Galarraga (19)	399	R
	Al Kaline+ (22)	399	R
54	Dale Murphy (18)	398	R
55	Joe Carter (16)	396	R
56	Jim Edmonds (17)	393	L
57	Graig Nettles (22)	390	L
58	Johnny Bench+ (17)	389	R
59	Dwight Evans (20)	385	R
60	Harold Baines (22)	384	L
61	Larry Walker (17)	383	L
62	Frank Howard (16)	382	R
	Jim Rice+ (16)	382	R
64	Albert Belle (12)	381	R
65	Orlando Cepeda+ (17)	379	R

	Tony Perez+ (23)	379	R
67	Matt Williams (17)	378	R
68	Norm Cash (17)	377	L
	Jeff Kent (17)	377	R
70	Adrian Beltre (16, 34)	376	R
	Carlton Fisk+ (24)	376	R
72	Rocky Colavito (14)	374	R
73	Gil Hodges (18)	370	R
74	Todd Helton (17, 39)	369	L
	Ralph Kiner+ (10)	369	R
76	Lance Berkman (15, 37)	366	B
77	Miguel Cabrera (11, 30)	365	R
78	Joe DiMaggio+ (13)	361	R
79	Gary Gaetti (20)	360	R
80	Johnny Mize+ (15)	359	L
81	Carlos Beltran (16, 36)	358	B
	Yogi Berra+ (19)	358	L
	Carlos Lee (14)	358	R
84	Greg Vaughn (15)	355	R
85	Luis Gonzalez (19)	354	L
	Lee May (18)	354	R
	Aramis Ramirez	354	R
88	Ellis Burks (18)	352	R
89	Dick Allen (15)	351	R
90	Chili Davis (19)	350	B
91	George Foster (18)	348	R
92	Ron Santo+ (15)	342	R
93	Mark Teixeira (11, 33)	341	B
94	Jack Clark (18)	340	R
95	Tino Martinez (16)	339	L
	Dave Parker (19)	339	L
	Boog Powell (17)	339	L
98	Don Baylor (19)	338	R
99	Joe Adcock (17)	336	R
100	Darryl Strawberry (17)	335	L
101	Moises Alou (17)	332	R

	Bobby Bonds (14)	332	R
103	Hank Greenberg+ (13)	331	R
	Derrek Lee (15)	331	R
105	Shawn Green (15)	328	L
	Mo Vaughn (12)	328	L
107	Jermaine Dye (14)	325	R
	Willie Horton (18)	325	R
109	Gary Carter+ (19)	324	R
	Lance Parrish (19)	324	R
111	Ron Gant (16)	321	R
112	Vinny Castilla (16)	320	R
	Troy Glaus (13)	320	R
114	Cecil Fielder (13)	319	R
115	Roy Sievers (17)	318	R
116	George Brett+ (21)	317	L
117	Ron Cey (17)	316	R
	Scott Rolen (17)	316	R
119	Jeromy Burnitz (14)	315	L
120	Torii Hunter (17, 37)	314	R
	Reggie Smith (17)	314	B
122	Ryan Howard (10, 33)	311	L
	Ivan Rodriguez (21)	311	R
124	Jay Buhner (15)	310	R
125	Edgar Martinez (18)	309	R
126	Greg Luzinski (15)	307	R
	Al Simmons+ (20)	307	R
	Miguel Tejada (16, 39)	307	R
129	Fred Lynn (17)	306	L
	Richie Sexson (12)	306	R
	Ruben Sierra (20)	306	B
132	David Justice (14)	305	L
	Reggie Sanders (17)	305	R
134	Steve Finley (19)	304	L
135	Rogers Hornsby+ (23)	301	R
136	Raul Ibanez (18, 41)	300	L
	Chuck Klein+ (17)	300	L

All-Time Career Batting Average Leaders

1	Ty Cobb+ (24)	0.3664	L
2	Rogers Hornsby+ (23)	0.3585	R
3	Shoeless Joe Jackson (13)	0.3558	L
4	Lefty O'Doul (11)	0.3493	L
5	Ed Delahanty+ (16)	0.3458	R
6	Tris Speaker+ (22)	0.3447	L
7	Billy Hamilton+ (14)	0.3444	L
	Ted Williams+ (19)	0.3444	L
9	Dan Brouthers+ (19)	0.3421	L
	Babe Ruth+ (22)	0.3421	L
11	Dave Orr (8)	0.342	R
12	Harry Heilmann+ (17)	0.3416	R
13	Pete Browning (13)	0.3415	R
14	Willie Keeler+ (19)	0.3413	L
15	Bill Terry+ (14)	0.3412	L
16	Lou Gehrig+ (17)	0.3401	L
	George Sisler+ (15)	0.3401	L
18	Jesse Burkett+ (16)	0.3382	L
	Tony Gwynn+ (20)	0.3382	L
	Nap Lajoie+ (21)	0.3382	R
21	Jake Stenzel (9)	0.3378	R
22	Riggs Stephenson (14)	0.3361	R
23	Al Simmons+ (20)	0.3342	R
24	Cap Anson+ (27)	0.3341	R
25	John McGraw+ (16)	0.3336	L
26	Eddie Collins+ (25)	0.3332	L
	Paul Waner+ (20)	0.3332	L
28	Mike Donlin (12)	0.3326	L

29	Sam Thompson+ (15)	0.3314	L
30	Stan Musial+ (22)	0.3308	L
31	Bill Lange (7)	0.3298	R
	Heinie Manush+ (17)	0.3298	L
33	Wade Boggs+ (18)	0.3279	L
34	Rod Carew+ (19)	0.3278	L
35	Honus Wagner+ (21)	0.3276	R
36	Tip O'Neill (10)	0.326	R
37	Hugh Duffy+ (17)	0.3255	R
	Bob Fothergill (12)	0.3255	R
39	Jimmie Foxx+ (20)	0.3253	R
40	Earle Combs+ (12)	0.3247	L
41	Joe DiMaggio+ (13)	0.3246	R
42	Babe Herman (13)	0.3245	L
43	Joe Medwick+ (17)	0.3236	R
44	Joe Mauer (10, 30)	0.323	L
45	Edd Roush+ (18)	0.3227	L
46	Sam Rice+ (20)	0.3223	L
47	Ross Youngs+ (10)	0.3222	L
48	Albert Pujols (13, 33)	0.3211	R
49	Kiki Cuyler+ (18)	0.321	R
50	Miguel Cabrera (11, 30)	0.3208	R
51	Charlie Gehringer+ (19)	0.3204	L
52	Chuck Klein+ (17)	0.3201	L
53	Mickey Cochrane+ (13)	0.3196	L
	Pie Traynor+ (17)	0.3196	R
55	Ken Williams (14)	0.3192	L
56	Ichiro Suzuki (13, 39)	0.3187	L
57	Kirby Puckett+ (12)	0.3181	R
58	Earl Averill+ (13)	0.3178	L
59	Vladimir Guerrero (16)	0.3176	R
	Arky Vaughan+ (14)	0.3176	L
61	Bill Everitt (7)	0.3174	L
62	Roberto Clemente+ (18)	0.3173	R
	Joe Harris (10)	0.3173	R

64	Chick Hafey+ (13)	0.317	R
65	Joe Kelley+ (17)	0.3169	R
66	Zack Wheat+ (19)	0.3167	L
67	Roger Connor+ (18)	0.3164	L
	Todd Helton (17, 39)	0.3164	L
	Lloyd Waner+ (18)	0.3164	L
70	George Van Haltren (17)	0.3163	L
71	Frankie Frisch+ (19)	0.3161	B
72	Goose Goslin+ (18)	0.316	L
73	Lew Fonseca (12)	0.3158	R
74	Bibb Falk (12)	0.3145	L
75	Cecil Travis (12)	0.3142	L
	Joey Votto (7, 29)	0.3142	L
77	Hank Greenberg+ (13)	0.3135	R
78	Jack Fournier (15)	0.3132	L
79	Elmer Flick+ (13)	0.313	L
80	Ed Morgan (7)	0.3128	R
81	Nomar Garciaparra (14)	0.3127	R
	Larry Walker (17)	0.3127	L
83	Bill Dickey+ (17)	0.3125	L
84	Derek Jeter (19, 39)	0.3124	R
85	Ryan Braun (7, 29)	0.3123	R
86	Dale Mitchell (11)	0.3122	L
	Manny Ramirez (19)	0.3122	R
88	Johnny Mize+ (15)	0.3121	L
	Joe Sewell+ (14)	0.3121	L
90	Fred Clarke+ (21)	0.312	L
	Deacon White+ (20)	0.312	L
92	Bug Holliday (10)	0.3119	R
93	Barney McCosky (11)	0.3118	L
94	Hughie Jennings+ (18)	0.3117	R
95	Edgar Martinez (18)	0.3115	R
96	Johnny Hodapp (9)	0.3114	R
	Matt Holliday (10, 33)	0.3114	R
	Freddie Lindstrom+ (13)	0.3114	R

99	Bing Miller (16)	0.3113	R
	Jackie Robinson+ (10)	0.3113	R
101	Baby Doll Jacobson (11)	0.3112	R
	Taffy Wright (9)	0.3112	L
103	Rip Radcliff (10)	0.311	

All-Time At Bats per Home Run Leaders

1	Mark McGwire (16)	10.61
2	Babe Ruth+ (22)	11.76
3	Barry Bonds (22)	12.92
4	Jim Thome (22)	13.76
5	Ryan Howard (10, 33)	13.96
6	Ralph Kiner+ (10)	14.11
7	Harmon Killebrew+ (22)	14.22
8	Sammy Sosa (18)	14.47
9	Adam Dunn (13, 33)	14.67
10	Ted Williams+ (19)	14.79
11	Manny Ramirez (19)	14.85
12	Albert Pujols (13, 33)	14.86
13	Alex Rodriguez (20, 37)	15.01
14	Juan Gonzalez (17)	15.11
	Dave Kingman (16)	15.11
16	Russell Branyan (14)	15.12
	Mickey Mantle+ (18)	15.12
18	Jimmie Foxx+ (20)	15.23
19	Mike Schmidt+ (18)	15.24
20	Jose Canseco (17)	15.27
21	Albert Belle (12)	15.36
22	Ron Kittle (10)	15.39
23	Carlos Delgado (17)	15.4
24	Ken Griffey (22)	15.56
25	Hank Greenberg+ (13)	15.69
26	Willie McCovey+ (22)	15.73
27	Frank Thomas+ (19)	15.74
28	Richie Sexson (12)	16.1
29	Jay Buhner (15)	16.17

	Cecil Fielder (13)	16.17
	Darryl Strawberry (17)	16.17
32	Mike Piazza (16)	16.18
33	Lou Gehrig+ (17)	16.23
34	Jim Gentile (9)	16.32
35	David Ortiz (17, 37)	16.37
36	Hank Aaron+ (23)	16.38
	Mike Napoli (8, 31)	16.38
38	Jason Giambi (19, 42)	16.45
39	Willie Mays+ (22)	16.49
40	Prince Fielder (9, 29)	16.6
41	Hank Sauer (15)	16.65
42	Eddie Mathews+ (17)	16.67
43	Willie Stargell+ (21)	16.69
44	Mark Teixeira (11, 33)	16.77
45	Rob Deer (11)	16.87
	Mo Vaughn (12)	16.87
47	Troy Glaus (13)	16.91
48	Mark Reynolds (7, 29)	16.92
49	Frank Howard (16)	16.98
50	Miguel Cabrera (11, 30)	17.04

All-Time Hits Leaders

1	Pete Rose (24)	4256
2	Ty Cobb+ (24)	4189
3	Hank Aaron+ (23)	3771
4	Stan Musial+ (22)	3630
5	Tris Speaker+ (22)	3514
6	Cap Anson+ (27)	3435
7	Honus Wagner+ (21)	3420
8	Carl Yastrzemski+ (23)	3419
9	Paul Molitor+ (21)	3319
10	Derek Jeter (19, 39)	3316
11	Eddie Collins+ (25)	3315
12	Willie Mays+ (22)	3283
13	Eddie Murray+ (21)	3255
14	Nap Lajoie+ (21)	3243
15	Cal Ripken+ (21)	3184
16	George Brett+ (21)	3154
17	Paul Waner+ (20)	3152
18	Robin Yount+ (20)	3142
19	Tony Gwynn+ (20)	3141
20	Dave Winfield+ (22)	3110
21	Craig Biggio (20)	3060
22	Rickey Henderson+ (25)	3055
23	Rod Carew+ (19)	3053
24	Lou Brock+ (19)	3023
25	Rafael Palmeiro (20)	3020
26	Wade Boggs+ (18)	3010
27	Al Kaline+ (22)	3007
28	Roberto Clemente+ (18)	3000
29	Sam Rice+ (20)	2987

30	Sam Crawford+ (19)	2961
31	Frank Robinson+ (21)	2943
32	Alex Rodriguez (20, 37)	2939
33	Barry Bonds (22)	2935
34	Jake Beckley+ (20)	2934
35	Willie Keeler+ (19)	2932
36	Rogers Hornsby+ (23)	2930
37	Al Simmons+ (20)	2927
38	Zack Wheat+ (19)	2884
39	Frankie Frisch+ (19)	2880
40	Omar Vizquel (24)	2877
41	Mel Ott+ (22)	2876
42	Babe Ruth+ (22)	2873
43	Harold Baines (22)	2866
44	Jesse Burkett+ (16)	2850
45	Brooks Robinson+ (23)	2848
46	Ivan Rodriguez (21)	2844
47	Charlie Gehringer+ (19)	2839
48	George Sisler+ (15)	2812
49	Ken Griffey (22)	2781
50	Andre Dawson+ (21)	2774
51	Johnny Damon (18)	2769
52	Vada Pinson (18)	2757
53	Luke Appling+ (20)	2749
54	Al Oliver (18)	2743
55	Ichiro Suzuki (13, 39)	2742
56	Goose Goslin+ (18)	2735
57	Tony Perez+ (23)	2732
58	Chipper Jones (19)	2726
59	Roberto Alomar+ (17)	2724
60	Lou Gehrig+ (17)	2721
61	Rusty Staub (23)	2716
62	Bill Buckner (22)	2715
63	Dave Parker (19)	2712
64	Billy Williams+ (18)	2711
65	Doc Cramer (20)	2705

66	Gary Sheffield (22)	2689
67	Fred Clarke+ (21)	2678
68	Luis Aparicio+ (18)	2677
69	Max Carey+ (20)	2665
	George Davis+ (20)	2665
71	Nellie Fox+ (19)	2663
72	Harry Heilmann+ (17)	2660
73	Ted Williams+ (19)	2654
74	Lave Cross (21)	2651
75	Jimmie Foxx+ (20)	2646
76	Jim O'Rourke+ (23)	2639
77	Rabbit Maranville+ (23)	2605
	Tim Raines (23)	2605
79	Steve Garvey (19)	2599
80	Ed Delahanty+ (16)	2597
81	Luis Gonzalez (19)	2591
82	Vladimir Guerrero (16)	2590
83	Julio Franco (23)	2586
84	Reggie Jackson+ (21)	2584
85	Ernie Banks+ (19)	2583
86	Richie Ashburn+ (15)	2574
	Manny Ramirez (19)	2574
88	Willie Davis (18)	2561
89	Steve Finley (19)	2548
90	George Van Haltren (17)	2544
91	Garret Anderson (17)	2529
92	Heinie Manush+ (17)	2524
93	Todd Helton (17, 39)	2519
94	Joe Morgan+ (22)	2517
95	Buddy Bell (18)	2514
96	Jimmy Ryan (18)	2513
97	Mickey Vernon (20)	2495
98	Fred McGriff (19)	2490
99	Ted Simmons (21)	2472
100	Joe Medwick+ (17)	2471

All-Time Runs Batted In Leaders

1	Hank Aaron+ (23)	2297
2	Babe Ruth+ (22)	2220
3	Cap Anson+ (27)	2075
4	Barry Bonds (22)	1996
5	Lou Gehrig+ (17)	1992
6	Alex Rodriguez (20, 37)	1969
7	Stan Musial+ (22)	1951
8	Ty Cobb+ (24)	1938
9	Jimmie Foxx+ (20)	1922
10	Eddie Murray+ (21)	1917
11	Willie Mays+ (22)	1903
12	Mel Ott+ (22)	1860
13	Carl Yastrzemski+ (23)	1844
14	Ted Williams+ (19)	1839
15	Ken Griffey (22)	1836
16	Rafael Palmeiro (20)	1835
17	Dave Winfield+ (22)	1833
18	Manny Ramirez (19)	1831
19	Al Simmons+ (20)	1828
20	Frank Robinson+ (21)	1812
21	Honus Wagner+ (21)	1733
22	Frank Thomas+ (19)	1704
23	Reggie Jackson+ (21)	1702
24	Jim Thome (22)	1699
25	Cal Ripken+ (21)	1695
26	Gary Sheffield (22)	1676
27	Sammy Sosa (18)	1667
28	Tony Perez+ (23)	1652
29	Ernie Banks+ (19)	1636

30	Harold Baines (22)	1628
31	Chipper Jones (19)	1623
32	Goose Goslin+ (18)	1610
33	Nap Lajoie+ (21)	1599
34	George Brett+ (21)	1596
35	Mike Schmidt+ (18)	1595
36	Andre Dawson+ (21)	1591
37	Rogers Hornsby+ (23)	1584
	Harmon Killebrew+ (22)	1584
39	Al Kaline+ (22)	1583
40	Jake Beckley+ (20)	1578
41	Willie McCovey+ (22)	1555
42	Fred McGriff (19)	1550
43	Willie Stargell+ (21)	1540
44	Joe DiMaggio+ (13)	1537
	Harry Heilmann+ (17)	1537
46	Tris Speaker+ (22)	1531
47	Jeff Bagwell (15)	1529
48	Sam Crawford+ (19)	1525
49	Jeff Kent (17)	1518
50	Carlos Delgado (17)	1512
51	Mickey Mantle+ (18)	1509
52	Albert Pujols (13, 33)	1498
53	Vladimir Guerrero (16)	1496
54	Dave Parker (19)	1493
55	Billy Williams+ (18)	1475
56	Ed Delahanty+ (16)	1466
	Rusty Staub (23)	1466
58	Eddie Mathews+ (17)	1453
59	Jim Rice+ (16)	1451
60	Joe Carter (16)	1445
61	George Davis+ (20)	1440
62	Luis Gonzalez (19)	1439
63	Jason Giambi (19, 42)	1436
64	Yogi Berra+ (19)	1430
65	David Ortiz (17, 37)	1429

66	Charlie Gehringer+ (19)	1427
67	Andres Galarraga (19)	1425
68	Joe Cronin+ (20)	1424
69	Jim Bottomley+ (16)	1422
70	Mark McGwire (16)	1414
71	Jose Canseco (17)	1407
72	Todd Helton (17, 39)	1406
	Robin Yount+ (20)	1406
74	Juan Gonzalez (17)	1404
75	Paul Konerko (17, 37)	1390
76	Ted Simmons (21)	1389
77	Dwight Evans (20)	1384
78	Joe Medwick+ (17)	1383
79	Lave Cross (21)	1378
80	Johnny Bench+ (17)	1376
81	Chili Davis (19)	1372
82	Garret Anderson (17)	1365
	Orlando Cepeda+ (17)	1365
84	Carlos Lee (14)	1363
85	Brooks Robinson+ (23)	1357
86	Darrell Evans (21)	1354
87	Bobby Abreu (17)	1349
88	Gary Gaetti (20)	1341
89	Johnny Mize+ (15)	1337
90	Mike Piazza (16)	1335
91	Duke Snider+ (18)	1333
92	Ivan Rodriguez (21)	1332
93	Ron Santo+ (15)	1331
94	Carlton Fisk+ (24)	1330
95	Carlos Beltran (16, 36)	1327
96	Al Oliver (18)	1326
97	Roger Connor+ (18)	1323
98	Ruben Sierra (20)	1322
99	Graig Nettles (22)	1314

All-Time Single Season Batting Average Leaders

1	Hugh Duffy+ (27)	0.4397	1894
2	Tip O'Neill (29)	0.4352	1887
3	Ross Barnes (26)	0.4286	1876
4	Nap Lajoie+ (26)	0.4265	1901
5	Willie Keeler+ (25)	0.4238	1897
6	Rogers Hornsby+ (28)	0.4235	1924
7	George Sisler+ (29)	0.4198	1922
8	Ty Cobb+ (24)	0.4196	1911
9	Tuck Turner (27)	0.4179	1894
10	Sam Thompson+ (34)	0.4146	1894
11	Fred Dunlap (25)	0.412	1884
12	Jesse Burkett+ (27)	0.4096	1896
	Ed Delahanty+ (31)	0.4096	1899
14	Ty Cobb+ (25)	0.4087	1912
15	Shoeless Joe Jackson (23)	0.4081	1911
16	George Sisler+ (27)	0.4073	1920
17	Ted Williams+ (22)	0.4057	1941
18	Jesse Burkett+ (26)	0.4054	1895
19	Ed Delahanty+ (27)	0.4042	1895
20	Ed Delahanty+ (26)	0.404	1894
21	Billy Hamilton+ (28)	0.4032	1894
22	Rogers Hornsby+ (29)	0.4028	1925
23	Harry Heilmann+ (28)	0.4027	1923
24	Pete Browning (26)	0.4022	1887
25	Rogers Hornsby+ (26)	0.4013	1922
	Bill Terry+ (31)	0.4013	1930
27	Hughie Jennings+ (27)	0.4012	1896

28	Ty Cobb+ (35)	0.4011	1922
29	Cap Anson+ (29)	0.3994	1881
30	Lefty O'Doul (32)	0.3981	1929
31	Harry Heilmann+ (32)	0.398	1927
32	Rogers Hornsby+ (25)	0.397	1921
33	Ed Delahanty+ (28)	0.3968	1896
34	Jesse Burkett+ (30)	0.3961	1899
35	Shoeless Joe Jackson (24)	0.3951	1912
36	Jack Clements (30)	0.3944	1895
37	Tony Gwynn+ (34)	0.3938	1994
38	Harry Heilmann+ (26)	0.3937	1921
39	Harry Heilmann+ (30)	0.3927	1925
	Babe Ruth+ (28)	0.3927	1923
41	Babe Herman (27)	0.3925	1930
	Joe Kelley+ (22)	0.3925	1894
43	Sam Thompson+ (35)	0.3922	1895
44	Al Simmons+ (25)	0.3916	1927
45	John McGraw+ (26)	0.391	1899
46	Ty Cobb+ (26)	0.3902	1913
47	Al Simmons+ (29)	0.3899	1931
48	George Brett+ (27)	0.3898	1980
49	Fred Clarke+ (24)	0.3897	1897
50	Tris Speaker+ (37)	0.3893	1925
51	Bill Lange (24)	0.3891	1895
52	Billy Hamilton+ (29)	0.3888	1895
53	Ty Cobb+ (34)	0.3886	1921
54	Ted Williams+ (38)	0.3881	1957
55	Rod Carew+ (31)	0.388	1977
	King Kelly+ (28)	0.388	1886
57	Cap Anson+ (42)	0.3878	1894
	Luke Appling+ (29)	0.3878	1936
59	Tris Speaker+ (32)	0.3877	1920
60	Lave Cross (28)	0.3875	1894
61	Deacon White+ (29)	0.3872	1877
62	Al Simmons+ (23)	0.3869	1925
63	Rogers Hornsby+ (32)	0.3868	1928

64	Tris Speaker+ (28)	0.3864	1916
65	Willie Keeler+ (24)	0.386	1896
66	Chuck Klein+ (25)	0.3858	1930
67	Hughie Jennings+ (26)	0.3856	1895
68	Willie Keeler+ (26)	0.385	1898
69	Arky Vaughan+ (23)	0.3848	1935
70	Rogers Hornsby+ (27)	0.3844	1923
71	Ty Cobb+ (32)	0.3843	1919
72	Nap Lajoie+ (35)	0.3841	1910
73	Ty Cobb+ (23)	0.3834	1910
74	Jesse Burkett+ (28)	0.383	1897
75	Tris Speaker+ (24)	0.3828	1912
76	Ty Cobb+ (30)	0.3827	1917
77	Lefty O'Doul (33)	0.3826	1930
78	Shoeless Joe Jackson (32)	0.3825	1920
79	Ty Cobb+ (31)	0.3824	1918
80	Babe Herman (26)	0.3814	1929
	Honus Wagner+ (26)	0.3814	1900
82	Joe DiMaggio+ (24)	0.381	1939
83	Al Simmons+ (28)	0.3809	1930
84	Rogers Hornsby+ (33)	0.3804	1929
	Paul Waner+ (24)	0.3804	1927
86	Billy Hamilton+ (27)	0.3803	1893
87	Tris Speaker+ (35)	0.3798	1923
88	Goose Goslin+ (27)	0.3794	1928
89	Freddie Lindstrom+ (24)	0.3793	1930
90	Larry Walker (32)	0.379	1999
91	Willie Keeler+ (27)	0.3789	1899
92	Lou Gehrig+ (27)	0.3787	1930
93	Pete Browning (21)	0.3785	1882
	John Cassidy (22)	0.3785	1877
95	Ty Cobb+ (38)	0.3783	1925
96	Babe Ruth+ (29)	0.3781	1924
97	Sam Crawford+ (31)	0.378	1911
98	Earl Averill+ (34)	0.3779	1936
	Tris Speaker+ (34)	0.3779	1922
100	Nap Lajoie+ (27)	0.3778	190

All-Time Single Season Home Run Leaders

1	Barry Bonds (36)	73	2001
2	Mark McGwire (34)	70	1998
3	Sammy Sosa (29)	66	1998
4	Mark McGwire (35)	65	1999
5	Sammy Sosa (32)	64	2001
6	Sammy Sosa (30)	63	1999
7	Roger Maris (26)	61	1961
8	Babe Ruth+ (32)	60	1927
9	Babe Ruth+ (26)	59	1921
10	Jimmie Foxx+ (24)	58	1932
	Hank Greenberg+ (27)	58	1938
	Ryan Howard (26)	58	2006
	Mark McGwire (33)	58	1997
14	Luis Gonzalez (33)	57	2001
	Alex Rodriguez (26)	57	2002
16	Ken Griffey (27)	56	1997
	Ken Griffey (28)	56	1998
	Hack Wilson+ (30)	56	1930
19	Jose Bautista (29)	54	2010
	Ralph Kiner+ (26)	54	1949
	Mickey Mantle+ (29)	54	1961
	David Ortiz (30)	54	2006
	Alex Rodriguez (31)	54	2007
	Babe Ruth+ (25)	54	1920
	Babe Ruth+ (33)	54	1928
26	Chris Davis (27)	53	2013
27	George Foster (28)	52	1977

	Mickey Mantle+ (24)	52	1956
	Willie Mays+ (34)	52	1965
	Mark McGwire (32)	52	1996
	Alex Rodriguez (25)	52	2001
	Jim Thome (31)	52	2002
33	Cecil Fielder (26)	51	1990
	Andruw Jones (28)	51	2005
	Ralph Kiner+ (24)	51	1947
	Willie Mays+ (24)	51	1955
	Johnny Mize+ (34)	51	1947
38	Brady Anderson (32)	50	1996
	Albert Belle (28)	50	1995
	Prince Fielder (23)	50	2007
	Jimmie Foxx+ (30)	50	1938
	Sammy Sosa (31)	50	2000
	Greg Vaughn (32)	50	1998
44	Albert Belle (31)	49	1998
	Barry Bonds (35)	49	2000
	Andre Dawson+ (32)	49	1987
	Lou Gehrig+ (31)	49	1934
	Lou Gehrig+ (33)	49	1936
	Shawn Green (28)	49	2001
	Ken Griffey (26)	49	1996
	Todd Helton (27)	49	2001
	Harmon Killebrew+ (28)	49	1964
	Harmon Killebrew+ (33)	49	1969
	Ted Kluszewski (29)	49	1954
	Willie Mays+ (31)	49	1962
	Mark McGwire (23)	49	1987
	Albert Pujols (26)	49	2006
	Frank Robinson+ (30)	49	1966
	Babe Ruth+ (35)	49	1930
	Sammy Sosa (33)	49	2002
	Jim Thome (30)	49	2001
	Larry Walker (30)	49	1997
63	Albert Belle (29)	48	1996

Adrian Beltre (25)	48	2004
Jimmie Foxx+ (25)	48	1933
Ken Griffey (29)	48	1999
Frank Howard (32)	48	1969
Ryan Howard (28)	48	2008
Harmon Killebrew+ (26)	48	1962
Dave Kingman (30)	48	1979
Alex Rodriguez (29)	48	2005
Mike Schmidt+ (30)	48	1980
Willie Stargell+ (31)	48	1971

All-Time Runs Batted in Leaders Single Season

1	Hack Wilson+ (30)	191	1930
2	Lou Gehrig+ (28)	184	1931
3	Hank Greenberg+ (26)	183	1937
4	Jimmie Foxx+ (30)	175	1938
	Lou Gehrig+ (24)	175	1927
6	Lou Gehrig+ (27)	174	1930
7	Babe Ruth+ (26)	171	1921
8	Hank Greenberg+ (24)	170	1935
	Chuck Klein+ (25)	170	1930
10	Jimmie Foxx+ (24)	169	1932
11	Joe DiMaggio+ (22)	167	1937
12	Sam Thompson+ (27)	166	1887
13	Lou Gehrig+ (31)	165	1934
	Manny Ramirez (27)	165	1999
	Al Simmons+ (28)	165	1930
	Sam Thompson+ (35)	165	1895
17	Babe Ruth+ (32)	164	1927
18	Jimmie Foxx+ (25)	163	1933
	Babe Ruth+ (36)	163	1931
20	Hal Trosky (23)	162	1936
21	Sammy Sosa (32)	160	2001
22	Lou Gehrig+ (34)	159	1937
	Vern Stephens (28)	159	1949
	Ted Williams+ (30)	159	1949
	Hack Wilson+ (29)	159	1929
26	Sammy Sosa (29)	158	1998
27	Juan Gonzalez (28)	157	1998

	Al Simmons+ (27)	157	1929
29	Jimmie Foxx+ (22)	156	1930
	Alex Rodriguez (31)	156	2007
31	Joe DiMaggio+ (33)	155	1948
	Ken Williams (32)	155	1922
33	Joe Medwick+ (25)	154	1937
	Babe Ruth+ (34)	154	1929
35	Tommy Davis (23)	153	1962
	Babe Ruth+ (31)	153	1926
	Babe Ruth+ (35)	153	1930
38	Albert Belle (31)	152	1998
	Lou Gehrig+ (33)	152	1936
	Rogers Hornsby+ (26)	152	1922
41	Lou Gehrig+ (29)	151	1932
	Mel Ott+ (20)	151	1929
	Al Simmons+ (30)	151	1932
44	Andres Galarraga (35)	150	1996
	Hank Greenberg+ (29)	150	1940
	Miguel Tejada (30)	150	2004
47	George Foster (28)	149	1977
	Rogers Hornsby+ (33)	149	1929
	Ryan Howard (26)	149	2006
50	Albert Belle (29)	148	1996

All-Time Fielding Percentage Leaders

1	Troy Tulowitzki (8, 28)	0.9853
2	Omar Vizquel (24)	0.9847
3	Jimmy Rollins (14, 34)	0.9831
4	J.J. Hardy (9, 30)	0.9825
5	Mike Bordick (14)	0.9821
6	Rey Sanchez (15)	0.9813
7	Cesar Izturis (13, 33)	0.9808
8	Larry Bowa (16)	0.9797
9	Jhonny Peralta (11, 31)	0.9796
10	Tony Fernandez (17)	0.9795
11	Cal Ripken+ (21)	0.9793
12	Stephen Drew (8, 30)	0.9786
13	Yunel Escobar (7, 30)	0.9783
14	Brendan Ryan (7, 31)	0.9782
	Ozzie Smith+ (19)	0.9782
16	Deivi Cruz (9)	0.9779
17	David Eckstein (10)	0.9778
18	Juan Castro (17)	0.9774
	Neifi Perez (12)	0.9774
	Jack Wilson (12)	0.9774
21	Frank Duffy (10)	0.9772
	Alex Rodriguez (20, 37)	0.9772
23	Spike Owen (13)	0.977
24	Orlando Cabrera (15)	0.9768
	Alan Trammell (20)	0.9768
26	Mark Belanger (18)	0.9767
	Michael Young (14, 36)	0.9767
28	Bucky Dent (12)	0.9764
29	Derek Jeter (19, 39)	0.9763

	Dick Schofield (14)	0.9763
31	Adam Everett (11)	0.9761
32	Rey Ordonez (9)	0.9757
33	Roger Metzger (11)	0.9755
34	Juan Uribe (13, 33)	0.9752
35	Jay Bell (18)	0.9751
	Asdrubal Cabrera (7, 27)	0.9751
37	Alex Gonzalez (13)	0.9749
	Khalil Greene (7)	0.9749
39	Barry Larkin+ (19)	0.9746
40	Alexei Ramirez (6, 31)	0.974
41	Kevin Elster (13)	0.9739
42	Royce Clayton (17)	0.9738
	Ozzie Guillen (16)	0.9738
	Marco Scutaro (12, 37)	0.9738
45	Rafael Belliard (17)	0.9737
46	Rich Aurilia (15)	0.9736
	Woody Woodward (9)	0.9736
48	Alcides Escobar (6, 26)	0.9735
49	Gary Disarcina (12)	0.9734
50	Jose Reyes (11, 30)	0.9732

Most Valuable Player Award Winners

Year	Player	Team	Pos.	Player	Team	Pos.
2013	Miguel Cabrera	Detroit	3B	A. McCutchen	Pittsburgh	CF
2012	Miguel Cabrera	Detroit	3B	Buster Posey	San Francisco	C
2011	Justin Verlander	Detroit	P	Ryan Braun	Milwaukee	LF
2010	Josh Hamilton	Texas	OF	Joey Votto	Cincinnati	1B
2009	Joe Mauer	Minnesota	C	Albert Pujols*	St. Louis	1B
2008	Dustin Pedroia	Boston	2B	Albert Pujols	St. Louis	1B
2007	Alex Rodriguez	New York	3B	Jimmy Rollins	Philadelphia	SS
2006	Justin Morneau	Minnesota	1B	Ryan Howard	Philadelphia	1B
2005	Alex Rodriguez	New York	3B	Albert Pujols	St. Louis	1B
2004	V. Guerrero	Anaheim	RF	Barry Bonds	San Francisco	LF
2003	Alex Rodriguez	Texas	SS	Barry Bonds	San Francisco	LF
2002	Miguel Tejada	Oakland	SS	Barry Bonds*	San Francisco	LF
2001	Ichiro Suzuki	Seattle	RF	Barry Bonds	San Francisco	LF
2000	Jason Giambi	Oakland	1B	Jeff Kent	San Francisco	2B
1999	Ivan Rodriguez	Texas	C	Chipper Jones	Atlanta	3B
1998	Juan Gonzalez	Texas	OF	Sammy Sosa	Chicago	OF
1997	Ken Griffey Jr.*	Seattle	OF	Larry Walker	Colorado	OF
1996	Juan Gonzalez	Texas	OF	Ken Caminiti*	San Diego	3B
1995	Mo Vaughn	Boston	1B	Barry Larkin	Cincinnati	SS
1994	Frank Thomas	Chicago	1B	Jeff Bagwell*	Houston	1B
1993	Frank Thomas*	Chicago	1B	Barry Bonds	San Francisco	OF
1992	Dennis Eckersley	Oakland	P	Barry Bonds	Pittsburgh	OF
1991	Cal Ripken Jr.	Baltimore	SS	Terry Pendleton	Atlanta	3B
1990	R. Henderson	Oakland	OF	Barry Bonds	Pittsburgh	OF
1989	Robin Yount	Milwaukee	OF	Kevin Mitchell	San Francisco	OF
1988	Jose Canseco*	Oakland	OF	Kirk Gibson	Los Angeles	OF
1987	George Bell	Toronto	OF	Andre Dawson	Chicago	OF
1986	Roger Clemens	Boston	P	Mike Schmidt	Philadelphia	3B

1985	Don Mattingly	New York	1B	Willie McGee	St. Louis	OF
1984	W. Hernandez	Detroit	P	Ryne Sandberg	Chicago	2B
1983	Cal Ripken Jr.	Baltimore	SS	Dale Murphy	Atlanta	OF
1982	Robin Yount	Milwaukee	SS	Dale Murphy	Atlanta	OF
1981	Rollie Fingers	Milwaukee	P	Mike Schmidt	Philadelphia	3B
1980	George Brett	Kansas City	3B	Mike Schmidt*	Philadelphia	3B
1979	Don Baylor	California	OF	Keith Hernandez	St. Louis	1B
				Willie Stargell	Pittsburgh	1B
1978	Jim Rice	Boston	OF	Dave Parker	Pittsburgh	OF
1977	Rod Carew	Minnesota	1B	George Foster	Cincinnati	OF
1976	T. Munson	New York	C	Joe Morgan	Cincinnati	2B
1975	Fred Lynn	Boston	OF	Joe Morgan	Cincinnati	2B
1974	Jeff Burroughs	Texas	OF	Steve Garvey	Los Angeles	1B
1973	Reggie Jackson*	Oakland	OF	Pete Rose	Cincinnati	OF
1972	Richie Allen	Chicago	1B	Johnny Bench	Cincinnati	C
1971	Vida Blue	Oakland	P	Joe Torre	St. Louis	3B
1970	Boog Powell	Baltimore	1B	Johnny Bench	Cincinnati	C
1969	H. Killebrew	Minnesota	1B/3B	Willie McCovey	San Francisco	1B
1968	Denny McLain*	Detroit	P	Bob Gibson	St. Louis	P
1967	Carl Yastrzemski	Boston	OF	Orlando Cepeda*	St. Louis	1B
1966	Frank Robinson*	Baltimore	OF	R. Clemente	Pittsburgh	OF
1965	Zoilo Versalles	Minnesota	SS	Willie Mays	San Francisco	OF
1964	Brooks Robinson	Baltimore	3B	Ken Boyer	St. Louis	3B
1963	Elston Howard	New York	C	Sandy Koufax	Los Angeles	P
1962	Mickey Mantle	New York	OF	Maury Wills	Los Angeles	SS
1961	Roger Maris	New York	OF	Frank Robinson	Cincinnati	OF
1960	Roger Maris	New York	OF	Dick Groat	Pittsburgh	SS
1959	Nellie Fox	Chicago	2B	Ernie Banks	Chicago	SS
1958	Jackie Jensen	Boston	OF	Ernie Banks	Chicago	SS
1957	Mickey Mantle	New York	OF	Hank Aaron	Milwaukee	OF
1956	Mickey Mantle*	New York	OF	Don Newcombe	Brooklyn	P
1955	Yogi Berra	New York	C	Roy Campanella	Brooklyn	C
1954	Yogi Berra	New York	C	Willie Mays	New York	OF
1953	Al Rosen*	Cleveland	3B	Roy Campanella	Brooklyn	C
1952	Bobby Shantz	Philadelphia	P	Hank Sauer	Chicago	OF
1951	Yogi Berra	New York	C	Roy Campanella	Brooklyn	C

1950	Phil Rizzuto	New York	SS	Jim Konstanty	Philadelphia	P
1949	Ted Williams	Boston	OF	Jackie Robinson	Brooklyn	2B
1948	Lou Boudreau	Cleveland	SS	Stan Musial	St. Louis	OF
1947	Joe DiMaggio	New York	OF	Bob Elliott	Boston	3B
1946	Ted Williams	Boston	OF	Stan Musial	St. Louis	1B
1945	Hal Newhouser	Detroit	P	Phil Cavarretta	Chicago	1B
1944	Hal Newhouser	Detroit	P	Marty Marion	St. Louis	SS
1943	Spud Chandler	New York	P	Stan Musial	St. Louis	OF
1942	Joe Gordon	New York	2B	Mort Cooper	St. Louis	P
1941	Joe DiMaggio	New York	OF	Dolph Camilli	Brooklyn	1B
1940	Hank Greenberg	Detoit	OF	Frank McCormick	Cincinnati	1B
1939	Joe DiMaggio	New York	OF	Bucky Walters	Cincinnati	P
1938	Jimmie Foxx	Boston	1B	Ernie Lombardi	Cincinnati	C
1937	C. Gehringer	Detroit	2B	Joe Medwick	St. Louis	OF
1936	Lou Gehrig	New York	1B	Carl Hubbell*	New York	P
1935	H. Greenberg*	Detroit	1B	Gabby Hartnett	Chicago	C
1934	M. Cochrane	Detroit	C	Dizzy Dean	St. Louis	P
1933	Jimmie Foxx	Philadelphia	1B	Carl Hubbell	New York	P
1932	Jimmie Foxx	Philadelphia	1B	Chuck Klein	Philadelphia	OF
1931	Lefty Grove	Philadelphia	P	Frankie Frisch	St. Louis	2B

Cy Young Award Winners

2013	Max Scherzer	Detroit	Clayton Kershaw	Los Angeles
2012	David Price	Tampa Bay	R.A. Dickey	New York
2011	J. Verlander *	Detroit	Clayton Kershaw	Los Angeles
2010	F. Hernandez	Seattle	Roy Halladay *	Philadelphia
2009	Zack Greinke	Kansas City	Tim Lincecum	SF
2008	Cliff Lee	Cleveland	Tim Lincecum	SF
2007	C.C. Sabathia	Cleveland	Jake Peavy *	San Diego
2006	Johan Santana	Minnesota	Brandon Webb	Arizona
2005	Bartolo Colon	Los Angeles	Chris Carpenter	St. Louis
2004	Johan Santana	Minnesota	Roger Clemens	Houston
2003	Roy Halladay	Toronto	Eric Gagne	Los Angeles
2002	Barry Zito	Oakland	Randy Johnson	Arizona
2001	Roger Clemens	NewYork	Randy Johnson	Arizona
2000	Pedro Martinez	Boston	Randy Johnson	Arizona
1999	Pedro Martinez	Boston	Randy Johnson	Arizona
1998	Roger Clemens	Toronto	Tom Glavine	Atlanta
1997	Roger Clemens	Toronto	Pedro Martinez	Montreal
1996	Pat Hentgen	Toronto	John Smoltz	Atlanta
1995	Randy Johnson	Seattle	Greg Maddux *	Atlanta
1994	David Cone	Kansas City	Greg Maddux *	Atlanta
1993	Jack McDowell	Chicago	Greg Maddux	Atlanta
1992	Denis Eckersley	Oakland	Greg Maddux	Chicago
1991	Roger Clemens	Boston	Tom Glavine	Atlanta
1990	Bob Welch	Oakland	Doug Drabek	Pittsburgh
1989	B. Saberhagen	Kansas City	Mark Davis	San Diego
1988	Frank Viola	Minnesota	Orel Hershiser *	Los Angeles
1987	Roger Clemens	Boston	Steve Bedrosian	Philadelphia
1986	Roger Clemens	Boston	Mike Scott	Houston
1985	B.Saberhagen	Kansas City	Dwight Gooden	New York

1984	W. Hernandez	Detroit	Rick Sutcliffe *	Chicago
1983	LaMarr Hoyt	Chicago	John Denny	Philadelphia
1982	Pete Vuckovich	Milwaukee	Steve Carlton	Philadelphia
1981	Rollie Fingers	Milwaukee	F. Velenzuela	Los Angeles
1980	Steve Stone	Baltimore	Steve Carlton	Philadelphia
1979	Mike Flanagan	Baltimore	Bruce Sutter	Chicago
1978	Ron Guidry *	NewYork	Gaylord Perry	San Diego
1977	Sparky Lyle	NewYork	Steve Carlton *	Philadelphia
1976	Jim Palmer	Baltimore	Randy Jones	San Diego
1975	Jim Palmer	Baltimore	Tom Seaver	New York
1974	Jim Hunter	Oakland	Mike Marshall	Los Angeles
1973	Jim Palmer	Baltimore	Tom Seaver	New York
1972	Gaylord Perry	Cleveland	Steve Carlton *	Philadelphia
1971	Vida Blue	Oakland	Ferguson Jenkins	Chicago
1970	Jim Perry	Minnesota	Bob Gibson	St. Louis
1969	Mike Cuellar	Baltimore	Tom Seaver	New York
	Denny McLain	Detroit		
1968	Denny McLain*	Detroit	Bob Gibson *	St. Louis
1967	Jim Lonborg	Boston	Mike McCormick	SF

One award for both leagues

Year	Player	Team
1966	Sandy Koufax *	Los Angeles (NL)
1965	Sandy Koufax *	Los Angeles (NL)
1964	Dean Chance	Los Angeles (NL)
1963	Sandy Koufax *	Los Angeles (NL)
1962	Don Drysdale	Los Angeles (NL)
1961	Whitey Ford	New York (AL)
1960	Vernon Law	Pittsburgh (NL)
1959	Early Wynn	Chicago (AL)
1958	Bob Turley	New York (AL)
1957	Warren Spahn	Milwaukee (NL)
1956	D. Newcombe	Brooklyn (NL)

All Hall of Fame Pitchers

Abs Era Ratio	Actual Actual ERA		GAMES	WINS	LOSSES	STRIKES	WALKS	League ERA
	1.82	Ed Walsh	430	195	126	1,736	617	
	1.89	Addie Joss	286	160	97	920	364	
	2.06	Mordecai Brown	481	239	130	1,375	673	
	2.13	Christy Mathewson	635	373	188	2,502	844	
	2.16	Rube Waddell	407	193	143	2,316	803	
	2.17	Walter Johnson	802	417	279	3,509	1,363	
	2.35	Eddie Plank	623	326	194	2,246	1,072	
	2.46	Chief Bender	459	212	127	1,711	712	
	2.52	Hoyt Wilhelm	1,070	143	122	1,610	778	
	2.56	Grover Alexander (bio)	696	373	208	2,198	951	
	2.62	Tim Keefe	599	342	225	2,543	1,234	
	2.63	Vic Willis	513	249	205	1,651	1,212	
	2.63	Cy Young	906	511	316	2,803	1,217	
	2.66	Joe McGinnity	465	246	142	1,068	812	
	2.67	Old Hoss Radbourn	528	309	195	1,830	875	
	2.68	Jack Chesbro	392	198	132	1,265	690	
	2.71	Mickey Welch	564	307	210	1,850	1,297	
	2.75	Whitey Ford	498	236	106	1,956	1,086	
	2.76	Sandy Koufax	397	165	87	2,396	817	
	2.81	John Clarkson	531	328	178	1,978	1,191	
	2.86	Jim Palmer	558	268	152	2,212	1,311	
	2.86	Tom Seaver	656	311	205	3,640	1,390	
0.91	2.87	Pud Galvin	697	360	308	1,799	744	3.14
	2.89	Stan Covelski	450	215	142	981	802	
	2.89	Juan Marichal	471	243	142	2,303	709	

	2.9	Rollie Fingers	944	114	118	1,299	492	
	2.91	Bob Gibson	528	251	174	3,117	1,336	
	2.95	Don Drysdale	518	209	166	2,486	855	
	2.95	Kid Nichols	620	361	208	1,868	1,268	
	2.98	Carl Hubbell	535	253	154	1,677	725	
	3.01	Goose Gossage	1,002	124	107	1,502	732	
	3.02	Dizzy Dean	317	150	83	1,163	453	
	3.06	Lefty Grove	616	300	141	2,266	1,187	
	3.06	Hal Newhouser	488	207	150	1,796	1,249	
0.75	3.07	Amos Rusie	462	245	174	1,934	1,704	4.07
0.95	3.08	Rube Marquard	536	201	177	1,593	858	3.24
	3.09	Warren Spahn	750	363	245	2,583	1,434	
	3.11	Gaylord Perry	777	314	265	3,534	1,379	
	3.15	Red Faber	669	254	213	1,471	1,213	x
	3.15	Eppa Rixey	692	266	251	1,350	1,082	x
	3.19	Nolan Ryan	807	324	292	5,714	2,795	
	3.22	Steve Carlton	741	329	244	4,136	1,833	
	3.23	Bob Lemon	460	207	128	1,277	1,251	
	3.24	Dazzy Vance	442	197	140	2,045	840	
	3.25	Bob Feller	570	266	162	2,581	1,764	
	3.26	Catfish Hunter	500	224	166	2,012	954	
	3.26	Don Sutton	774	324	256	3,574	1,343	
	3.27	Jim Bunning	591	224	184	2,855	1,000	
	3.31	Bert Blyleven	692	287	250	3,701	1,322	
	3.34	Lefty Gomez	368	189	102	1,468	1,095	
	3.34	Fergie Jenkins	664	284	226	3,192	997	
	3.35	Phil Niekro	864	318	274	3,342	1,809	
	3.41	Robin Roberts	676	286	245	2,357	902	
	3.5	Dennis Eckersley	1,071	197	171	2,401	738	
0.92	3.53	Burleigh Grimes	616	270	212	1,512	1,295	3.83
	3.54	Early Wynn	691	300	244	2,334	1,775	
	3.59	Waite Hoyt	674	237	182	1,206	1,003	
0.96	3.6	Herb Pennock	617	240	162	1,227	916	3.73
	3.64	Jesse Haines	555	210	158	981	871	x
0.85	3.67	Ted Lyons	594	260	230	1,073	1,121	4.27
	3.8	Red Ruffing	624	273	225	1,987	1,541	x

Hall of Fame Members by Postion

Name (Year inducted)

PITCHERS (74)

Alexander, Grover C..1938
Bender, Charles A. "Chief"..1953
Blyleven, Rik Aalbert "Bert"*..2011
Brown, Mordecai P 1949
Brown, Raymond..2006
Bunning, James P. D*...1996
Carlton, Steven N.*..1994
Chesbro, John D 1946
Clarkson, John G..1963
Cooper, Andy 2006
Coveleski, Stanley A 1969
Day, Leon...1995
Dean, Jay H. "Dizzy" 1953
Dihigo, Martin 1977
Drysdale, Donald S 1984
Eckersley, Dennis*..2004
Faber, Urban C. "Red" 1964
Feller, Robert W. A 1962
Fingers, Roland G.*...1992
Ford, Edward C. "Whitey"*...1974
Foster, Willie H 1996
Galvin, James F. "Pud"...1965
Gibson, Robert* 1981

Rogan, Wilber J 1998
Ruffing, Charles H. "Red"..1967
Rusie, Amos W 1977
Ryan, Lynn Nolan* 1999
Seaver, George T.* 1992
Smith, Hilton 2001
Spahn, Warren E 1973
Sutter, Howard Bruce*...2006
Sutton, Donald H.*..1998
Vance, Arthur C. "Dazzy" 1955
Waddell, George E. "Rube".......................................1946
Walsh, Edward A..1946
Welch, Michael F 1973
Wilhelm, James Hoyt 1985
Williams, Joe "Smokey Joe".....................................1999
Willis, Victor, G..1995
Wynn, Early..1972
Young, Denton T. "Cy" 1937

CATCHER (16)

Bench, Johnny L.* 1989
Berra, Lawrence P. "Yogi"* 1972
Bresnahan, Roger P 1945
Campanella, Roy..1969
Carter, Gary E..2003
Cochrane, Gordon S..1947
Dickey, William M..1954
Ewing, William B. "Buck"..1939
Ferrell, Richard B...1984
Fisk, Carlton*...2000
Gibson, Joshua 1972
Hartnett, Charles L. "Gabby" 1955

Lombardi, Ernest...1986
Mackey, Biz..2006
Santop, Louis 2006
Schalk, Raymond W 1955

FIRST BASEMEN (22)

Anson, Adrian C. "Cap"..1939
Beckley, Jacob P...1971
Bottomley, James L..1974
Brouthers, Dennis "Dan"..1945
Cepeda, Orlando M.*..1999
Chance, Frank L...1946
Connor, Roger 1976
Foxx, James E 1951
Gehrig, H. Louis...1939
Greenberg, Henry B...1956
Kelly, George L...1973
Killebrew, Harmon C 1984
Leonard, Walter F. "Buck" 1972
McCovey, Willie L.*..1986
Mize, John R..1981
Murray, Eddie C.*...2003
Pérez, Tony*...2000
Sisler, George H 1939
Suttles, Mule 2006
Taylor, Ben..2006
Terry, William H...1954

SECOND BASEMEN (20)

Alomar, Roberto * 2011
Carew, Rodney C.* 1991
Collins, Edward T 1939
Doerr, Robert P.* 1986
Evers, John J 1946
Fox, Nelson J 1997
Frisch, Frank F 1947
Gehringer, Charles L 1949
Gordon, Joseph L. "Flash" 2009
Grant, Frank 2006
Herman, William J 1975
Hornsby, Rogers 1942
Lajoie, Napoleon "Larry" 1937
Lazzeri, Anthony M 1991
Mazeroski, William S.* 2001
McPhee, Bid 2000
Morgan, Joe L.* 1990
Robinson, Jack R 1962
Sandberg, Ryne* 2005
Schoendienst, Albert F.* 1989

THIRD BASEMEN (16)

Baker, J. Franklin 1955
Boggs, Wade* 2005
Brett, George H.* 1999
Collins, James J 1945
Dandridge, Raymond E 1987
Johnson, William J. "Judy" 1975
Kell, George C 1983
Lindstrom, Frederick C 1976
Mathews, Edwin L 1978

Molitor, Paul* 2004
Robinson, Jr. Brooks C.* 1983
Santo, Ronald E 2012
Schmidt, Michael J.* 1995
Traynor, Harold J. "Pie" 1948
White, Deacon 2013
Wilson, Jud 2006

SHORTSTOPS (24)

Aparicio, Luis E.* 1984
Appling, Lucius B. "Luke" 1964
Bancroft, David J 1971
Banks, Ernest* 1977
Boudreau, Louis 1970
Cronin, Joseph E 1956
Davis, George S 1998
Jackson, Travis C 1982
Jennings, Hugh A 1945
Larkin, Barry L.* 2012
Lloyd, John H 1977
Maranville, Walter J. 1954
Reese, Harold H 1984
Ripken, Calvin E. Jr. "Cal"* 2007
Rizzuto, Philip F 1994
Sewell, Joseph W 1977
Smith, Ozzie* 2002
Tinker, Joseph B 1946
Vaughan, Joseph F. "Arky" 1985
Wagner, John P. "Honus" 1936
Wallace, Roderick J 1953
Ward, John M 1964
Wells, Willie Sr 1997

Yount, Robin R.*..1999

LEFT FIELDERS (21)

Brock, Louis C.* 1985
Burkett, Jesse C 1946
Clarke, Frederick C 1945
Delahanty, Edward J 1945
Goslin, Leon A. "Goose"... 1968
Hafey, Charles J. "Chick" 1971
Henderson, Rickey N. H.*... 2009
Irvin, Monford "Monte"* 1973
Kelley, Joseph J.. 1971
Kiner, Ralph M.* 1975
Manush, Henry E. "Heinie" 1964
Medwick, Joseph M.. 1968
Musial, Stanley F.* 1969
O'Rourke, James H... 1945
Rice, James E. "Jim"* 2009
Simmons, Aloysius H 1953
Stargell, Wilver D. "Willie" 1988
Wheat, Zachariah D.. 1959
Williams, Billy L.* 1987
Williams, Theodore S... 1966
Yastrzemski, Carl M. "Yaz"* 1989

CENTER FIELDERS (23)

Ashburn, Don R. "Richie" 1995
Averill, H. Earl 1975
Bell, James T. "Cool Papa" 1974
Brown, Willard 2006
Carey, Max G 1961
Charleston, Oscar M 1976
Cobb, Tyrus R 1936
Combs, Earle B 1970
DiMaggio, Joseph P 1955
Doby, Lawrence E 1998
Duffy, Hugh 1945
Hamilton, William R 1961
Hill, Pete 2006
Mantle, Mickey C 1974
Mays, Willie H.* 1979
Puckett, Kirby 2001
Roush, Edd J 1962
Snider, Edwin D. "Duke" 1980
Speaker, Tristram E 1937
Stearnes, Turkey 2000
Torriente, Cristóbal 2006
Waner, Lloyd J 1967
Wilson, Lewis R. "Hack" 1979

RIGHT FIELDERS (24)

Aaron, Henry L.* 1982
Clemente, Roberto W 1973
Crawford, Samuel E 1957
Cuyler, Hazen S. "Kiki" 1968
Dawson, Andre N.* 2010
Flick, Elmer...1963
Gwynn, Anthony K. 2007
Heilmann, Harry E 1952
Hooper, Harry B 1971
Jackson, Reginald M.* 1993
Kaline, Albert W.* 1980
Keeler, William H. "Willie" 1939
Kelly, Michael J. "King" 1945
Klein, Charles H 1980
McCarthy, Thomas F 1946
Ott, Melvin T 1951
Rice, Edgar C. "Sam" 1963
Robinson, Frank* 1982
Ruth, George H. "Babe" 1936
Slaughter, Enos B 1985
Thompson, Samuel L 1974
Waner, Paul G 1952
Winfield, David M.* 2001
Youngs, Ross M 1972

DESIGNATED HITTERS (1)

Thomas, Frank 2014

List of Players that should be inducted into the Hall of Fame

Players

Barry Bonds
Shoeless Joe Jackson
Richie Allen
Mark McGuire
Ken Griffey Jr
Jim Thome
Albert Pujols
Alex Rodriguez
Larry Walker
Cesar Cedeno
Darrel Evans
Tim Raines
Reggie Smith
Jeff Bagwell
Dwight Evans
Fred Lynn
Eric Davis
Bobby Bonds
Ken Williams
Norm Cash
Jim Wynn
Frank Howard
Lance Berkman

Jim Edmonds
Raphael Palmeiro
Jack Clack
David Oritz
Orlando Cepeda
Manny Ramirez
Sammy Sosa
Todd Helton
Gary Sheffield
Vladimir Guerrero
Gil Hodges
Darryl Strawberry
Edgar Martinez
Kirk Gibson
Juan Gonzalez
Boog Powell
Miguel Cabrera
Tip O'neil
Fred McGriff
Bobby Abreu
Keith Hernandez
Greg Luzinski
Pedro Guerrero
Carlos Delgado
Craig Nettles
Rick Monday
Dale Murphy
Ellis Burks
Rico Carty
Tony Oliva
Cy Williams
Brian Giles
Jason Giambi

George Foster
Ivan Rodriguez
Bobby Grich
Ryan Howard
Gary Gaetti
Mike Piazza
Al Oliver
Bill Dahlen
Charlie Keller
Chipper Jones
Alan Trammel
Dave Parker

List of Pitchers that should be inducted into the Hall of Fame

Pitchers

Roger Clemons
Pedro Martinez
Smokey Joe Wood
Randy Johnson
Kevin Brown
Andy Messersmith
Fred Toney
Eddie Cicotte
Dean Chance
Dutch Leonard
Vida Blue
Mike Cueller
Sam McDowell
Mel Stottlemyre
Ron Guidry
Wilbur Wood
Dave McNally
Mariano Rivera
John Hiller
Dan Quisenberry
Sparky Lyle
Don McMahon
Ron Perranoski
Tug Mcgraw
Brett Saberhagen

List of Players that should not be in the Hall of Fame

(Based on "Absolute Numbers Theory")

Pete Rose
Bid McPhee
John Evers
Pie Traynor
Pee Wee Reese
George Kell
George Kelly
Billy Herman
Deacon White
Richard Ferrell
Fred Lindstrom
Lloyd Waner
David Bancroft
Rabbit Maranville
Red Schoendist
Joe Sewell
John Ward
Ray Schalk
Phil Rizutto
Nellie Fox

List of Pitchers that should not be in the Hall of Fame

(Based on "Absolute Numbers Theory")

Rube Marquard
Herb Pennock
Pud Galvin

Conclusion

These are the findings of some of the greatest player rankings in the history of baseball based on an "Absolute Numbers" theory. All players were ranked according to how well they performed in relation to the average player of their era. I don't guarantee by any means that this is an all-inclusive list of the best players in baseball only that it showed the relative rankings of the players that were reviewed. As more relevant players are discovered they will be added to the lists for further comparisons.

This book was written in about 2 weeks of intense work after being inspired by a picture that I found of my father in a baseball uniform from 1948.

Made in the USA
Middletown, DE
20 September 2022